"The materials provided in the text will guide administrators and district personnel in making "school- and districtwide reforms" that benefit students and support teachers."

—Grace Maes
Reading Specialist & Literacy Coach
Mt. Diablo Unified School District

"As a bilingual literacy coach working primarily with English learners, it is so helpful to have a resource that addresses a critical component of language development with practical strategies."

—Kathy Flores
Literacy Coach
Cambridge Elementary, Mt. Diablo Unified School District

"*Nourishing Vocabulary* is a book that should be in the hands of every teacher. It is a complete resource, full of ideas for implementing a 'comprehensive' vocabulary program across the grade levels. These activities are quick to implement and effective."

—Sarah Schroeder
Teacher
Kensington, CA

"As a high school ESL teacher, I was intrigued by the innovative strategies given for the older student."

—Jana Perkins
ESL Teacher & Literacy Coach
Bay Area Public High School

"If you want a resource for teaching vocabulary that is well-researched, complete, filled with effective teaching strategies, AND easy-to-use, look no further. Lubliner and Scott have assembled such a resource and done it compactly with a positive metaphor that unites all the content. When we nourish vocabulary growth meaningfully, we are also feeding the academic growth of the child. The vocabulary pyramid is a unifying theme that links all the incredibly useful information in this book.

Lubliner and Scott have done an excellent job of marshalling the best ideas—including their own research—on vocabulary development and teaching. This book will definitely be on my own bookshelf and recommended to colleagues and students."

—Dana L. Grisham
Interim Associate Dean
CSU East Bay

"Shira Lubliner and Judith Scott have researched and written a treatise that shows teachers, especially those working with mandated programs, how to integrate social studies and science instruction into their curriculum."

—Vivian Boyd
Director, Curriculum and Instruction
Mt. Diablo Unified School District

"As a literacy coach, I was particularly interested in the variety of problem-solving strategies and cue cards found in this book."

—Kathy O'Brien
Reading First Literacy Coach
Mt. Diablo Unified School District

"With district and state mandates, and teachers restricted by the constraints of our daily schedules, it is refreshing to find simple strategies that we can implement in our limited time."

—Lynne Cheney
5th Grade Teacher
Mt. Diablo Unified School District

"At last, a book that exemplifies best practices in vocabulary instruction while using research to substantiate their use."

—Dr. Valerie Helgren-Lempesis
Graduate Reading Coordinator
CSU East Bay

"*Nourishing Vocabulary* lays a clear theoretical foundation for vocabulary instruction. The book provides effective doable strategies. In addition, the scripted examples of instruction help teachers with explicit, comprehensive language. The lesson plans are research-based, systematic, and practical. Teachers don't have to reinvent the wheel!"

—Patricia Preut
Reading Specialist, National Presenter, Consultant
Mt. Diablo Unified School District, Developmental Studies Center

Nourishing Vocabulary

*We dedicate this book to all our children, Shira's first grandchild—Noah,
and grandchildren yet to come: May your lives be filled with wonderful words.*

Shira Lubliner • Judith A. Scott

Nourishing Vocabulary

Balancing Words and Learning

CORWIN PRESS
A SAGE Company
Thousand Oaks, CA 91320

For information:

Corwin Press
A SAGE Company
2455 Teller Road
Thousand Oaks, California 91320
www.corwinpress.com

SAGE Pvt. Ltd.
B 1/I 1 Mohan Cooperative
   Industrial Area
Mathura Road, New Delhi 110 044
India

SAGE Ltd.
1 Oliver's Yard
55 City Road
London EC1Y 1SP
United Kingdom

SAGE Asia-Pacific Pte. Ltd.
33 Pekin Street #02-01
Far East Square
Singapore 048763

Printed in the United States of America.

Library of Congress Cataloging-in-Publication Data

Lubliner, Shira, 1951-
Nourishing vocabulary: balancing words and learning/Shira Lubliner and Judith A. Scott.
   p. cm.
Includes bibliographical references and index.
ISBN 978-1-4129-4245-4 (cloth)
ISBN 978-1-4129-4246-1 (pbk.)
   1. Vocabulary—Study and teaching. I. Scott, Judith A. II. Title.

LB1574.5.L833 2008
372.6'1—dc22   2007052911

This book is printed on acid-free paper.

08   09   10   11   12   10 9 8 7 6 5 4 3 2 1

Acquisitions Editor:	Hudson Perigo
Editorial Assistant:	Lesley Blake
Production Editor:	Veronica Stapleton
Copy Editor:	Helen Glenn Court
Typesetter:	C&M Digitals (P) Ltd.
Proofreader:	Gail Naron Chalew
Indexer:	Rick Hurd
Cover Designer:	Scott Van Atta

Contents

Foreword

This book is about *nourishing our students' minds*. This well-crafted book by Lubliner and Scott is an exceptional resource when teaching students vocabulary and concepts. This link between vocabulary and concept development is important to consider here, for when we teach vocabulary we are teaching concepts. Through the routines and activities here, students explore their thinking, and who doesn't like to think about and for themselves? *What do you know?* The activities in this book guide students in a search for what they bring to the vocabulary, and then students get underway to organize the ideas they are studying. Students' abilities to categorize and organize their thinking hierarchically are key to critical thinking, and by exploring vocabulary deeply, students see inside the language to uncover ideas and concepts. This vocabulary instruction also teaches study habits in your discipline by guiding teachers to identify, prioritize, and present vocabulary activities that are interwoven with strategies students will use throughout the year. This book nourishes my thinking and puts a smile on my face!

In that last sentence is the link I want to make in this foreword: the link between the need to teach students vocabulary for logic or thinking (the cognitive), and to teach for students' motivation in learning (feelings, the visceral, the physical). These aspects add up to confidence, confidence that we have in teaching, and confidence that students have in learning. I'll return to the word *confidence* a little later, but for now, consider the idea that students are nourished by the cognitive and physical workings of words and vocabulary instruction.

When we experience a word, there are the physical and the cognitive parts, perhaps like the yin and yang of a word. There in the history or morphology of the vocabulary lies the more complete involvement students can have learning about words, and their meanings. For example, the story of the word *nourish*, the metaphor for vocabulary learning in this book, began with organic and physical aspects from the Latin word for *nurse* and the derived Indo-European root *(s)nāu*, "to swim," and "to let flow." As the thinking of speakers evolved, the mind connection to the word *nourish* was made. This we see in the surfacing of the word in Old French, 1000 AD to 1300 AD. Today, the word *nourish* has a cognitive denotation in addition to the physical manifestations of the word. Likewise, as students' thinking evolves, they make mind connections as in a cognitive denotation for nourish. Students' ideas and thinking are nourished, as in a healthy diet, nurtured, as ideas exist in the garden of our minds. Vocabulary instruction is nourishment for students' minds.

Before school, vocabulary is nourished at home, and we know how important home language use and interaction are; from researchers like Hart and Risley (1995) we learn that by school age, some children have heard 30 million more words than other children. Teachers also recognize how students respond intellectually and socially to various narrative styles and structures (McCabe, 1997). Culture, feelings, intellect, and interests can join in these early years to form a base for the vocabulary students learn.

Vocabulary development is intertwined with reading achievement, and the relationship between vocabulary and literacy is reciprocal. Vocabulary learning and instruction are closely linked to literacy learning, and this too is an organic link in which students' knowledge of phonics and spelling interacts with their vocabulary knowledge. In beginning literacy, students' oral language and limited phonics and spelling knowledge feed a slow movement through easy reading materials, while sound and spelling forge their orthographic knowledge. Until the time that literacy is a communication that serves the rapid transmission of information, listening—or, as Edmund Henderson said, "language through the ear hole"—is the primary avenue in learning vocabulary. Once students' orthographic knowledge is in command of single-syllable and most two-syllable words, literacy can become the primary avenue for vocabulary learning. The reciprocal relationship between reading and oral language becomes weighted in the direction of literacy feeding oral language: nearly all of the new vocabulary that students learn from the late intermediate and advanced levels of reading, for most, from high school on, comes from literacy.

In literacy development and instruction, vocabulary is part of the word study equation: word study = phonics + vocabulary + spelling. For intermediate and advanced readers, phonic study is influenced by the complexity of the words and the subsequent changes that are made in pronunciation with changes in syntactic function—that is, *invite/invitation* and *confide/confidence*—and the change in the pronunciation of the vowels with changes in syntactic role; that is, verb/noun. Phonics is important as directed by vocabulary and spelling. Vocabulary and spelling join in the study at these upper levels in the study of morphology, and as you will see in this book, grammar study in English and the language arts can be integrated into word study when words are studied deeply. Students' study of morphology begins with easy prefixes and suffixes and gradually includes the harder affixes as well as the roots. Can we help students see that the word *confidence* is a noun with three parts: *con* + *fid* + *ence*, that there is in this word a prefix that means *with* + a root related to words like *fidelity* + *ence*, a noun-forming suffix? Can we also have them look inside of the word root for related words semantically: *allegiance, accuracy, faith, fealty,* and *loyalty*? The same deep word study in vocabulary instruction applies equally well in science in words like *epi-+dermal*, or *hydro-+electr+-ic*.

Students' development suggests how to teach vocabulary; some students need the oral support through the ears, and others read with enough proficiency to use their eyes to bring vocabulary to life. The strategies taught in this book, with the rich set of templates in Appendix B, make it easy to bring eyes and ears together for students of different reading proficiencies and language backgrounds; your partner studies of vocabulary are a match for the routine and cue cards the authors have created. The chapter on instruction with students learning English, and the teaching experiences with English learners presented in other chapters are informative and soulful because you'll feel for students when there are instructional mismatches, and thoughtful as we look into how to teach students vocabulary as they learn a new language.

What we are doing in vocabulary development is teaching students to see into words, and we are teaching them ways to organize the ideas related to the words. Vocabulary study is a thoughtful process that students use to organize the information in their content area studies. The structural study of words in the morphology is a way of getting the ideas in front of students so that they are prepared to experience the ideas and information in their content studies. Examining related words morphologically and conceptually leads to the internalization of the vocabulary and the generalizations of pattern and meanings.

In teaching vocabulary, educators are on the cutting edge of understanding human thought. The interaction of vocabulary and thinking is truly one of the fundamental areas of language study by scientists and philosophers. For many years, we have wondered if language influences thought or thought influences language. *Cogito, ergo sum,* Latin for "I think, therefore I am" was what Descartes said about the importance of thinking, and, by the way, it is through language that we share ideas and thinking. Vygotsky, the psychologist, demonstrated that learning and language have social roots and ecologies that affect how and what we learn. About the same time, the famous language philosopher Wittgenstein began his career thinking that language could be structured with a logical order and precision of expression that left no ambiguity in the logic or truth of one's ideas. By the end of his career, the rigor of truth and logic through language was supplanted by a social view of language as a series of language games. Similarly, the famous behaviorist B. F. Skinner, of all people, made a vocabulary connection between thinking and feeling in one of his last articles in which he traced the etymologies of eighty words to show how the meaning of words evolved over time from statements of physical conditions to more abstract principles and ideas. He observed of the study of the history of words, that "etymology is the archaeology of thought" (1989, p. 13). Teaching each day, educators probably have an answer to this weighty question. I think that most educators sense that vocabulary encourages thinking, and that thinking nurtures vocabulary and language development. You will find this book an important resource for teaching thinking through vocabulary. I think this book will bring a smile to your face, too, because you will feel a new confidence teaching vocabulary in interesting ways that encourage learning.

Donald Bear

January 2008

REFERENCES

Hart, B., & Risley, R. T. (1995). *Meaningful differences in the everyday experiences of young American children.* Baltimore: Brookes Publishing Company.

McCabe, A. (1997). *Chameleon readers: All kinds of good stories.* New York: Webster-McGraw-Hill.

Skinner, B. F. (1989). The origins of cognitive thought. *American Psychologist, 44,* 13–18.

Acknowledgments

Corwin Press would like to thank the following individuals for reviewing the manuscript:

Teresa P. Cunningham
Principal, Laurel Elementary School
Johnson County School System
Laurel Bloomery, TN

Stephanie Malin
Elementary Instructional Coach
Beaverton School District
Beaverton, OR

Karen Landress, NBCT, MEd, MA, CCC-SLP
Speech/Language Pathologist
Merritt Island, FL

Mary Amato, NBCT
Literacy Coach
Alexander Graham Bell School
Chicago, IL

About the Authors

 **Shira Lubliner** (EdD, University of San Francisco) has been an educator for more than thirty years, working as a classroom teacher and a private school principal, and is currently an associate professor of teacher education at California State University, East Bay. She is the author of numerous articles and several books, including *A Practical Guide to Reciprocal Teaching* (2001), and *Getting Into Words: Vocabulary Instruction that Strengthens Comprehension* (2005). Shira presents workshops for teachers on vocabulary instruction and reading comprehension throughout the country. She is the past president of California Professors of Reading/Language Arts.

 **Judith A. Scott** (PhD, University of Illinois) has been a vocabulary researcher for twenty years and is the graduate director for the PhD program in the Department of Education at the University of California, Santa Cruz. Her work blends vocabulary instruction with effective teacher education within the context of language, literacy, and culture. She directs a $1.4 million federal grant to integrate word consciousness into standards-based, literature-rich writing workshop classrooms as part of the V.I.N.E. (Vocabulary Innovations in Education) project. Judith is the lead author of *The Word-Conscious Classroom: Building the Vocabulary Readers and Writers Need* (2008) and numerous articles. In 2006, the International Reading Association recognized her extensive work with teachers and schools with the presentation of the John Chorlton Manning Public School Service Award.

Introduction

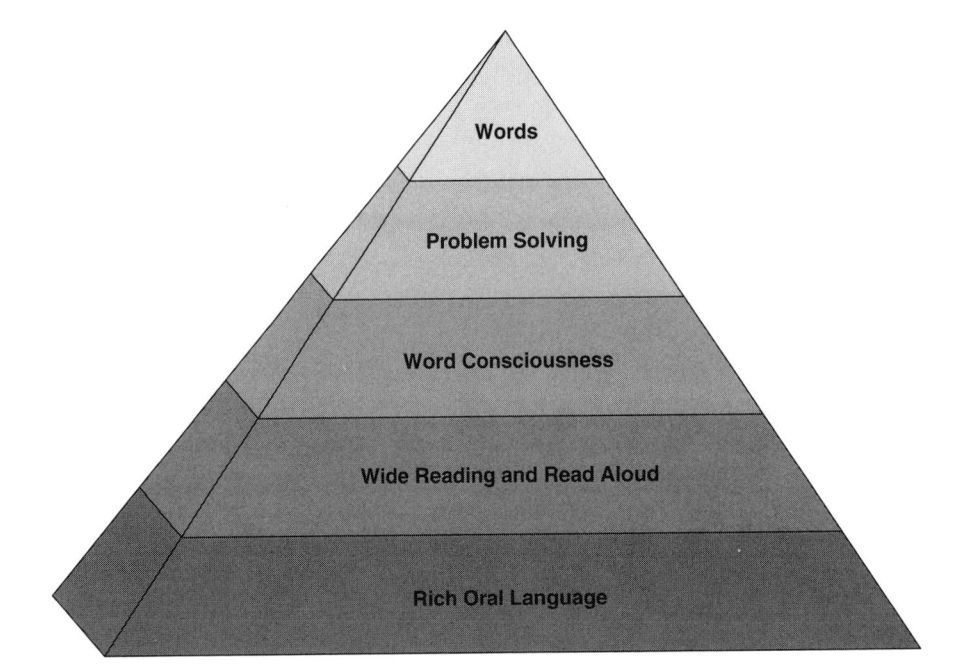

We decided to name this book *Nourishing Vocabulary* to emphasize the fundamental nature of vocabulary instruction. Teaching vocabulary is more than conveying information about words; it is the nourishment of children's minds with meaningful ideas and rich language. We use the metaphor of the food pyramid to illustrate this message. We all know that a balanced diet of essential nutrients is necessary for children's health. An educational diet composed of rich language experiences is equally important to nurture children's intellectual growth and development.

How are our children being nourished in terms of their vocabulary development? A number of studies dating back to the 1970s have documented the lack of vocabulary instruction in schools (Durkin, 1978–1979; Roser & Juel, 1982; Scott, Jamieson-Noel, & Asselin, 2003). The publication of the National Reading Panel Report (2000) changed the educational climate and renewed interest in vocabulary instruction. Educators began to notice that vocabulary might be an aspect of the achievement gap, and vocabulary was designated as one of five key topics in the federally funded Reading First program. Despite the emerging consensus regarding the importance of vocabulary, there is little evidence that children of the twenty-first century are receiving more vocabulary instruction than in past years, nor is there evidence that research-based instructional practices are often followed in classrooms (Biemiller, 2001; Scott et al., 2003; Watts, 1995).

In addition, a heavy emphasis on decoding instruction and rigid adherence to mandated reading programs have narrowed the curriculum in the early grades. When teachers follow the pacing guides and adhere to program fidelity, they often feel as though they are left with little time to devote to reading aloud, discussion, and independent reading. Consequently, many of the activities that are most effective in developing children's language and vocabulary have been pushed out of the curriculum. It seems easy to conclude that, when it comes to vocabulary instruction, many American children have been placed on a starvation diet!

An Overview of the Vocabulary Pyramid

1

THE VOCABULARY PYRAMID

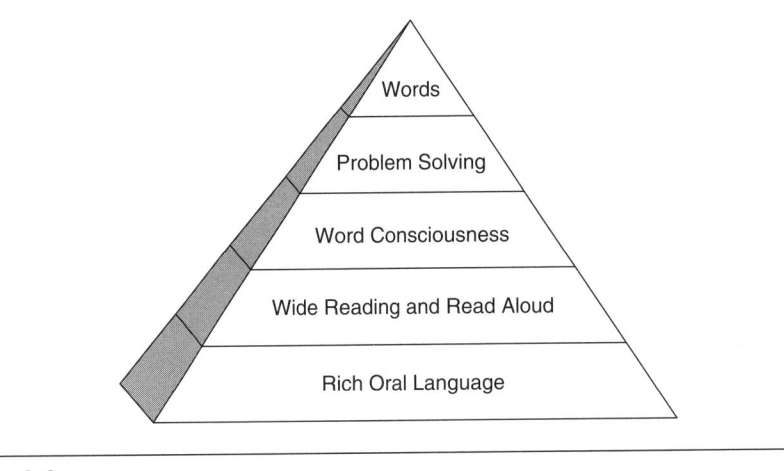

Figure 1.1

When you think about eating, you may think about hamburgers, good wine, and chocolate cake. We know that isn't a balanced diet, however, and most of us are at least aware of what a good diet should look like. It's the one we want our children to eat—with six to eight glasses of water, full of fresh fruit and vegetables, a sampling of complex carbohydrates, and minimal fatty proteins. What we want to convey in this book is the analogy that word learning is (1) essential for a healthy academic life, (2) has several components that can be compared to the food pyramid (before it was recently tipped on its side) in terms of frequency and daily diet, and (3) has a scope that goes beyond learning simple definitions. Learning definitions for words is merely the tip of the pyramid!

The purpose of a strong vocabulary program is to provide students with a solid foundation for participating fully in their school experiences. Providing students with a healthy breakfast enables them to concentrate more fully on their learning. Providing students with a healthy word diet enables them to comprehend and communicate more fully.

RICH ORAL LANGUAGE

Let's start with the base of the pyramid: rich oral language. This is the foundation of our program. Compare it to drinking six to eight glasses of water every day. Although water isn't generally considered part of the food pyramid, it is essential to healthy living. Water keeps your skin hydrated, is necessary for general well-being and health, and keeps all your systems flowing smoothly. Rich oral language lubricates the system of word learning. It is an essential element of communication.

What does rich oral language look like and why is it important?

Scenario

A three-year-old picks up a rusty nail on the sidewalk.

Adult #1:   "What do you have? Let me have that!" (end of conversation)

Adult #2:   "What do you have? Oh, a rusty nail! That's dangerous, so please be careful. Can I please have that? See the sharp point at the end? It can puncture your skin and, because it's rusty, it may have nasty germs on it that can make you sick. It's not a good idea to pick up rusty sharp objects like that."

Can you see how the second adult extends the knowledge of the child through conversation in this scenario? And, in the course of the conversation, the adult has introduced words—such as *rusty, dangerous, sharp, puncture, nasty, germs,* and *objects*—within a meaningful context.

Words are primary in how we, as humans, communicate. We have both receptive and expressive vocabularies. The more extensive our expressive vocabulary, the more precisely we can convey our message to other people through written and spoken language. The more extensive our receptive vocabulary, the more likely we will be to encounter known words when we read. The child associated with the understand others and to adult in the second scenario above is more likely to understand and use the words she hears in context. Thus, when that child attempts to read and comes across the word *rusty* in a book, she can map the sounds she hears with a known word in memory. If another child hasn't had experience with the word *rusty*, he is in the more difficult position of figuring out a meaning for the word as well as decoding it. It is only when you know a word that you are likely to use it in writing and speech.

Whether we cut short or extend conversations presents differential patterns in word learning. Exposing children to the type of words found in rich oral discussions can make a difference in their academic success. Children exposed to varied vocabulary and rich discussions in homes or preschools, the type of discussion that stimulates children's thinking, have higher literacy scores in kindergarten, fourth, and seventh grade (Dickinson & Tabors, 2001). In addition, this type of environment can compensate for differences in the match between language used in homes and that used in schools (Dickinson & Tabors, 2001).

Perhaps you can see now why we put rich oral language at the base of the pyramid. Teachers and parents who engage children in discussions about the world are developing not only their understanding of the way the world works, but also an understanding of the words used to describe and explain that world.

WIDE READING AND READ ALOUD

The second foundational level of our program is active and explicit exposure to written language found in novels, picture books, poems, and informational texts. Reading aloud to students of all ages exposes them to the richness of language not found in everyday oral communication. This is the breads and cereals level of vocabulary learning, the base of the old food pyramid. We suggest at least six good-sized helpings of read aloud and independent reading throughout each day.

Not all words occur equally often in English. Some words, like *have* and *go*, are incredibly common and are a part of the 100 most common words that make up about 50 percent of the material we read. Other words, such as *exoskeleton*, occur fewer than once per one million words of text. Then there are the words in between, not incredibly common but seen regularly in text and used somewhat often in speech, such as *universe* and *risk*. Most of us use relatively few words when we talk. The language in children's books, on the other hand, is often rich and powerful (Hayes & Ahren, 1988).

The words *intricate, baffling, chalice, acquired, incalculable, inscriptions, decipher, appealed, substantial, grail, unprecedented, exceeds*, and *intrinsic* all appear on the first page of the children's book, *Greenwitch*, a 131-page novel by Susan Cooper. How often do you use such words at the dinner table? Exposure to words in stories and discussions around the words help students expand their vocabularies (Elley, 1989; Penno, Wilkinson, & Moore, 2002; Robbins & Ehri, 1994). Stopping to explain or discuss the words, as well as reading the stories several times, helps consolidate this word knowledge (Biemiller, 2004; Elley, 1989; Penno et al., 2002; Robbins & Ehri, 1994).

Independent reading is also important. Students learn both unknown words and partially known words when they read texts independently, with similar gains for each (Schwanenflugel, Stahl, & McFalls, 1997). A meta-analysis of incidental word learning found, on average, that simply reading will enable students to learn 15 percent of the unknown words they encounter. These averages are tempered by grade level, reading level, and the density of text, but even fourth graders had the probability of learning 7 percent of the unknown words that they read independently. So, fourth-grade students reading 100,000 words independently (in books where 95 percent of the words are familiar) are learning approximately 350 words from the mere act of reading this many words (Swanborn & de Glopper, 1999).

WORD CONSCIOUSNESS

Word consciousness is an appreciation and understanding of the power and uses of words as tools of communication. It is the metacognitive or metalinguistic knowledge that a learner brings to the task of word learning (Anderson & Nagy, 1992; Graves & Watts-Taffe, 2002; Scott & Nagy, 2004). When we've talked about word consciousness in other books and articles, we've talked about "marinating" children in rich language experiences. Part of this is exposure to massive amounts of rich oral and written language. Another aspect, however, is making students aware of how the language of schools might differ from their home language, learning how to express themselves more powerfully in academic language as an addition to their home language, and gaining knowledge of how language patterns work in general. This is the fruits and vegetables level of the pyramid that deserves significant attention in a word learning program. Many of us need to add this element, like fruits and vegetables, to our daily diet. Much like developing art appreciation and music appreciation, developing an appreciation for the power of words and consciousness awareness of words is an attitude and stance that permeates our interactions regarding language each and every day.

Chances of learning words increase if students pay attention to the words they encounter in reading, in listening, and in the world around them. This conscious attention can be fostered by teachers and parents when they nurture students' awareness about words as tools of communication, and awareness of how the English language packages word meanings. Knowledge about words is something that adult native speakers use almost automatically to figure out new word meanings (Nagy & Scott, 1991). However, there are elements of morphology, syntax, and the understanding of linguistic characteristics of words that can help students learn about sets of words and how to identify particular linguistic patterns. Learning words in sets by becoming conscious of these patterns will help students acquire not just specific words but also a facility to learn words in general (Scott & Nagy, 2004). Developing word consciousness involves coaching students in how words function and in how different words function differently to convey meaning. When someone wants to go with another person to lunch, a coworker might say to a colleague, "Can I come too?" or, on a more formal occasion, "Would it be appropriate if I attended as well?" However, a young child might say, "I wanna go!" Knowing when and how to use these different forms of language, as well as grasping the subtle differences conveyed by the syntax and word choice, is part of understanding the complexity of language. Helping students become conscious of these differences, and helping them realize how words are related to one another morphologically and semantically, is critical to both understanding and using sophisticated academic language (Baumann, Kame'enui, & Ash, 2003; Graves, 2000; Graves & Watts-Taffe; Scott, 2004; Scott & Nagy, 2004).

PROBLEM SOLVING

The problem-solving level of word learning is the dairy and eggs level of our program. It deserves a few servings each day and adds protein to our diet.

There are several strategies available for figuring out unknown words. For some words, you can use word parts to figure out the meaning (such as *houseboat, jumped, unhappy*). In other contexts, the author defines the word in the text. It is also sometimes appropriate to use a dictionary. We need to teach these problem-solving strategies to students so that they can use them independently when they encounter words they don't know. In addition, we need to explicitly teach students how to read and use tools such as dictionaries and a thesaurus.

When we focus on word learning, we often tell teachers to teach context clues. However, learning how to use context clues is not as simple and straightforward as it might seem. Using such clues involves making inferences, figuring out which meaning of a word is appropriate and which aspect of the text is salient to the word in question. Problems also arise because context can be misleading at times (Robbins & Ehri, 1994; Schatz & Baldwin, 1986). However, there are ways to focus students' attention on problem-solving techniques that are worth doing on a regular basis. These techniques should be taught explicitly and then developed throughout the year.

Dictionaries can provide explicit information about a word's meaning that is normally only implicit in context. However, like dairy and egg products, they can be overused. The weakness of dictionaries is that they are poor tools for teaching school-aged children the meanings of new words. Miller and Gildea (1987) studied the sentences children generated when given definitions of unfamiliar words and concluded that this widely used task is pedagogically useless. For example, students take a definition such as the one for *erode*, meaning: "to eat out or eat away dirt," and create a sentence such as, "My family erodes a lot." Even when definitions were revised to enhance clarity and accuracy, student generated sentences were judged acceptable only half of the time (McKeown, 1993). Scott and Nagy (1997) found that the difficulty children experienced in interpreting definitions was primarily due to their failure to take the syntax or structure of definitions into account. Their errors reflected the selection of a fragment of a definition as the meaning of an unknown word, and half of the students were unable to make basic distinctions, such as whether the word was a noun or a verb, from a dictionary entry. Therefore, it seems important to teach students to use this tool well and to use it in small doses.

WORDS

Words are the meat of any vocabulary program. As important as it is to teach individual word meanings, we hope that you now realize the base that underlies this teaching. When we think of learning vocabulary, the individual word level is often the only one used or developed. Our program sees explicit teaching of individual words as critical, particularly in relationship to content area material. However, a diet of meat alone is not only boring but also unhealthy. We suggest that a balanced vocabulary diet contains problem-solving strategies, word consciousness, read alouds, wide reading, and rich oral language in addition to a singular focus on individual words. In fact, the more these elements can be combined in a complex and spicy meal, the more interesting word learning will become to our students.

We will come back to this basic pyramid throughout the book as a metaphor for how much and how often various activities should occur in different grades. In the next section, we'll discuss why we think this metaphor works in greater depth, given our current understanding of the nature of word learning.

The Nature of Word Learning 2

Page Number	Principle Number	Basic Principle
7	1	Word learning is multidimensional.
9	2	Words come in different types of packages.
10	3	Word learning is incremental.
11	4	Students need to develop problem-solving strategies for figuring out unknown words.

Figure 2.1   Basic Principles

If you recognize and understand the nature of word learning, you will be in a better position to teach vocabulary appropriately. This is much like knowing a few of the basic facts about cooking. Many cooks realize that you need a leavening agent to make bread rise, that egg yolk or oil will ruin a meringue, and that mixing fat, flour, and liquid properly eliminates the problem of lumpy gravy. These reactions are based on chemistry. Understanding these principles will enhance the outcome of your food, and practice and experience allow you to experiment, making basic substitutions, as long as you don't violate the principles related to the chemistry of cooking.

Similarly, understanding basic principles about word learning can enhance the outcome of your vocabulary program. In this section, we explain some of these principles. Understanding them will help you adjust the guidelines and information in this book to fit your students and your individual context for teaching and learning.

BASIC PRINCIPLE #1: WORD LEARNING IS MULTIDIMENSIONAL

Words are often thought of as solitary units. However, we think of words as complex and multidimensional. What does that mean? First, it means that there are several different levels of word knowledge that range from knowing a word well enough to define it on a test to vaguely understanding it. In addition, you can think of words as objects suspended in a three-dimensional matrix of knowledge with links to knowledge about the world, links to knowledge about linguistic features of the word, and links to knowledge about other words. For instance, the word *articulate* can be defined as a verb meaning "to express thoughts coherently," and as such might be used in the sentence, "It's important to articulate your feelings." In addition to knowing this definition, you may recognize that *articulate* can also be an adjective, as in "She gave an articulate speech for commencement." You might also know the antonym, *inarticulate*, and realize that the prefix *in-* means "not." As a sophisticated language user, you are probably aware of instances when you would use the word *articulate* rather than the word *talk*, though articulation is a type of talking. However, *articulation* can also refer to the ways in which community college credits transfer to a university. *Articulate* and *articulation* would be connected in this matrix of knowledge, along with *articulated*, *articulating*, and *articulates*. Other words with related meanings might be attached as well, words such as *pronunciation*, *clear*, *coherent*, *lucid*, *eloquent*, and *enunciate*. In some places, *articulated buses* (long buses with a pivotal joint in the middle) are used. They might also be attached to this network of knowledge related to the word *articulate*. From this brief example, we hope you are able to see how words are not isolated units, but rather complex entities that often have multiple meanings depending on the context (Nagy & Scott, 2000).

Different words also have different stylistic registers. A stylistic register conveys when and how a word is used in context. *Articulate* is a less common word than *talk* and a more common one than *enunciate*. It is likely to be used in a more formal or academic setting to pass judgment on another person's ability to communicate clearly and is the type of word one might include in a letter of recommendation. A paragraph containing the word *articulate* is more likely to also contain words such as *speech*, *concepts*, and *audience* rather than those like *bellow*, *rats*, and *umbrellas*. Although the phrases "Way ta go!" "Good job on your talk," and "You were very articulate" may express virtually identical intent, they are used in different registers. The word *articulate* also conveys more precise feedback on elements of the speech appreciated by the speaker than the other two.

A word like *articulate* may be very familiar to you and less familiar to your ten-year-old son. Words are known to different degrees by different people. In addition, one person may be able to pronounce *articulate* but not be able to distinguish it from other semantically similar words, such as *eloquent*, but another might know the definition and be able to use it well in appropriate contexts.

How This Relates to Teaching Within the Nourishing Vocabulary Program

One aim of a comprehensive vocabulary program should be to provide multidimensional knowledge about words. Activities that focus on where, how, and when to use words or phrases, activities that focus on gradations of meaning, and activities that help student make distinctions between words are useful in developing the complex network of knowledge that surrounds words.

BASIC PRINCIPLE #2: WORDS COME IN DIFFERENT TYPES OF PACKAGES

We all realize that nouns, verbs, adjectives, and adverbs behave slightly differently in English, and that instruction may vary depending on the type of word being explained. However, even these simple categories have levels of complexity. A noun can be a *count noun*, a *mass noun*, or an *abstract noun*. Count nouns are things you can count, like *windows, peanuts, clocks,* and *shoes*. Mass nouns are things you can't count, like *sunshine, traffic, dust,* or *sugar*. You can see and touch count nouns and some mass nouns (concrete objects) but you can't see or touch abstract nouns such as *government, friendship, grief,* or *courage*.

To explain a concrete noun, we often pull in information about the superordinate category of a word. For instance, you might explain to a child that a *pelican* is a type of bird (superordinate category) with a large pouch under its beak used for catching fish (descriptors). This type of explanation also works well for many verbs. For example, *jogging* can be defined as "running at a slow and steady pace." But, you can show a picture of concrete nouns, while the visual explanation of concrete verbs requires a video. Abstract concepts are, by definition, not easily pictured. These include verbs that can't be pictured such as *need, owe, love,* or *fear*.

This is a superficial treatment of the complexity of English nouns and verbs, and we haven't even covered adverbs and adjectives. However, in the interest of space, we refer you to other resources both on the Internet and in books in Appendix A.

Michael Graves (1986) recognized that teaching words that represent new concepts for students should be distinguished from teaching words that are close synonyms for known concepts. Although it is relatively easy to teach a word like *feline* for which a common synonym (*cat*) exists, it is much harder to teach words that represent new or difficult concepts, such as *gravity* or *democracy*. When you are teaching new or difficult concepts, both the label and conceptual knowledge must be developed. For instance, if a Spanish-speaking child knows about cats, it is a relatively simple process to tie both English words, *cat* and *feline*, to *el gato*, the familiar Spanish word for a cat. But, teaching about the arctic habitat, for instance, may involve developing both new conceptual information and new labels.

Another type of word learning involves learning about nuances of meaning in words that fall along a continuum. For example, there is a continuum for describing temperature that ranges from *hot* to *cold*. Along the continuum are words like *frigid, chilly, cool, warm, scorching, torrid,* and *blistering*. These words are not synonyms for *hot* and *cold*, but describe gradations of *hot* and *cold*. Although *torrid* or *frigid* may be new words, and are not synonymous with known words, they are related to these known concepts and their definitions depend on understanding that they are extreme ends of the continuum. (We won't even go into the metaphorical uses of these words!)

Graves (1986) also points out that words can have multiple meanings, and that often students are not learning new words, but expanding the network of knowledge about words that they know. Thus a student may know the word *break*, as in *breaking bones* or *breaking china cups*, but not realize that waves can *break* on the shore.

The idea of building an associative network of knowledge around words helps us think about the type of instruction that will be most appropriate. When people learn new word meanings, they could be building a new concept and creating new links (as in the case of *gravity*); attaching a new label to a known concept (such as gluing *feline* onto the concept of *cat*); recognizing nuances of words (for example, *frigid, cool, scorching*); or expanding the domain of a label (that is, recognizing new meanings for a known word).

How This Relates to Teaching Within the Nourishing Vocabulary Program

Paying attention to the type of words that are being taught will influence the depth and breadth of your teaching. Concrete nouns can be taught through pictures and concrete verbs can be taught through demonstration or video, but abstract nouns and verbs can only be conveyed through other words. When we are teaching words, we need to recognize whether the words are new concepts, new labels for old concepts, an expansion of meaning for a known word, or an expansion within a known category of words. The last three types are going to be more easily learned than words that represent entirely new concepts. However, developing conceptual knowledge builds world knowledge and this is one of the ultimate goals of schooling.

BASIC PRINCIPLE #3: WORD LEARNING IS INCREMENTAL

It is fairly well established that the networks of knowledge described in the first principle continue to develop over time (Stahl, 2003). Although there may be some variation due to differences in types of words, for many words there appears to be an initial fast mapping of new words into general categories or associations. However, it takes multiple exposures to the word to build up enough knowledge to be able to use it comfortably. As a word is encountered repeatedly over time, information about it builds up and the word moves up the continuum toward known.

Repeating a word supports students' understanding of its meaning as well as how it can be used in various contexts. If we really want students to know a word, we need to keep coming back to it. McKeown, Beck, Omanson, and Pople found that "for virtually every instructional goal, more encounters with a word yields better outcomes than fewer encounters" (1985, p. 534).

The different contexts in which a word occurs will provide different types of information to the word learner. As an example, a common word like *red* provides a different mental image in the phrases *a red-headed Irishman* and *a stream of bright red blood*.

How This Relates to Teaching Within the Nourishing Vocabulary Program

As teachers, we need to provide multiple exposures to words. Pointing out instances of the same word, even if it is in a different form, can help consolidate word knowledge.

BASIC PRINCIPLE #4: STUDENTS NEED TO DEVELOP PROBLEM-SOLVING STRATEGIES FOR FIGURING OUT UNKNOWN WORDS

Several strategies are available for figuring out unknown words. For some words, you can use word parts to figure out the meaning (that is, *houseboat, jumped, unhappy*). In some texts, particularly textbooks created for school-age populations, the author defines the word in the text using appositives (see sidebar). At other times an appropriate strategy is to go to a reference text, such as a dictionary.

> An *appositive* is a noun or noun phrase that renames another noun right beside it. Example: An exoskeleton, or hard outer shell, protects the insect.

To problem solve word meanings, students need to recognize when they don't know a word, and then to draw on their knowledge of the world (semantic knowledge), knowledge of how English packages words (linguistic knowledge), and knowledge of ways to figure out word meanings (strategic knowledge). Just as they need to learn to use a variety of cues in early reading, word learners also need to learn to cross-check these clues.

How This Relates to Teaching Within the Nourishing Vocabulary Program

We need to teach word learning strategies to students as well as teach them how to read dictionary definitions well. Activities that focus on problem solving using word parts, understanding appositives, thinking about what they already know about words, using context wisely, and understanding how dictionary definitions convey meaning are all important strategies to enhance word learning.

SUMMARY

These four basic principles will take you a long way in developing and planning an appropriate vocabulary diet in your classroom: (1) word learning is multidimensional, (2) words come in different types of packages, (3) word learning is incremental, and (4) students need to develop problem-solving strategies for figuring out unknown words. These allow you to examine the word-learning activities you might implement in your classroom more critically. Does your instruction help students develop multidimensional words schemas? Are you differentiating between words that require a significant amount of teaching (words that represent new concepts), and words that are synonyms for known words? Are you coming back to words multiple times? Are you teaching students how to use their semantic, linguistic, and strategic knowledge to figure out word meanings? Given these four principles and an understanding of the types of word-learning tasks in the vocabulary pyramid, are you providing a nutritional balance of word learning in your classroom? If not, this book is designed to help you achieve this balance.

Before we began our description of ways to achieve a nutritional balance of word learning in classrooms, there are two other areas to address. The first involves the overall goal of a balanced vocabulary program, and the second, the ways one might go about choosing words to teach.

Developing an Overall Vocabulary Plan 3

This chapter provides useful background knowledge for articulating overall goals in vocabulary instruction. The following factors are important to consider as you plan for your students and your school.

THE VOCABULARY GAP

Most of you may be aware of the vocabulary gap between particular segments of the population in the United States. Several research studies have documented that some children enter school knowing only a fraction of the words commonly found in schools compared to the number of school-related terms that their privileged peers know (Biemiller, 2004; Chall, Jacobs, & Baldwin, 1990; Hart & Risley, 1995) and that these differences increase over time. Several factors contribute to these differences, such as the amount and type of verbal communication in English and exposure to written forms of English, instruction given in an unfamiliar register, and students' willingness to embrace such a register. Regardless of the causes, it is clear that this gap widens throughout the years and can result in huge differences in word knowledge.

Estimates vary widely, but a conservative estimate is that an average native speaker of English knows 4,000 to 5,000 base words when he or she enters kindergarten (Biemiller & Slonin, 2001), and learns about 2,000 to 3,000 new words each year (Anglin, 1993; Beck & McKeown, 1991; Nagy & Herman, 1987; Stahl & Nagy, 2006). Much of this learning comes from exposure to the language of books, because oral language tends to rely on a smaller set of words.

Now, consider the consequences of limiting exposure to new vocabulary words by focusing narrowly on decoding and fluency in primary classrooms. Those children who most need exposure to the academic forms of language found in schools are not getting that exposure when they only hear or read stories containing sentences like *Nan sat in the van*. An environment that limits students' exposure to rich language has dire consequences for children who depend on classroom instruction to develop the language skills necessary for success in school.

THE BIG PROBLEM OF SMALL VOCABULARIES

Text difficulty escalates rapidly as children move into the upper grades. Although they may have mastered decoding skills, children who depend on schools for literacy are often overwhelmed by the challenge posed by textbooks and novels with complex language and vast numbers of unknown words. Upper-grade textbooks are characterized by extensive use of academic vocabulary—words that express complex ideas in disciplines such as social studies, science, and math. Fictional texts that students read in the upper grades are equally challenging. Novels and stories contain many rare words that are not commonly used in casual discourse. Children with small vocabularies face very big problems as they progress through school.

ENGLISH LEARNERS

English language learners (ELLs) are confronted by even greater challenges than native English-speaking students with limited vocabularies. Depending on the age of entry into American schools, English learners face a vocabulary gap that may exceed tens of thousands of words (Graves, 2004; Nagy & Anderson, 1984; Nagy & Herman, 1987). Well-meaning teachers may be reluctant to push English learners, concerned that academic pressure will raise the students' affective filter (Krashen, 1994) and increase their stress level. Many of the texts designed for English learners set low expectations in terms of vocabulary, often identifying as few as ten instructional words per unit of instruction. Students who are taught ten words per week are likely to learn fewer than 400 words in a school year (Snow & Kim, 2007). At that rate, English learners' progress in school is likely to be agonizingly slow. Students may not know English well enough to acquire vocabulary from reading, limiting their exposure to grade-level academic content. Spanish-speaking students face particularly challenging circumstances due to their isolation in highly segregated schools and communities (Gándara, Rumberger, Maxwell-Jolly, & Callahan, 2003). These students may encounter few opportunities to hear or speak English outside of the classroom. We believe that English learners need intensive vocabulary instruction designed to accelerate vocabulary acquisition in English if they are to succeed in American schools. Too often, instruction falls short. English learners remain in supportive language settings for years, never attaining the vocabulary and language proficiency necessary for academic success.

Fifteen-year-old José was born in Mexico, but he has attended school in this northern California neighborhood since kindergarten. José speaks English fluently, but his academic vocabulary is limited and he reads at approximately the fourth-grade level. Despite ten years of attendance in American schools, José remains in a sheltered English class that is classified as far below basic. He rarely speaks English outside of the classroom, preferring to socialize with other Spanish-speaking students and returning to a home where no English is spoken. After many years of academic failure, José does not expect to pass the California high school exit exam. He drops out of school as soon as he turns sixteen.

THE CHALLENGE OF ACCELERATING VOCABULARY ACQUISITION

Accelerating students' vocabulary acquisition is a challenge that entails reconceptualizing vocabulary instruction. Our goal in writing this book is to help teachers identify and overcome instructional challenges, providing students with a well-balanced diet of vocabulary instruction. We will begin by identifying the vocabulary-related challenges that are common to many classrooms and schools: choosing words to teach (and not to teach), finding sufficient time to devote to vocabulary instruction, teaching enough words, expanding instruction to encompass all subjects in the curriculum, using research-based methods of instruction, and articulating vocabulary instruction between grade levels.

Choosing Words to Teach (and Not to Teach)

Judy was reading a fourth-grade textbook on California the other day and came across two words, *tomol* and *wot,* that the publisher had pulled out for focus in the vocabulary sidebar and defined within the text. Neither word is in the dictionary available on her computer, nor have either of the authors, both university reading professors, ever heard or used these words. It turns out, according to this book, that *tomol* is a word in the Chumash language for the type of canoes that members of that California coastal tribe built and used in the eighteenth century. *Wot* is the Chumash word for "leader." On the same page were words such as *astonish* and *plentiful.*

The class reading this book is a relatively typical fourth-grade class. There are thirty-three students with one fifth-year teacher. Of these students, four are identified as limited English proficient and have either Spanish or Mixtec as their native language, another three have been transitioned and are now considered fluent English proficient, six additional students were born and raised in California but speak Spanish primarily in their home, one is Vietnamese, three are African American and more than 60 percent of the students qualify for the free or reduced lunch program. If I were their teacher, would I single out words such as *tomol* and *wot* for additional instructional focus? Why or why not? And what principles underlie that decision?

We explicitly value the introduction of both the language and the culture of the Chumash people. However, these words are defined in the text and give students the opportunity to use relatively simple problem-solving techniques to discover the meaning of the words. In addition, there are more than 500,000 word-level entries in the current version of the *Oxford English Dictionary* (2004). Of those, we commonly use about 5,000 in everyday oral conversations. Some words occur so rarely that we may only hear or see them once or twice in a lifetime of reading (this includes words such as *tomol* and *wot*). Other words occur more frequently but are not your common everyday words (this includes words such as *astonish, serendipitous,* and *microorganism*).

As a teacher, your instructional time is limited. Do you really want to spend much time with words that students will rarely see again?

> **Key principle for choosing words to teach:**
>
> *If you are taking the time to teach this word, make sure it's a word that students really need to know.*

Part of this equation would entail an understanding of how often this word might be seen or used in grade-level texts. Another part is whether the word can be understood as a different label for a known concept, and whether this different label is useful or important beyond the text being read. Although there have been attempts to categorize words by difficulty ratings, words are squiggly characters and such ratings are often compromised by multiple meanings for words and metaphoric use of language. One widely acclaimed source for an estimation of a word's difficulty is the *Living Word Vocabulary* (Dale & O'Rourke, 1981), which provides a grade-level ranking for a large corpus of words (words are ranked as known by at least two-thirds of the sample of students in designated grades four through sixteen). These estimates have been reworked by Biemiller (2004, 2005), who claims that children learn words in a relatively predictable and consistent order. This makes some sense if you consider that words occur more or less frequently in English. Counts of word frequency can be found in indices such as *The Educator's Word Frequency Guide* (Zeno, Ivens, Millard, & Duvvuri, 1995), which estimates the frequency of words that school-aged children encounter, based on more than 60,000 sample grade-level texts. Using such an index can help a publisher decide which words are worth instructional time. Unfortunately, a recent examination of the vocabulary lists for each grade level from one prominent publisher revealed little evidence that word frequency or a developmental sequence was followed. In fact, the identification of vocabulary words for instruction appeared to be quite arbitrary. An analysis of several stories in the fifth-grade reading anthology revealed no evidence of word selection based on difficulty or frequency indices. Fifty percent of the words on the vocabulary list were ranked at the twelfth-grade level or higher (LWV) in terms of difficulty, with an average frequency (WF) of less than two exposures in the fifth-grade reading corpus. Analyses of other stories revealed a similar pattern—that is no pattern—in terms of word selection. Word selection decisions appeared to be entirely random at every grade level.

This becomes a tremendous problem when teachers are pressured to follow the teacher's guide without deviation. Recently, Shira worked with teachers in a large urban school district on vocabulary instruction. At the end of the first day of the workshop, a teacher asked, "How can we use your methods and maintain program fidelity?" Shira was puzzled and inquired as to what she meant by "program fidelity." The teacher replied, "It means that you have to follow the teacher's guide exactly. You can't change anything. So, we have to teach the words in the basal vocabulary list whether they are worth teaching or not."

We were taken aback by the degree to which the teachers are being pressured to relinquish their own judgment regarding literacy instruction, including the teaching of vocabulary. Thus the first challenge that teachers face in designing a nourishing vocabulary program is to balance teacher judgment with publisher recommendations in choosing words to teach. This also means that district and state personnel must give teachers the flexibility to do so.

A Tale of Three Teachers

Mrs. Rogers teaches fifth grade in an upper-income suburban elementary school. A probationary teacher, Mrs. Rogers is careful to follow the mandated curriculum, teaching each page of the reading anthology based on the teacher's guide, including the words on the weekly vocabulary list. Mrs. Rogers is humiliated when the principal informs her that there have been a number of parental complaints regarding the teaching of "absurdly easy" vocabulary words.

Mr. Valdez teaches a class of fifth-grade students who are classified as fluent English speakers, despite very low vocabulary and reading comprehension scores. Although he is under a great deal of pressure to follow the scripted reading curriculum, Mr. Valdez understands that his students need to learn a much broader array of vocabulary than the words listed for instruction. The principal observes Mr. Valdez teaching additional words from the story and asks why he is not following the script and is teaching vocabulary that isn't listed in the teacher's guide.

Ms. Chang teaches fifth grade in a very diverse urban school. Some of her students are gifted; others have learning disabilities. Ms. Chang also has a number of students from different language backgrounds who receive English language development support. Ms. Chang attempts to follow the reading and language arts curriculum, but finds many of the activities, particularly vocabulary instruction, problematic. Her high-performing students find the words too easy. In fact most of Ms. Chang's English-only students already know most of the words that are listed for instruction. Her English learners don't know the words on the vocabulary lists but they are missing many other more fundamental vocabulary words Ms. Chang wants them to learn. She finds the vocabulary guidelines in the reading program of little value.

All three teachers are required to use the same reading program, and are expected to follow the same guidelines for vocabulary instruction, despite immense differences in their students. None of the teachers find that the mandated vocabulary curriculum meets the needs of their students.

Finding Enough Time to Devote to Instruction

Developing students' vocabulary is important and requires a sizable investment of instructional time. Children who depend on schools for literacy need comprehensible and comprehensive instruction to narrow the vocabulary-induced achievement gap. How much time is necessary? Vocabulary should be taught all day, every day! As we discuss in this book, vocabulary instruction includes a wide range of activities. such as explicitly teaching words, teaching problem solving skills, teaching word consciousness, reading aloud, and using rich oral language in classroom discourse. We suggest finding time for vocabulary instruction by embedding word learning activities in every facet of instruction. Thus the second challenge that teachers face in designing a nourishing vocabulary program is devoting enough time to vocabulary instruction.

Teaching Enough Words

During the course of our vocabulary workshops, teachers often ask, "How many words should I teach?" "A lot!" we reply. For children who depend on schools for literacy to catch up with their privileged classmates, they need to learn a huge number of words. But the pace of vocabulary instruction suggested by publishers is not likely to accelerate students' vocabulary acquisition rate (Snow & Kim, 2007). An analysis of several stories in a commonly used reading anthology reveals the extent of the problem. The teacher's guide provides a vocabulary list consisting of only seven words out of a pool of more than thirty words that might be difficult for children in a particular story. The review list for the entire theme includes thirty-two words, resulting in a vocabulary program designed to teach students fewer than 200 words in a school year. Although the reading program provides many worthwhile activities, the slow pace of instruction is a serious concern, particularly in the case of children who need accelerated vocabulary instruction to catch up with their peers.

Reading program consultants often advise teachers to limit weekly vocabulary instruction to a few words and to teach these words thoroughly. This approach, known as rich vocabulary instruction, requires up to twenty instructional minutes per word (Beck, McKeown, & Kucan, 2002; Beck, Perfetti, & McKeown, 1982; McKeown, Beck, Omanson, & Perfetti, 1983). Spending a lot of time on a few words may be effective with some students, particularly those with well-developed vocabularies. These students learn as many as 3,000 words per year, most from independent reading (Nagy, 1985, 1988; Nagy & Anderson, 1984; Nagy, Anderson, & Herman; 1987). Limiting instruction to a few words, taught in great depth, is more risky for children who depend on schools for literacy. Without the skills and motivation to read widely, less literate children will probably not acquire the vocabulary they need outside of the classroom. If they lack adequate vocabulary to support comprehension, they will find reading very frustrating. These children may resist reading, read less, learn fewer words from texts than their advantaged peers, and progress more slowly. As Stanovich (1986) points out, when it comes to vocabulary, the rich get richer and the poor grow poorer. Thus the third challenge that teachers face in designing a nourishing vocabulary program is teaching enough words to accelerate students' vocabulary development.

Expanding Instruction to Encompass All Subjects in the Curriculum

Vocabulary instruction typically takes place in the reading and language arts block in elementary school and English class in middle school and high school. Teachers select five to fifteen words, often identified in the basal reader teacher's guide, which students are expected to learn for the weekly vocabulary test. Vocabulary instruction limited to reading and the language arts does not provide exposure to enough words to expand children's vocabularies, particularly those of children who depend on schools for literacy. Teachers can greatly expand the scope of vocabulary instruction by teaching vocabulary in social studies, math, and science, in addition to language arts. When content area teachers resist the inclusion of vocabulary in their instruction, the following explanation may help: content area instruction focuses on key concepts; concepts have labels; labels are words. Content area instruction will be more effective when students master the essential conceptual and linguistic tools that underpin the discipline. Providing students with a well-balanced diet of vocabulary instruction and rich language experiences in each area of the curriculum helps to accelerate vocabulary development. Thus the fourth challenge that teachers face in designing a nourishing vocabulary program is expanding vocabulary instruction to encompass all subjects in the curriculum.

Whose Job Is This, Anyway?

Ms. Steinberg is chair of the English department in a large urban high school. She works very hard to develop the students' vocabulary, and encourages the other English teachers to incorporate research-based methods into their instruction. Ms. Steinberg knows that some of the students, particularly those who depend on schools for literacy, need more intensive vocabulary instruction. But she does the best she can during her fifty-minute English period.

One afternoon Ms. Steinberg is surprised to receive a visit from Mr. Wu, chair of the science department. Mr. Wu hands her a list of words and explains that the students do not know the vocabulary needed to comprehend their science books. He informs Ms. Steinberg that the science teachers would appreciate her help in ensuring that the English teachers provide additional vocabulary instruction in the science words. Ms. Steinberg is stunned.

Using Research-Based Methods of Instruction

When instructional time is limited, it is easy for teachers to fall back on familiar, if not very effective, methods of teaching vocabulary—asking students to look words up in the dictionary, write the words in sentences, and memorize the definitions for the weekly vocabulary test. These activities continue despite a convergence of evidence that definitional approaches are not effective in promoting vocabulary growth (Miller & Gildea, 1987; Nagy, 1985; Scott & Nagy 1997). Recent research has identified a number of more effective methods of teaching vocabulary that include direct and indirect methods of instruction (NICHHD, 2000; Stahl & Nagy, 2006). We use the vocabulary pyramid as a blueprint, incorporating direct methods, such as explicit interactive word instruction, and indirect methods, such as teaching problem-solving skills and fostering word consciousness, reading aloud to students and encouraging wide reading, and immersing students in rich oral language. Designing effective vocabulary instruction entails limiting definitional activities to the smallest part of the pyramid or eliminating them altogether. Thus the fifth challenge that teachers face in designing a nourishing vocabulary program is identifying and implementing research-based instructional methods.

Articulating Vocabulary Instruction Across Grade Levels

There are a vast number of words: as many as 88,500 distinct word families appear in the texts that students read (Nagy, Anderson, & Herman, 1987). Beck, McKeown, and Kucan (2002) have narrowed the scope to approximately 7,000 word families that are particularly useful to students. Hiebert has identified Word Zones for the 5,586 most frequent words (www.textproject.org). Between 5,000 and 7,000 is a manageable number of words to teach, if instruction were systematic and articulated between grade levels. However, word selection appears to be quite arbitrary in most reading programs, based on words that happen to appear in basal stories. For example, the word *habitat* appears on vocabulary lists at several grade levels in one commonly used reading program. Although *habitat* is an important concept, and it is important to provide multiple exposures to words, building conceptual knowledge over time, a word like *habitat* may be taught multiple times, but other essential vocabulary words may never appear on vocabulary lists at all. This arbitrary approach does not make good use of precious instructional time. A systematic way to identify words that students do not know, in the texts that are used at each grade level, with carefully sequenced word lists can help ensure that instruction focuses on as many important words and concepts as possible. Thus the sixth challenge that teachers face in designing a nourishing vocabulary program is the articulation of vocabulary instruction across grade levels.

VOCABULARY-MALNOURISHED CHILDREN IN ELEMENTARY SCHOOL

All children enter school with oral language skills that enable them to communicate with their families and communities. However, home languages differ considerably. Some children grow up in non-English-speaking homes and face the challenge of acquiring an entirely new language. Others speak forms of English that differ from the language spoken in schools and must learn a new communication style. When there is a close match between the child's home language and that of the school, literacy acquisition of the type of language found in schools is likely to be easier. Children from professional homes speak just like their teachers, making communication smooth and effortless. Children whose language differs from that of their teachers may encounter barriers as they enter school. They may feel estranged if their home language is belittled as slang or poor English. Teachers can help by accepting home languages as equally valid means of communication, while teaching children to communicate in a second language, formal English.

Limited ability to speak and understand formal English may inhibit school success, but written language presents an even greater challenge. When children enter school with little exposure to the language of books, they may be malnourished in the types of words typically found in schools. The language and vocabulary found in books are substantially different from the language of oral communication. For example, Hayes and Ahrens (1988) found that children's books have 30.9 rare words per thousand, compared to 17.3 rare words per thousand in the speech of college-educated adults. Thus, an important component of the vocabulary diet involves hearing and discussing the powerful language used in rich children's literature. The more often parents read to their young children, the greater the exposure to relatively rare vocabulary and complex language. Children who have been read to regularly have an immense advantage over children with little exposure to books.

VOCABULARY-MALNOURISHED STUDENTS IN MIDDLE AND HIGH SCHOOL

Over a period of years, virtually all children acquire the vocabulary they need for oral communication, particularly the language needed to fulfill social needs. By the time they reach middle school, most students have acquired what we call *teen speak* as their primary spoken language. This unique conversation style, often incomprehensible to adults, allows teenagers to communicate effortlessly with one another, using the fewest possible words. This oddly truncated form of English works well for oral communication because it is highly contextualized and draws on gestures, facial expressions, and shared experiences to convey meaning. The following example is a conversation between two teenage girls, discussing the events of the previous weekend.

Teen A:	What's with that? (gestures toward another girl who is glaring at them)
Teen B:	There was this party and Mike and me, you know . . . (giggles). She saw us and she flipped, no joke.
Teen A:	What did you say?
Teen B:	I was like . . . whatever. She was so pissed!
Teen A:	What'd Mike say?
Teen B:	He told me she's just some breezy.
Teen A:	Are you guys a thing now?
Teen B:	Yeah . . . we're like this (laughs and crosses fingers).
Teen A:	I'm not gonna lie, he's pretty cute.
Teen B:	Uh-huh.

The teenagers' conversation consists of sentence fragments, punctuated with words and phrases such as *you know*, *like*, and *whatever*. Because of their shared social experiences, the girls are able to fill in gaps in coherence with inferences, allowing them to communicate with a minimum number of words. Despite the lack of coherence to outside observers, conversation flows smoothly between the teenagers, regarding the familiar topic (boy-girl relationships).

When the same topic appears in literature, such as Shakespeare's play *Romeo and Juliet,* the teenagers' language skills prove entirely inadequate. Although they are familiar with the topic of the story (boy-girl relationship) and discuss it endlessly in regard to their own experiences, they are often unable to comprehend the text. The archaic language and unfamiliar vocabulary render English literature incomprehensible to students who depend on school for literacy.

Juliet: What's he that follows there, that would not dance?

Nurse: I know not.

Juliet: Go ask his name: if he be married. My grave is like to be my wedding bed.

Nurse: His name is Romeo, and a Montague; The only son of your great enemy.

Juliet: My only love sprung from my only hate!
           Too early seen unknown, and known too late!
           Prodigious birth of love it is to me,
           That I must love a loathed enemy.

(Shakespeare, *Romeo and Juliet,* Act I, Scene 5)

There are also vast differences between informal written communication between teenagers and the demands that schools place on students in terms of academic reading and writing. The following is an example of a text message, the preferred form of written communication for many young people.

CaX043:   hey!

fan29:   whatz ^

CaX043:   nm, I got a question. . . .

fan29:   k

CaX043:   do u think that u'd want 2 hang out with sarah smtime?

fan29:   pffff, I doont no. lol jeeez. wiierd question.

CaX043:   its just that I think she likes u or somtin.

fan29:   Why doesnnt she call me then?

CaX043:   bc she's SHY! god. ur sooooo unundestandin sometimes! uch.

Note that the text contains many misspellings and unfamiliar abbreviations, making it very difficult for adults to understand. Teenagers, on the other hand, find text messages a practical and efficient way to communicate. Text messages are a world apart from the formal writing required in school. When teens are asked to write a persuasive essay or analytical paper, they find it difficult to express themselves in formal English. Without an academic vocabulary and writing skills, students may be unable to produce acceptable written work necessary for success in higher education.

The Scope of the Problem

The number of students whose limited vocabulary puts them at risk for academic failure appears to be increasing. More children are living in poverty than a decade ago, a societal problem that is closely associated with underdeveloped vocabulary. The percentage of students receiving free and reduced-price lunch in California, for example rose from 40.7 percent in the 1992–1993 school year to 49.1 percent in 2004–2005 (Education Data Partnership, 2005). The population of English learners in California schools also increased, from 22.2 percent in 1992–1993 to 25.2 percent in 2004–2005. We can anticipate a great deal more growth in the population of English learners in California, as the percentage of ELLs in kindergarten in 2004–2005 was 37.5 percent.

Even our most successful students show evidence of academic malnourishment. More than 60 percent of students accepted into the California State University system (the top 33 percent of California high school graduates) require remedial instruction in English, math, or both. More than 60 percent of the freshmen accepted to the University of California Irvine (the University of California accepts the top 12.5 percent of California high school graduates) failed the writing proficiency exam. Ninety-five percent of the students placed in ESL classes at UC Irvine have lived in the United States for more than eight years (Scarcella, 2002). Although the border states such as California may not represent the nation as a whole, schools throughout the country are trying to find ways to improve educational outcomes for children who depend on schools for literacy.

WHY YOU NEED THIS BOOK

The introduction to *Nourishing Vocabulary* focuses on the challenges that confront teachers in addressing the vocabulary-related achievement gap. Schools charged with the nourishment of young learners are prompted by publishers to overfeed children with some components of literacy such as decoding and fluency, while scrimping on vocabulary instruction. Children who depend on schools for literacy and English learners bring much to school but do not typically have the breadth or depth of knowledge about words as their privileged peers. They receive instruction in only a few words per week, and rarely catch up. The consequences of the vocabulary achievement gap are devastating. Limited vocabulary development is strongly correlated with poor reading comprehension and general academic failure (Chall, Jacobs, & Baldwin, 1990; Stanovich, 1986).

What can you do about the vocabulary-related achievement gap? The first step, which you have already taken in purchasing this book, is learning about the scope of the problem and determining to make a difference in the lives of students who need you the most. The second step is changing your mind-set regarding vocabulary instruction to embrace the word *acceleration* and the idea that vocabulary instruction must be embedded in every facet of the school curriculum. The program described in this book is designed to nourish students with rich language experiences. Children who depend on schools for literacy need to learn more words, and learn them more quickly than their peers if they are to succeed in school. The goal of instruction is to accelerate vocabulary development on a massive scale, providing broad exposure to words and related concepts. Methods are comprehensive, including the teaching of words and problem-solving skills, fostering of word consciousness, and exposure to vocabulary through daily reading aloud, wide reading, and rich oral language. Instruction is designed to narrow the vocabulary gap by teaching vocabulary all day, every day, across the curriculum, and throughout the school. This book will provide you with the tools you need to be a nourishing vocabulary teacher. As you learn to prepare well-balanced lessons that integrate language and content, you will be providing students with the vocabulary they need to thrive in school.

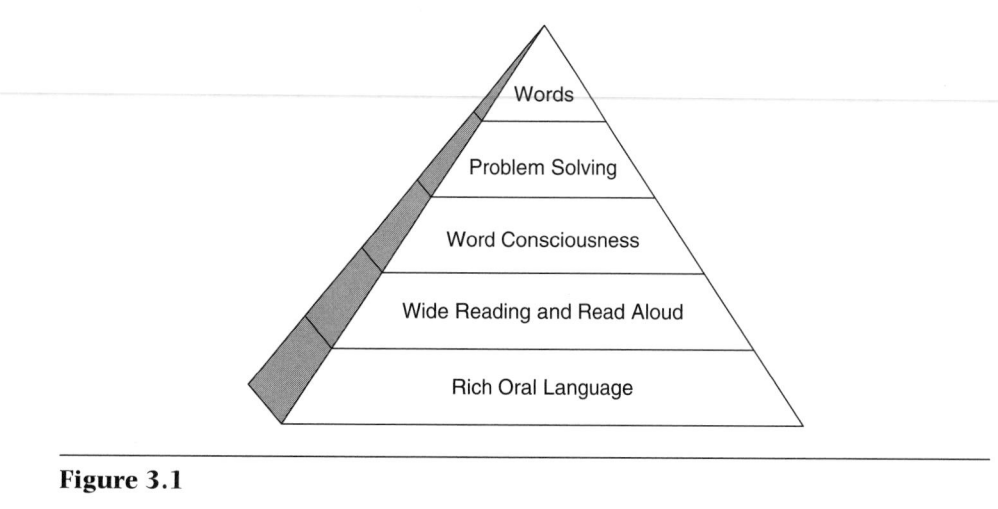

Figure 3.1

NOURISHING VOCABULARY MENU

Figure 3.2 includes a menu of instructional activities designed to address each component of the nourishing vocabulary pyramid. To avoid excessive overlap, most activities are presented in only one chapter despite the fact that they can be modified to meet the needs of students of different ages and proficiency levels. For example, many of the activities designed for English learners (Chapter 7) work equally well for upper elementary students (Chapter 5). Word sorting and feature analysis activities recommended for secondary students (Chapter 6) are appropriate for younger students when the words are selected from texts that children read or that teachers read aloud to them. Don't limit yourself to a single chapter! We suggest that you read the entire book and select a balanced assortment of Nourishing Vocabulary activities.

Vocabulary Component	Chapter Number: Page Number	Instructional Activity	Description
Words	6:96	Feature analysis	Used to review vocabulary and content
	6:89–91 7:112–114 7:118	Word sorts, SAT word sorts 2,000 most common word sorts Antonyms	Used to categorize words according to a particular semantic relationship
	6:85–86, 103, 104	Graphic organizers	Used to organize content and vocabulary
Problem solving: Self-monitoring	5:48 6:82	Stoplight vocabulary Word knowledge chart	Methods to help students evaluate their level of word knowledge
Problem solving: Clarifying strategies	5:58 6:93 7:121	Problem-solving cue card Cognates: teacher narrative	Guides students' efforts to use clarifying strategies to figure out word meaning instructional sequence for teaching Spanish-speaking students to use cognates
Problem solving: Word parts	5:58 5:57 5:59 6:105 7:123 6:100	Word part chart and sort, root web Adjective and adverb sort Root and affix chart Prefix and suffix chart Word family web Spanish prefixes News and views	Designed to build morphological awareness and knowledge of word parts Helps Spanish-speaking students acquire English vocabulary Designed to help students use Greek and Latin roots to make sense of texts
Problem solving: Context	5:51, 6:96 7:118 7:124 5:69	Context cue card Cloze Collocation frame Word frame Digging into the dictionary	Guides students' efforts to use context cues to figure out word meaning text with missing words, designed to increase students' skill at using context cues Used to practice collocations: words that belong together instructional protocol and activity used to teach dictionary skills
Word consciousness	5:63 5:65 6:103	Schema building Semantic web	Method to develop semantically related networks of words and concepts A graphic organizer of semantically related words
Wide reading and read aloud	4:40 & 5:72	Read-aloud lesson plan	Used to enhance students' vocabulary learning during read aloud
Rich oral language	5:74 & 6:87	Semantic word wall	Words from all content areas posted on a word wall to encourage use in classroom discourse
Assessment	8:148	Glossary of vocabulary assessments	Various measures of vocabulary growth

Figure 3.2   Nourishing Vocabulary Menu Assessments

NOURISHING VOCABULARY PLANNING TEMPLATES

Figure 3.3 includes a list of planning templates that can be used to organize vocabulary-enriched units and lessons across the curriculum. The planning templates are designed to be flexible scaffolds, not rigid scripts. We encourage you to experiment. Feel free to incorporate a variety of planning templates and modify them to meet the needs of your students. Reproducible templates are included in Appendix B.

Template	Level	Chapter Number: Page Number	Purpose
Planning matrix	primary (K)	4:31	Planning nourishing vocabulary instruction across the curriculum
Vocabulary-enriched lesson plan	primary (K)	4:32	Planning primary lessons that address multiple components of the vocabulary pyramid
Scaffolded discourse template	primary (K)	4:36	Planning vocabulary instruction based on oral discourse
Read-aloud lesson plan	primary (K)	4:42	Planning vocabulary instruction based on read aloud
Read-aloud lesson plan	upper elementary	5:72	Planning vocabulary instruction based on read aloud
Planning matrix	upper elementary	5:77	Planning nourishing vocabulary instruction across the curriculum
Vocabulary-enriched lesson plan	upper elementary	5:78	Planning upper elementary lessons that address multiple components of the vocabulary pyramid
Vocabulary-enriched lesson plan	secondary	6:83	Planning secondary lessons that address multiple components of the vocabulary pyramid
Unit plan: Science	secondary	6:95	Planning a vocabulary-enriched science unit for secondary students
Vocabulary-enriched lesson plan: Science	secondary	6:97	Planning vocabulary-enriched science lessons for secondary students
News and views	secondary	6:100	Planning vocabulary-enriched current events instruction for secondary students
Vocabulary-enriched cross-curricular lesson plan	secondary	6:100	Planning integrated vocabulary-enriched instruction for secondary students
Mini-lesson plan	ELL, struggling readers	7:129	Planning vocabulary mini-lessons designed to meet the needs of students below grade level
Unit planning template	all	9:154	Planning nourishing vocabulary instruction across the curriculum

Figure 3.3   Nourishing Vocabulary Templates

Planning Instruction for Primary Students 4

Vocabulary Component	Page Number	Description
Words	29	Choosing core and extended vocabulary to teach
	36	Common antonyms
Problem solving: Self-monitoring Clarifying strategies Word parts	38 39 39	Teaching problem-solving skills to young children Teaching word parts Problem-solving cue card
Word consciousness	38	Teaching word consciousness to young children
Wide reading and read aloud Read-aloud lesson plan	40–42	Scaffold teachers use to enhance students' vocabulary learning during read aloud
Rich oral language Scaffolded discourse template	36	Planning vocabulary instruction based on rich oral discourse
Planning Planning matrix Vocabulary-enriched lesson plan	29 31	Planning nourishing vocabulary instruction across the curriculum Planning primary lessons that address multiple components of the vocabulary pyramid

Figure 4.1   Planning Instruction for Young Children

The first several years of schooling are critical in terms of children's vocabulary development. Instruction that encompasses the full range of early reading skills in addition to broad vocabulary exposure lays a foundation for future academic success. Some experts recommend a narrow focus on phonics and sight words in the primary grades, with little time devoted to vocabulary until third grade or later (Shanahan, 2006). This approach allows the vocabulary-related achievement gap to continue growing unchecked for several years after children enter school. Gradually the texts get harder and it becomes evident that children cannot read if they do not understand the words (Becker, 1977; Chall, Jacobs, & Baldwin, 1990). This pattern of neglecting vocabulary until it is all but too late must change. We recommend that primary reading instruction be revamped to ensure that vocabulary receives as much attention as other components of the literacy curriculum.

A well-balanced program of vocabulary instruction is based on the nourishing vocabulary pyramid, with components of instruction listed from the top down (see Figure 4.2).

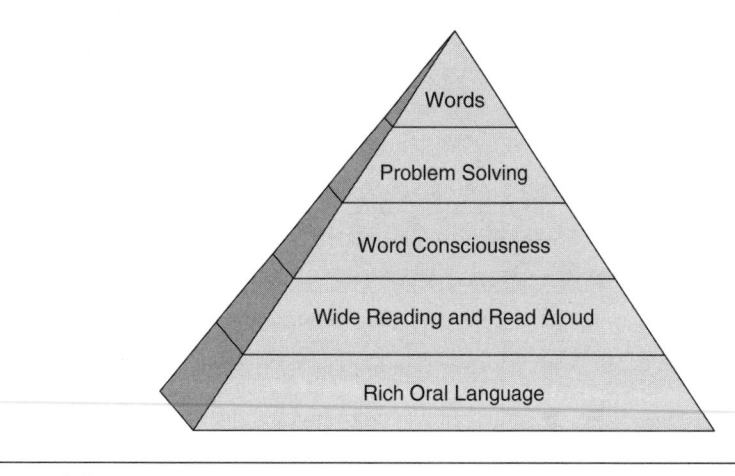

Figure 4.2

We suggest that you begin by carefully selecting uncommon, but important words from grade-level texts and provide direct vocabulary instruction based on these words. You will help your students become proficient and independent learners by teaching problem-solving skills that enable them to monitor their comprehension of words and to implement effective clarifying strategies in response to unfamiliar words encountered during reading. Children thrive in a warm, vocabulary-rich classroom, where word consciousness is developed as they interact playfully with language. We suggest that instruction focus on building word knowledge and world knowledge across content areas, helping children construct word schemata—rich networks of related words and concepts. Because young children do not read well enough to acquire the vocabulary they need through independent reading, we recommend reading aloud daily, selecting books with high interest themes and many rare words. Children should also be encouraged to develop vocabulary through wide reading as soon as they acquire independent reading skills. The most important and nourishing food group in the primary grades is rich oral language, the foundation of the nourishing vocabulary pyramid. We suggest immersing children in rich oral language by talking frequently with them about the content of instruction and encouraging them to use rich language in speaking and writing. Most important, we recommend that all of the components of the vocabulary pyramid be included each day, providing children with a well-balanced and nourishing diet of instruction.

Creating a well-balanced vocabulary program for young students requires a completely different mindset. Most primary teachers have been trained to use limited language, rarely varying their discourse beyond the 2,000 most common words. When student teachers in one of Shira's classes tried to incorporate rich oral language into instruction, their cooperating teachers reprimanded them: "Do you think the children can understand when you use big words?" The student teachers quickly learned to limit themselves to the type of limited discourse their cooperating teachers deemed appropriate. The children thus lost an important vehicle for vocabulary growth. Children do not benefit when we dumb down the language curriculum. As the vignettes in this chapter illustrate, children can understand an extensive number of sophisticated words when teachers structure classroom discourse to support comprehension. The goal of a program based on the vocabulary pyramid is to accelerate children's vocabulary acquisition.

PLANNING VOCABULARY AND CONTENT INSTRUCTION IN ALL SUBJECT AREAS

Vocabulary acceleration starts as soon as children enter school. We begin with the mandated curriculum in reading and the language arts, social studies, math, and science, identifying content objectives in each subject area and selecting books filled with rich vocabulary to read aloud to the children. After the content objectives have been identified, teachers examine the texts and identify vocabulary words that will be the focus of instruction.

Choosing Words to Teach

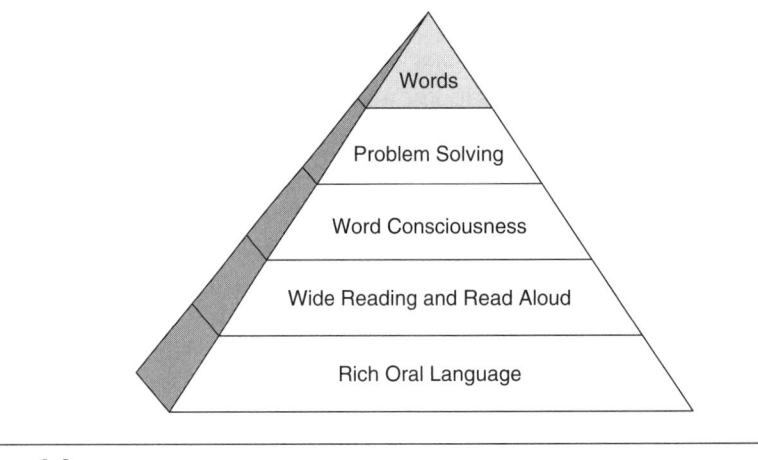

Figure 4.3

Core vocabulary words identified for explicit instruction from grade level texts are:

- Words that most children don't already know
- Words that are important to comprehension
- Words that appear multiple times in grade-level texts

Extended vocabulary words related to core vocabulary are:

- Morphological extensions that belong to the same word family (have prefixes and/or suffixes).
- Extensions are semantically related and can be used to discuss core vocabulary.

Choosing words to teach entails careful consideration of the vocabulary of the children and the vocabulary demands of the texts that will be used for instruction. *Core vocabulary* words are selected from the texts in each content area and are listed on the planning matrix. *Extended vocabulary* words are added to increase the scope of vocabulary exposure. It is important to note that vocabulary words are derived from texts that teachers read aloud to young children (see sidebar).

A series of kindergarten vignettes illustrates the process of planning and delivering nourishing vocabulary instruction.

Ms. Wolfe teaches kindergarten in a diverse urban school. She knows that many of her students have limited vocabulary and will need a great deal of instruction if they are to catch up with their more privileged peers. Ms. Wolfe uses the planning matrix (Figure 4.6) to ensure that vocabulary is embedded in every facet of her instruction. She begins with the mandated curriculum in reading and language arts, social studies, math, and science, identifying content objectives in each subject area and selecting books filled with rich vocabulary to read aloud to the children. Ms. Wolfe prepares to select vocabulary words by carefully reviewing the texts that she will use for instruction. She begins with the reading and language arts story, *The Three Billy Goats Gruff*, and selects seven core vocabulary words that appear in the story that most of her students are unlikely to know: *terrifying, troll, roar, permission, plank, hooves,* and *disappeared*. Ms. Wolfe decides that she will engage the children in a discussion of the goats' movement across the bridge. She adds six extended vocabulary words that can be used to describe movement: *stroll, trot, stomp, lumber, slither,* and *dart*. She also decides to focus on superlatives (*big, bigger, biggest*) and ordinal words (*first, second, third*) that are used in the story and can be reinforced in the other content areas. Ms. Wolfe lists the core and extended vocabulary words for reading and the language arts on the planning matrix (Figure 4.4) and identifies the vocabulary objectives for the lesson.

Ms. Wolfe reviews the social studies chapter, "Our Neighborhood," and identifies challenging words that appear in the text: *neighborhood, grocery, pharmacy, bakery, dry cleaner, cash register, employer, employee, equipment, customer, purchase, emergency,* and *fire engine, fire house, fire fighter*. She adds extended vocabulary words describing firefighters' movement (*run, leap, stomp, climb*) that she will use to discuss the story with the children, noting that these are some of the same words used to describe the Billy Goats Gruff. She decides to incorporate superlatives describing fire fighters (*strong, stronger, strongest . . .*) into the social studies lesson, providing the children with additional reinforcement of vocabulary taught during reading and the language arts.

Having completed her reading and language arts and social studies content and her vocabulary objectives, Ms. Wolfe turns her attention to the math book. She identifies content vocabulary in the series of lessons about shapes (*shape, circle, triangle, square, rectangle, object, angle*) and extended vocabulary that can be used to accelerate students' learning (*circular, triangular, rectangular, container*). Once again, she decides to include superlatives and ordinal words, providing her students with additional reinforcement of vocabulary introduced in reading and the language arts.

Ms. Wolfe considers the dinosaur unit she has planned for science and selects ten words that will be the focus of her instruction: *brontosaurus, tyrannosaurus rex, triceratops, ferocious, fierce, gentle, tiny, gigantic, huge, extinct*. She lists words that will be used to describe dinosaur movement and superlatives that can be used to compare and contrast different dinosaurs. She adds the science vocabulary, which completes the planning matrix.

Ms. Wolfe notes that if her vocabulary instruction were limited to reading and the language arts, her students would be exposed to only thirteen distinct words in the literature-based unit. However, her decision to add vocabulary objectives to social studies, science, and math will expose her students to forty-nine vocabulary words plus additional words describing movement, ordinal words, and superlatives. Ms. Wolfe knows that children will learn only a percentage of the words that have been introduced in a single unit. However, with repeated exposures and extended practice, many of these words will be learned to a level of mastery. In addition to increasing the volume of words that are explicitly taught, Ms. Wolfe will provide the children with many opportunities to practice emergent problem-solving skills and to develop word consciousness. By teaching vocabulary across the curriculum she will nearly quadruple her students' exposure to words and word learning strategies, enhancing the likelihood of accelerated vocabulary acquisition. It is clear that Ms. Wolfe has devoted a great deal of thought to the section in the planning matrix labeled Connections across subject areas. She plans to provide multiple exposures to words in different subject areas, a practice that is likely to increase the effectiveness of her vocabulary instruction. Ms. Wolfe knows that the more connections she builds across subject areas, the more likely the children are to acquire and retain new vocabulary. A cross-curricular planning matrix template is included in Appendix B.

Reading and Language Arts	Social Studies	Math	Science
Content Objectives Oral comprehension: retell story *The Three Billy Goats Gruff*	*Content Objectives* Explain the function and importance of the places in our neighborhood	*Content Objectives* Identify shapes and their attributes (*circle, triangle, square, rectangle*), sort and classify differently shaped objects	*Content Objectives* Identify dinosaurs and their attributes (*brontosaurus, tyrannosaurus rex, triceratops*)
Vocabulary Objectives Demonstrate comprehension of core vocabulary words used in the story: *terrifying, troll, roar, permission, plank, hooves, disappeared* Teach extended vocabulary related to story: *stroll, trot, stomp, lumber, slither, dart* Teach superlatives: *big, bigger, biggest, ugly, uglier, ugliest* Teach ordinal words: *first, second, third, last, then, finally, in the end*	*Vocabulary Objectives* Demonstrate comprehension of core vocabulary words used in the story: *grocery store, pharmacy, bakery, dry cleaner, shoe store, fire house* Teach extended vocabulary related to the story: *cash register, employer, employee, equipment, customer, purchase, emergency, fire engine, firehouse, firefighter*, ways firefighters move (*run, leap, stomp, climb*) Teach superlatives related to firefighters: *fast, faster, fastest, strong, stronger, strongest*	*Vocabulary Objectives* Demonstrate comprehension of core content words: *shape, circle, triangle, square, rectangle, object, container, angle, circular, triangular, rectangular* Teach prefix *tri* (3) Teach superlatives related to the objects: *big, bigger, biggest, small, smaller, smallest* Teach ordinal words: *first second, third, last*	*Vocabulary Objectives* Demonstrate comprehension of core content words: *brontosaurus, tyrannosaurus rex, triceratops* Teach extended vocabulary: *ferocious, fierce, gentle, tiny, gigantic, huge, extinct* Teach words related to how dinosaurs move: *stomp, lumber, slither, leap* Teach superlatives related to dinosaurs: *big, bigger, biggest, ugly, uglier, ugliest, fast, faster, fastest*
Connections across subject areas	Superlatives (*big, bigger, biggest, strong, stronger, strongest*), prefix *tri*, movement (*stroll, trot, stomp, lumber, slither, dart, run, leap, climb*), ordinal words (*first, second, third, last, then, finally, in the end*)		

Figure 4.4 Kindergarten Cross-Curricular Planning Matrix

Planning Vocabulary-Enriched Lessons

Now that Ms. Wolfe has completed the planning matrix, she is ready to plan individual lessons. She will design lessons that address each component of the vocabulary pyramid, always focusing on rich oral language as the vehicle of instruction. Figure 4.5 is a plan for the reading and language arts lesson, introducing *The Three Billy Goats Gruff* that Ms. Wolfe teaches to her kindergarten students. Note that she takes time to assess her students' existing word knowledge and carefully develops background knowledge about goats and trolls. She embeds vocabulary instruction in activities that occur before, during, and after reading; plans engaging discussions based on oral discourse; and develops assessments that will measure the students' vocabulary learning.

A vignette describing Ms. Wolfe's lesson follows Figure 4.7. A blank copy of the lesson planning matrix is included in Appendix B.

Note: We understand that teachers are extremely busy and may not always have time to write out complete lesson plans. The lesson planning matrix and lesson plan forms are provided as a model that can be used to develop vocabulary-rich lessons.

Vocabulary-Enriched Reading and Language Arts Lesson Plan

Lesson Date: _____ Text: _____ Chapter: _____

Standards and Objectives: Oral comprehension; retell story *The Three Billy Goats Gruff*

Vocabulary Objectives: Students will learn vocabulary from story (*terrifying, troll, roar, permission, plank, hooves, disappeared*), words related to the way we move our bodies (*stroll, trot, stomp, lumber, slither, dart*), superlatives (*big, bigger, biggest, ugly, uglier, ugliest*), and ordinal words (*first, second, third, last, then, finally, in the end*).

WORDS identify words, assess students' vocabulary knowledge	Core: *terrifying, troll, roar, permission, plank, hooves, disappeared* Ext: ways of moving our bodies: *stroll, trot, stomp, lumber, slither, dart* Ext: superlatives: *big, bigger, biggest, ugly, uglier, ugliest* Ext: ordinal words: *first, second, next, then, finally, in the end*
SCHEMA teach key concepts, build word schema	Develop goat and troll schemata: What do you know about goats, trolls? What do they look like? How big are they? How do they move? Show picture of billy goats and troll; point to their beards, horns, ears, hooves, tail, and so on.
INSTRUCTIONAL SEQUENCE	
BEFORE READING	Introduce story, preteach red-light words.
DURING READING problem-solving strategies, content	Read aloud story *The Three Billy Goats Gruff* Prob: Teach word structure: use of superlative suffixes (er, est) with words *large, small, tiny, pretty, ugly,* to describe characters in the story When rereading text, ask questions such as "Do you know that word?" and "Where have you heard that word before?"
AFTER READING organize and review content, process vocabulary connections to writing	Discuss story with a focus on plot elements. Model retelling first segment of the story, encourage children to retell subsequent parts of the story.

RICH ORAL LANGUAGE	Reread the story *The Three Billy Goats Gruff*, stopping to discuss core vocabulary. Use ordinal words (*first, second, third, last, then, finally, in the end*) and superlatives (*big, bigger, biggest*) to describe what happened in the story. Ask children to pretend to be trolls, make terrifying face, show different ways of moving (*strolling, trotting, stomping across the bridge*) Leaving the classroom: ask children whether they would like to pretend to be trolls that stomp or goats that trot.
Assessment	Superlatives: Provide pictures of goats and trolls of different sizes. Children color the big goat or trolls red, the bigger goats or trolls blue, the biggest goats or trolls green. Assess for accuracy. Ordinal words: Sequence chart. Children put pictures from the story in the correct order and retell the story using ordinal words.

Figure 4.5   Vocabulary-Enriched Reading and Language Arts Lesson Plan

Rich Oral Language

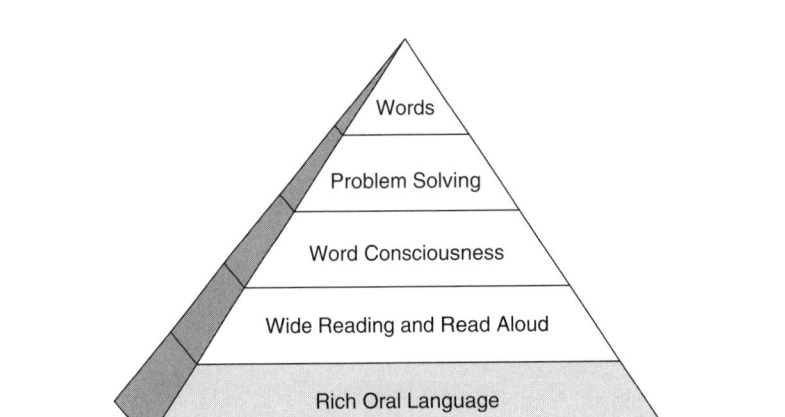

Figure 4.6

Rich oral language is the foundation of the vocabulary acceleration program. The following vignette illustrates nourishing vocabulary methods in a kindergarten class as Ms. Wolfe reads the story *The Three Billy Goats Gruff* aloud and leads a discussion, using core and extended vocabulary related to *The Three Billy Goats Gruff.*

Ms. Wolfe:	How did the Billy Goats Gruff go across the bridge?
Children:	Trip trap, trip trap.
Ms. Wolfe:	That's right! The Billy Goats' hooves clattered on the wooden planks of the bridge, like this (taps the table with blocks to simulate the sound). Let's pretend that this carpet is the bridge. Can you pretend to be billy goats crossing the bridge?
Children:	(Children get up and walk across the carpet.)

(Continued)

(Continued)

Ms. Wolfe:	Good! You are strolling slowly across the bridge (taps blocks slowly). Now, pretend you are in a hurry (taps blocks with a faster rhythm). Benji, it looks you are trotting across the bridge.
Benji:	Yeah! I'm a big billy goat!
Ms. Wolfe:	Okay, now pretend that you see a terrifying sight: it's the troll. You are terrified (she makes a terrified face). How would you cross the bridge now? (She taps the blocks very fast as the children run across the carpet pretending to be terrified.) Okay, boys and girls, the terrifying troll has disappeared. You can sit down. Now, let's pretend that YOU are trolls. How would you cross the bridge if you were a troll?
Children:	(Children make scary faces and stomp across the carpet.)
Ms. Wolfe:	Great! Anna, are you stomping across the bridge, like a troll?
Anna:	Yeah, I'm a scary troll! (Anna stomps again.)
Ms. Wolfe:	Okay, great job! You are certainly terrifying trolls! Now, let's pretend you are elephants. How do elephants cross the bridge?
Children:	(Children get up and pretend to lumber across the carpet like elephants.)
Ms. Wolfe:	Jamil, are you lumbering across the bridge?
Jamil:	Yeah, I'm a daddy elephant.
Ms. Wolfe:	Jamil, what are you doing with your arms?
Jamil:	I'm making the elephant's nose.
Ms. Wolfe:	Great! You're making the elephant's trunk with your arms. Everyone look! Jamil is a daddy elephant, lumbering across the bridge and swinging his trunk.

Ms. Wolfe engages the children in a discussion that draws on story content and vocabulary. She has the children act out different kinds of motion, provides auditory cues (tapping blocks on the table), gestures (making faces), and uses the new vocabulary words multiple times. She also capitalizes on spontaneous word learning opportunities, teaching words such as *the elephant's trunk* (Jamil's contribution). Ms. Wolfe continues to use extended vocabulary throughout the day, including words such as *trot, stomp, lumber, dart,* and *slither.* Whenever the children leave the classroom they select a type of motion to go from place to place. For example, the children decide to lumber like elephants on their way to lunch and stomp like trolls back from recess.

During math time, Ms. Wolfe teaches the children to identify the attributes of triangle-, rectangle-, and circle-shaped objects, using attribute blocks. She maximizes the effectiveness of vocabulary instruction by planning classroom discourse to include words such as *shape, object, size, angle, container, triangle-triangular, rectangle-rectangular,* and *circle-circular.* Ms. Wolfe supports the children's vocabulary acquisition by providing comprehensible input, a phrase borrowed from the English language development literature (Krashen, 1994). She uses pictures, realia, and gestures to help children comprehend the sophisticated vocabulary that she embeds in content area instruction. The following example from a math lesson demonstrates the difference between unplanned classroom discourse and discourse that is designed to provide comprehensible input and exposure to rich vocabulary.

Normal discourse: The teacher says . . .

"Let's put the shapes into the boxes. The triangles go here (puts a triangle in a box), the rectangles go here (puts a rectangle in another box), and the circles go here (puts a circle in a third box)."

Rich oral discourse: Ms. Wolfe says . . .

"Look at the pile of attribute blocks on the table (points to the blocks). Let's sort these objects by shape. This object is circular (the teacher holds up a circle and runs her finger around the circumference). Circles are round. First we will put a circle in the container (puts a circle in the appropriate container). This object is rectangular (holds up a rectangle and points to the four angles). Rectangles have four angles. Next, we will put a rectangle in the container (puts a rectangle in the appropriate container). This object is triangular (holds up a triangle and points to the angles.) Triangles have three angles. Last, we will put the triangle into the container (puts the triangle into the appropriate container). Now, let's sort these objects by shape and put them in the containers. The circular objects go in this container (puts a circle in the box), the rectangular objects go in this container (puts a rectangle in another box), and the triangular objects go in this container (puts a triangle in a third box)."

After the children have sorted the objects by shape, Ms. Wolfe discusses the size of the objects, using superlatives. She asks the children to identify the small, smaller, and smallest circles, the big, bigger, and biggest triangles, and so forth. Ms. Wolfe also provides a framework for word family instruction by using related words in her discourse with the children. For example, she discusses the attribute blocks using the words *circle* and *circular, rectangle* and *rectangular, triangle* and *triangular* to build broader vocabulary knowledge.

Rich oral discourse provides children with exposure to many more words than conventional discourse, but changing the way you speak to your students is not easy. We suggest posting a list of core and extended vocabulary on the classroom wall in the early stages of instruction and writing sample phrases, using the new words. Over time, incorporating rich vocabulary into your discourse becomes natural and requires less detailed planning. Figure 4.7 demonstrates the use of a scaffolded discourse template to develop rich oral discourse. A blank scaffolded discourse template is provided in Appendix B.

There are countless opportunities throughout the day to develop children's vocabulary through rich oral language. Teachers can embed instruction with activities that children enjoy such as the opposites game. The teacher begins by modeling a pair of antonyms children are certain to know, such as *big* and *little*. Then the teacher invites the children to respond to the prompt *happy*. When a child responds with the correct antonym, *sad*, it is his or her turn to generate the next antonym pair. Children sometimes have trouble coming up with a word that has an opposite, but with practice, they gain proficiency at the opposites game. The following list of antonyms could be developed with students and posted in the room as support for the game. Additional antonym pairs are provided in Chapter 8 and in Appendix B.

Subject: Reading	Vocabulary	Scaffolded Discourse
Story/Content	*terrifying, troll, roar, permission, plank, hooves, disappeared, trot*	A *terrifying* troll lived under the *planks* of the bridge. The Billy Goats Gruff wanted *permission* to cross the bridge to eat the grass on the other side. The littlest goat *trotted* across the bridge. The troll heard the *clatter* of his *hooves* and *roared* that he would eat the littlest Billy Goat Gruff.
Words related to goats, trolls	*hooves, beard, horns, shaggy fur, trot, terrifying, roar*	Goat: Look at the picture: the goats have little *hooves, beards, horns,* and *shaggy fur.* Troll: Look at the picture of the troll. Isn't he a *terrifying* sight? Imagine how the goats felt. They must have been *terrified* by the troll.
Problem-solving skills: superlatives, ordinal words	*big, bigger, biggest, ugly, uglier, ugliest, first, second, third, last, then, finally, in the end*	Color the picture of the *biggest* goat green. Which troll was the *ugliest*? Which goat crossed the bridge *first, second, and third*? What was the *first* thing that happened in the story? What happened *next, last*?
Classroom directions	*permission, stroll, trot, stomp, lumber*	Whose turn is it to be *first, second,* and *third. . .*in line? Would you like to *stroll, trot, stomp,* or *lumber* to music? Let's *lumber* like elephants on our way to lunch and then we'll *stomp* like trolls on the way back. You have *permission* to go to recess.
Other		

Figure 4.7   Scaffolded Discourse Template: *The Three Billy Goats Gruff*

Common Antonyms

big-little	*slow-fast*
happy-sad	*before-after*
pretty-ugly	*young-old*
good-bad	*poor-rich*
hot-cold	*light-dark*
day-night	*win-lose*
up-down	

Building on this activity, you can discuss shades of meaning for other words you encounter (for a further description of this activity, see Scott, Skobel, & Well, 2008). Many of these pairs are points on a continuum. Along the continuum are many other words. *Frigid* is not just an antonym of *cold*, it means "very cold"; *warm* is less hot than *boiling*. When you read aloud from books, you can identify and collect these gradations as well as develop other antonym pairs such as *warm-cool* and *blistering-frigid*.

Another vocabulary game that can be played in an oral context is the describing game. The teacher begins this game by modeling the process as follows.

Ms. Wolfe:	Let's think of words to describe this picture (holds up a picture of a golden retriever). Cute . . .
Theresa:	Soft?
Ms. Wolfe:	Good! Who can think of other words to describe the dog?
Max:	Yellow.
Danny:	Big.
Susie:	Furry.
Ms. Wolfe:	Okay! We have a cute, soft, yellow, big, furry dog. That describes the dog's appearance very well. Now, let's try to imagine his temperament— does he look like a nice dog? What words could we use to describe his temperament?

The activity continues with the children generating additional words to describe the dog. Note that the teacher uses rich words such as *appearance* and *temperament* to extend the children's vocabulary. Once the children have gained proficiency with the describing game, the teacher initiates play without a picture. The teacher encourages the children to think of an imaginary creature such as a dragon and to describe its appearance, temperament, and behavior. Each time the game is played other imaginary creatures are described.

A familiar game that can be used to build vocabulary is twenty-one questions. The teacher begins by telling the students that she is thinking of something and the children are given twenty-one chances to correctly identify the mystery item. Guesses must be answered either yes or no. Usually, the children guess randomly and are not very successful in their initial efforts. The teacher points out that they will do much better if they begin by asking what she refers to as big questions. She teaches the children to sort possible items into categories such as person, place, or thing, animal, mineral, or vegetable; living or not living; and to use categories as the basis of their questions. With a little practice, the children soon learn to question efficiently and are more often successful. The game can also be played with items that are found in books that are read in class or content that has been studied. For example, after completing the story *The Three Billy Goats Gruff*, the teacher could tell the children that she is thinking of something in the story. The children have twenty-one questions to figure out the identity of the mystery item (the bridge). The game provides an enjoyable opportunity to review the content of the story. Twenty-one questions is an excellent sponge activity that can be used without props whenever there are a few minutes to spare.

Children enjoy the imaginative and playful aspects of games such as the opposites game, the describing game, and twenty-one questions. They develop word consciousness and gain valuable experience using vocabulary expressively.

TEACHING PROBLEM-SOLVING SKILLS AND WORD CONSCIOUSNESS TO YOUNG CHILDREN

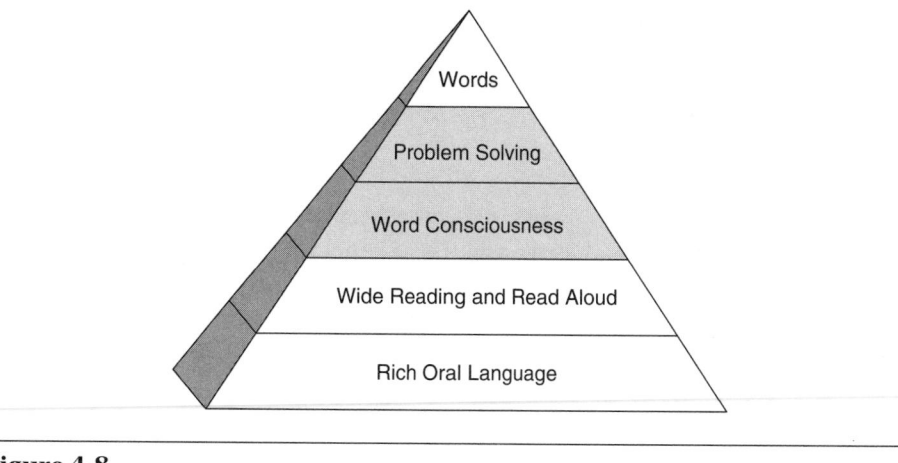

Figure 4.8

The previous examples show how classroom discourse can be a vehicle for teaching problem-solving skills and word consciousness to young children. The teacher fosters the development of word consciousness by expanding the children's awareness of how meaning is packaged into words in English (that is, gradations of temperature, size, emotion, and so on) and engaging them in playful discussions featuring rich vocabulary. The children are exposed to problem-solving skills in much the same way. Instruction takes place during read aloud as children are taught to identify and figure out the meaning of unknown words using their growing understanding of possible meanings. The purpose of instruction is to provide young children with emergent problem-solving skills that can be applied to written texts when they are older. The following strategies underlie problem-solving discussion in the primary classroom (see Figure 4.9).

In this vignette, Ms. Wolfe, the kindergarten teacher, is embedding problem-solving skills and word consciousness in a math lesson. She reviews shapes with the children and leads a discussion of the prefix *tri-*, providing a foundation for using word parts as a problem-solving strategy. By drawing the children's attention to the morphological features of words and how words are used, Ms. Wolfe helps develop emergent word consciousness in her kindergarten students.

NOURISHING VOCABULARY
PROBLEM-SOLVING CUE CARD

MONITOR
- Think about the meaning of words as you read.
- Notice when you don't understand a word so that you can fix the problem.

MANAGE THE PROBLEM
Choose a problem-solving approach. Read the sentence and think about the unfamiliar word: which of these clarifying strategies might help?

- TRY <u>MEMORY</u>: Have you ever seen or heard the word before? How was it used?
- TRY <u>TOPIC CUES</u>: What do you know about the topic that helps you figure out the word?
- TRY <u>WORD PARTS</u>: Use your knowledge of prefixes, suffixes, base words, or roots to help you fix the problem.
- TRY <u>TEXT CLUES</u>: If you are reading a textbook, use chapter titles, subtitles, headings, and boldface print to get information that might help you understand the word. Remember that key words are often defined in the text.
- TRY <u>CONTEXT</u>: See context cue cards.

MIX THE STRATEGIES
- Use more than one clarifying strategy to figure out a word.
- Always come back to context: make sure that the meaning of the word makes sense in the sentence.

MONITOR AGAIN AND MOVE ON
- Double check: does it make sense?
- When you know enough about the word to understand the text, continue reading.
- If you can't figure out the word, put a Post-it on the page and look it up later if you need to know the exact meaning.

Figure 4.9   Nourishing Vocabulary Problem-Solving Cue Card

Ms. Wolfe:	Who can describe this object for me (puts a red, triangle-shaped transparency on the overhead)?
Rudi:	It's red.
Xavier:	It's a triangle.
Amy:	It's a big one.
Ms. Wolfe:	Right! It's a large, red triangle. It has three sides, doesn't it? What do we call the space inside the triangle where two of the sides come together (points to one of the angles)?
Rudi:	Point?
Ana:	Angle?
Ms. Wolfe:	That's right; you remembered! The space inside the point of the triangle is called an angle. Let's count the angles in the triangle (points to each angle as she speaks) one . . . two . . . three . . . The triangle has three angles. Now, I have a question for you. What sound do you hear at the beginning of the word triangle?
Children:	/t/ . . . /tr/ . . . /tri/ . . .

(Continued)

(Continued)

Ms. Wolfe:	Right! Triangle begins with the sound /tri/. Now, I'm going to show you some pictures of other things that begin with the same sound. What's this (holds up a picture of a tricycle)?
Children:	It's a tricycle. I have a tricycle. I got one for my birthday. I know how to ride a big bicycle.
Ms. Wolfe:	Okay, you're right! It's a tricycle. How many wheels does it have?
Children:	Three!
Ms. Wolfe:	Good! Now, let's look at this picture of a tripod. It's used to hold a camera very still when you take a picture. Do you see three of something in this picture?
Children:	Three poles? Three legs. It has three legs.
Ms. Wolfe:	Yes, a tripod has three legs. Now, look at this (holds up a picture of a triceratops dinosaur).
Children :	(Shout excitedly.) Triceratops . . . a dinosaur . . . It has three horns.
Ms. Wolfe:	Great! You remembered that this kind of dinosaur is called a triceratops and that it has three horns. Now listen carefully (points to the picture of each object as she says the word): triangle . . . tricycle . . . tripod . . . triceratops . . . Can you hear the same sound at the beginning of each word? The prefix *tri-* means three: (points to each picture) three angles, three wheels, three legs, three horns.

It is important to note the overlap of concepts and vocabulary from different subject areas that contributes to the success of this lesson. The children have already learned about the attributes of shapes in their math lesson and have learned about dinosaurs in earlier science instruction, enabling them to readily identify the meaning of the prefix *tri-* in relation to the words *triangle* and *triceratops*. Rich oral language pervades the lesson, as the teacher engages the children in discussion and uses pictures of familiar objects to increase the success of the word learning experience.

ACCELERATING VOCABULARY DEVELOPMENT THROUGH READ ALOUD

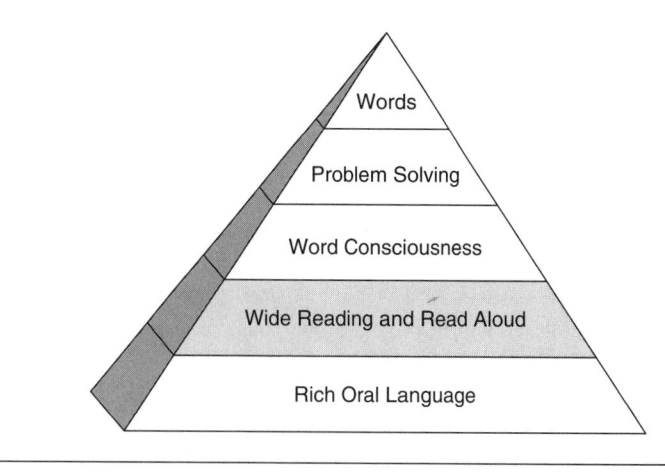

Figure 4.10

We suggest that teachers begin a read-aloud program by selecting high-interest books that are thematically related to the content objectives in one or more subject areas. For example, Ms. Wolfe selects stories such as *The Dinosaur Who Lived in My Backyard* (Hennessy, 1990) and the informational text *Dinosaurs, Strange and Wonderful* (Pringle, 1995) to reinforce content and vocabulary related to a science unit on dinosaurs. She reads the stories aloud several times over a period of days, stopping to discuss vocabulary and story concepts. Ms. Wolfe selects a variety of fiction and nonfiction books aligned to content standards in each subject area, to read aloud to the children.

It is important that books selected for read aloud are high interest and contain plenty of rich vocabulary. A variety of reading genres should be included in the read-aloud program, particularly informational texts. Children are often exposed almost exclusively to narrative texts in the primary grades, which contributes to comprehension difficulties with informational texts encountered in the upper grades.

It is important to emphasize that texts included in commercial reading programs are often unsuitable for the purpose of developing children's vocabulary. Recently, Shira was asked to provide a professional development workshop for teachers in a large urban school district. The district personnel asked her to use their adopted reading program as a basis of her presentation. She carefully inspected kindergarten, first-, and second-grade stories and found an overwhelming emphasis on decodable texts, with very limited vocabulary. She found it difficult to locate texts that had enough rich vocabulary to model the methods of vocabulary instruction included in this book. Even the stories designated for read aloud had been stripped of challenging words. She suggested that the teachers locate the original stories and read them aloud to the children, in lieu of the bland, simplified versions included in the teachers' guides.

We do not mean to suggest that commercial reading programs are lacking in all instructional value. On the contrary, most programs provide useful suggestions for teaching reading mechanics and other literacy topics. But a balanced literacy diet is incomplete without vocabulary! Vocabulary-rich read-aloud books provide children with vocabulary, language, and exposure to world knowledge that they will need to comprehend upper-grade texts. Read aloud is also used to model problem-solving skills. Teachers think aloud as they read, pausing to demonstrate how to monitor comprehension and use clarifying strategies to make sense of challenging words. As children's decoding skills and fluency develop, teachers help them apply problem-solving skills to texts that children read themselves.

The following read-aloud lesson plan (Figure 4.11) can be used to guide your thinking as you prepare to read aloud stories to your students.

YOUNG CHILDREN WITH SPECIAL NEEDS AND ENGLISH-LANGUAGE LEARNERS

Instruction based on the vocabulary pyramid provides a great deal of support to children with special needs and English-language learners. Children are

Read-Aloud Lesson Plan

Lesson Date: _____ Text: _Dinosaurs Strange and Wonderful_____ Author: Pringle, C._____

Genre: Informational Text_____ Subject Area: Science_____

Words	triceratops, velociraptor, stegosaurus, brontosaurus, tyrannosaurus, mysterious, mystery, imagine, reptiles, skeleton, discovered, fossils, paleontologists, plates, horns, jaws, teeth, claws
Word schema: dinosaur	Types of dinosaurs: triceratops, velociraptor, stegosaurus, brontosaurus, tyrannosaurus, meat eater, plant eater Body parts of dinosaurs: plates, horns, jaws, teeth, claws Learning about dinosaurs: skeleton, fossil, paleontologist Discovered dinosaur-related words: imagine, terrifying, huge, gigantic, enormous (words that describe the idea of big)
Instructional sequence	
	BEFORE READING Picture walk, preteach red-light vocabulary DURING READING Point to pictures of dinosaurs when reading their names AFTER READING Discuss prefix tri- Root word saur (Greek word for lizard)
Rich oral language	Types of dinosaurs and their body parts: A triceratops has three horns. Which kind of dinosaurs were meat eaters? What did a tyrannosaurus look like? The tyrannosaurus was a meat eater so he had strong jaws, razor-sharp teeth for biting and chewing, and deadly claws for ripping. Learning about dinosaurs and related words: Look at this picture of a dinosaur fossil. I discovered this wonderful book about dinosaurs. What do paleontologists do? Would you like to be a paleontologist when you grow up? Imagine how terrifying it would be to be chased by a huge, hungry tyrannosaurus! Which dinosaur is the most gigantic?

Figure 4.11   Read-Aloud Lesson Plan

immersed in a supportive, language-rich environment that provides them with frequent opportunities to acquire vocabulary through read aloud and classroom discourse. Teachers enhance the value of read aloud with picture walks (showing children the pictures in a story), gestures, and realia to introduce key concepts and vocabulary before reading. Support personnel such as resource teachers, English-language teachers, and reading specialists have an important role to play in the education of children with special needs and should be involved in planning carefully integrated instruction. Whenever possible, children should receive support inside the regular classroom to avoid the

fragmentation that often results when children are pulled out for special education services (Allington & Cunningham, 1996).

Children with special needs and English learners benefit greatly when their parents are involved in literacy instruction. Almost all parents want their children to succeed in school and most appreciate it when schools and teachers reach out to them. Valuing the home culture and the knowledge that students do bring with them into the classroom helps parents connect with the classroom. When parents are literate, teachers can provide texts and suggestions for developing children's vocabulary and content knowledge through read aloud. When translations are available, parents of English learners can be encouraged to read stories to their children in their native language before the stories are read in class in English. Exposure to texts in the child's native language provides background knowledge that supports comprehension and encourages vocabulary acquisition in English. When reading aloud by parents is not an option, books on tape and buddy readers are possibilities. There are many ways to support nonliterate parents in their quest to help their students. One school holds monthly Family Literacy Nights, at which a storyteller, a teacher, or a parent reads aloud from selected picture books in the evening. Children and parents bring pillows and arrive in their pajamas to sit on the floor of the multipurpose room to listen to the stories. The goal is to create an inviting environment for families.

Supporting Children With Special Needs

Resource Specialists

- Work closely with resource specialists to provide seamless vocabulary and content instruction.

Parents

- Send home texts or books on tape/CD to be read at home before they are introduced in class.
- Provide suggestions for developing vocabulary and Content knowledge through discussion.

ELL Strategies

- Use pictures, gestures, and realia to ensure comprehensible input.
- Preteach vocabulary.
- Preview texts in native language.

TRANSITION FROM PRIMARY TO UPPER ELEMENTARY INSTRUCTION

The methods presented in this chapter are designed for young children who do not yet read well enough to learn vocabulary from reading. Oral discourse is the primary vehicle of vocabulary instruction. Gradually children's reading capacity increases and they become capable of learning vocabulary from texts that they read themselves. This transition typically occurs between the end of first grade and third grade, however it may be delayed in the case of struggling readers. As children enter the upper elementary grades the vocabulary curriculum widens and incorporates a wide range of instructional activities. Teachers may wish to adapt these activities for primary vocabulary instruction by presenting them in an oral context.

Planning Instruction for Upper Elementary Students 5

Vocabulary Component	Page Number	Instructional Activity	Description
Words	46	Choosing words to teach	Identifying core and extended vocabulary words from texts
Problem solving: Self-monitoring	48	Stoplight vocabulary Word knowledge chart	Used to help students evaluate their level of word knowledge
Problem solving: Clarifying strategies	50	Problem-solving cue card	Guides students' efforts to use clarifying strategies to figure out word meaning
Problem solving: Word parts	56 58 57 59	Word part chart Word part sort Root web Adjective and adverb sort	Designed to build morphological awareness and knowledge of word parts
Problem solving: Context	51	Context cue card	Guides students' efforts to use context cues to figure out word meaning
	69	Digging into the dictionary	Instructional protocol and activity used to teach dictionary skills
Word consciousness	63	Schema building	Method to develop semantically related networks of words and concepts
	65	Semantic web	A graphic organizer of semantically related words

Figure 5.1   Planning Instruction for Upper Elementary Students   *(Continued)*

(Continued)

Vocabulary Component	Page Number	Instructional Activity	Description
Wide reading and read aloud	72	Read-aloud lesson plan	Used to enhance students' vocabulary learning during read aloud
Rich oral language	74	Semantic word wall	Words from all content areas posted on a word wall to encourage use in classroom discourse
Putting it all together	77	Planning matrix	Planning nourishing vocabulary instruction across the curriculum
	78	Vocabulary-enriched lesson plan	Planning upper elementary lessons that address multiple components of the vocabulary pyramid

Figure 5.1 Planning Instruction for Upper Elementary Students

Source: Lubliner, S. (2005b). *Getting into words: Vocabulary instruction that strengthens comprehension* (pp. 80–88). Baltimore: Paul H. Brookes Publishing Co., Inc. Reprinted by permission.

This chapter focuses on the design of effective, nutritious vocabulary instruction for upper elementary students. *Upper elementary* is defined as the level at which students read well enough to acquire vocabulary from texts. Some students reach this level as early as second or third grade. Many students, however, do so only in fourth grade or later. Upper-elementary-level activities are also appropriate for middle school students whose reading proficiency is not yet adequately developed for secondary vocabulary acquisition activities. We begin with a discussion of word selection guidelines.

CHOOSING WORDS TO TEACH

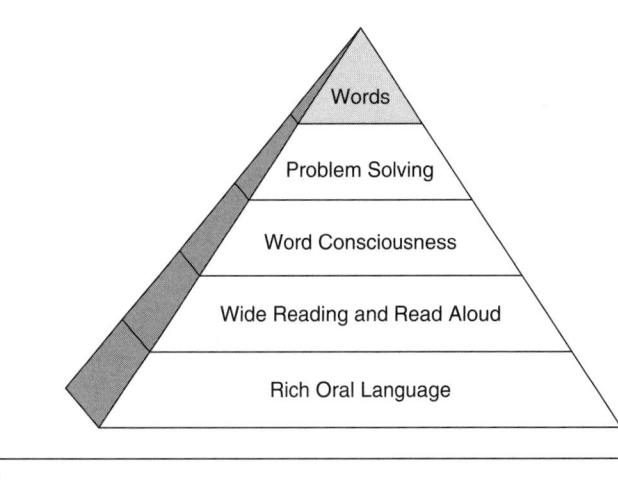

Figure 5.2

Designing systematic vocabulary instruction for upper elementary students is particularly challenging given the vast numbers of words that appear in grade-level texts and the widely varying vocabularies of the students. There are no universally accepted word lists that can be used as a basis of instruction and textbooks are of limited value in identifying vocabulary words. So, how do we choose words to teach upper elementary students? Following the guidelines provided in the sidebar, teachers review their textbooks and literature, selecting core vocabulary words that are important in each subject area. A limited number of core vocabulary words are identified for each unit because providing in-depth instruction and multiple exposures requires a sizeable investment of instructional time. Once such words have been identified, an extended vocabulary list composed of semantically or morphologically related words or words needed to discuss the topic are added. For example, a fourth-grade vocabulary list might include the core word *investigate.* Extended vocabulary words—such as *investigates, investigated, investigating, investigation,* and *investigator*—are added to accelerate learning.

> *Core vocabulary* words identified for explicit instruction from grade-level texts are:
>
> - Words that most children don't already know
> - Words that are important to comprehension
> - Words that appear multiple times in grade-level texts
>
> *Extended vocabulary* words related to core vocabulary are:
>
> - Morphological extensions that belong to the same word family (have prefixes and/or suffixes).
> - Extensions that are semantically related and can be used

THE INTERSECTION OF WORDS AND METACOGNITION

Because instructional time is limited, it is extremely important to concentrate teaching on vocabulary words that students do not already know. An effective method to accomplish this goal is a metacognitive method called stoplight vocabulary (Lubliner, 2005b). Before starting a new chapter or text, the teacher lists prospective vocabulary words on a stoplight vocabulary sheet and gives a copy to each student. The teacher asks the students to honestly evaluate their own level of word knowledge for each word. Students work independently, coloring the stoplights red for an unknown word, yellow for a partially known word, and green for a word that is known well and can be used independently in speaking and writing.

The following is an example of stoplight vocabulary based on a fifth-grade social studies textbook (Lubliner, 2005b; see Figure 5.3). A full-sized version of a stoplight vocabulary sheet is included in Appendix B.

The teacher collects the stoplight vocabulary sheets and determines which words have been colored red, yellow, and green by the majority of students. Red-light words are completely unknown and will require the greatest investment of instructional time. Teachers provide direct, intensive instruction for red-light words. Yellow-light words are partially known, suggesting that students may be able to understand them in context. Teachers can facilitate the learning of yellow-light words through problem solving instruction. Green-light words are words that students already know and can use expressively.

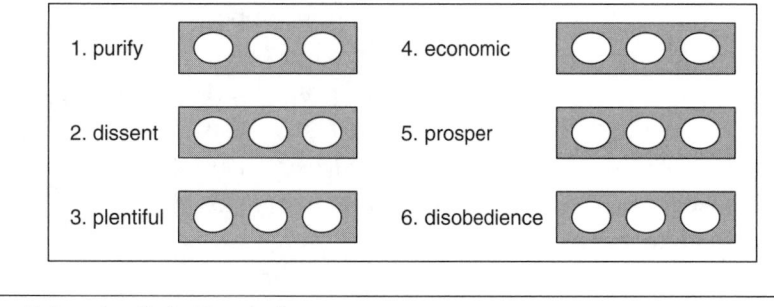

Figure 5.3   Stoplight Vocabulary

Source: Lubliner, S. (2005b). *Getting into words: Vocabulary instruction that strengthens comprehension* (pp. 80–88). Baltimore: Paul H. Brookes Publishing Co., Inc. Reprinted by permission.

Teaching green-light words to the entire class is not an efficient use of instructional time; however, teachers may need to provide mini-lessons to struggling readers and English learners who have not yet mastered these words.

A variation on stoplight vocabulary is the word knowledge chart. The teacher lists challenging vocabulary words from the textbook on a piece of chart paper. The word list is posted on an easel facing the wall, to ensure students' privacy. The students take turns placing red, yellow, and green stick-on dots next to each word listed on the chart paper. They place red dots next to completely unknown words, yellow dots next to partially known words, and green dots next to words that they know well and can use independently. The teacher scans the word knowledge chart for red-light words and provides direct instruction, preteaching these words before reading the text.

PROBLEM-SOLVING SKILLS

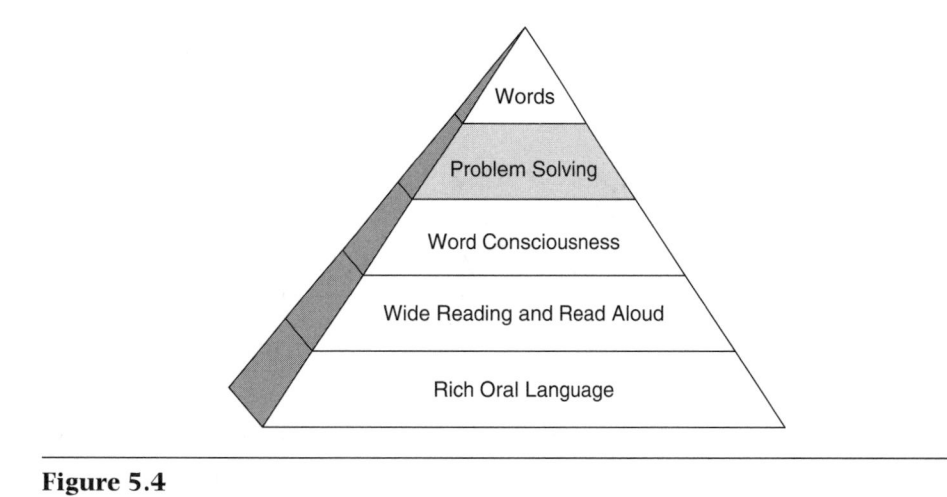

Figure 5.4

Developing students' problem-solving skills is a critical and complex endeavor. Teachers must build motivation, teach metacognitive skills, and help students internalize effective clarifying strategies. The problem-solving cue card is used as a basis of instruction (see Figure 5.5). Teachers begin by introducing and explicitly teaching each strategy. Modeling is provided with specially constructed texts, followed by guided practice and instruction designed to help students transfer strategic skills to natural texts.

The strategies in the first group are listed under the category *monitor* and are designed to build metacognitive skills. Students are prompted to "think about the meaning of words as you read" and "notice when you don't understand a word so that you can fix the problem." Self-monitoring is often a problem for struggling students who are unable to identify most of the words that they do not know. When students are given explicit instruction and plenty of practice monitoring their comprehension of words and texts, their ability to self-monitor improves substantially (Lubliner & Smetana, 2005).

The second group of strategies falls under the category *manage the problem*. It includes *memory*, a strategy designed to encourage students' lexical access as they reach purposefully into memory for partially learned words. *Try topic cues* prompts students to review their prior knowledge of the topic and consider the unknown word in relationship to that knowledge structure. For example, a student faced with the unknown word *blizzard* could use prior knowledge about snow and dangerous storms to figure out the approximate meaning of the word.

Try word parts is a strategy based on morphology. Students are prompted to use knowledge of prefixes, suffixes, base words, and roots to construct word meaning. Students must have developed morphological awareness (the ability to notice word parts) and knowledge of high-frequency affixes and roots in order to use this strategy effectively.

Try text clues directs students' attention to text features that contribute to the construction of word meaning. For example, textbook authors routinely use chapter titles, section titles, boldface print, and highlighting to indicate the main ideas discussed in the text. When students pay attention to text features, they are often able to discern the meaning of unknown words in relationship to the topic.

The final management strategy, *try context*, is complex. So we have developed an additional cue card that can be used as a basis for instruction (page 51).

Once students have learned each of the management strategies, instruction shifts to effective strategy implementation. *Mix the strategies* reminds students that strategies often work better in tandem than in isolation and encourages them to use more than one strategy to figure out word meaning. For example, morphological analysis might provide partial word knowledge; however combining morphology with context increases the likelihood that the construction of meaning will make sense.

Finally, students are encouraged to *monitor again and move on*. They double check word meaning and make sure that they understand the text well enough to continue reading. If they are unable to figure out the meaning of an unknown word, students are prompted to put a Post-it in the text and look up the word later if they need to know the exact meaning (Lubliner, 2005b).

**NOURISHING VOCABULARY
PROBLEM-SOLVING CUE CARD**

MONITOR

- Think about the meaning of words as you read.
- Notice when you don't understand a word so that you can fix the problem.

MANAGE THE PROBLEM

Choose a problem-solving approach. Read the sentence and think about the unfamiliar word: which of these clarifying strategies might help?

- TRY <u>MEMORY</u>: Have you ever seen or heard the word before? How was it used?
- TRY <u>TOPIC CUES</u>: What do you know about the topic that helps you figure out the word?
- TRY <u>WORD PARTS</u>: Use your knowledge of prefixes, suffixes, base words, or roots to help you fix the problem.
- TRY <u>TEXT CLUES</u>: If you are reading a textbook, use chapter titles, subtitles, headings, and boldface text to get information that might help you understand the word. Remember that key words are often defined in the text.
- TRY <u>CONTEXT</u>: See context cue cards.

MIX THE STRATEGIES

- Use more than one clarifying strategy to figure out a word.
- Always come back to context. Make sure that the meaning of the word makes sense in the sentence.

MONITOR AGAIN AND MOVE ON

- Double check: does it make sense?
- When you know enough about the word to understand the text, continue reading.
- If you can't figure out the word, put a Post-it on the page and look it up later if you need to know the exact meaning.

Figure 5.5   Nourishing Vocabulary Problem-Solving Cue Card

A Focus on Context: The Nourishing Vocabulary Context Cue Card

Using context cues to construct the meaning of unknown words is one of the hallmarks of a proficient reader. However, context is tricky and doesn't always work. The nourishing vocabulary context cue card (see Figure 5.6) is designed to help students learn to use a range of context cue substrategies effectively. We suggest that context be taught as form of hypothesis testing. Students begin by considering the unknown word in the text and generate a hypothesis regarding word meaning. They try each context cue and check to see whether the hypothesized meaning makes sense so that the hypothesis can be confirmed or rejected. Let's take a closer look at each type of context cue.

Students find context cues easiest to use when information is located in close proximity to the target word. Learning to check for double-comma cues (appositives) is a quick and easy strategy that students master readily. The following is an example of a double-comma cue: "The triceratops, a dinosaur with three horns, was not a meat-eater." Note that the definition of triceratops is provided in the same sentence, set off by double commas.

NOURISHING VOCABULARY
CONTEXT CUE CARD

Looking at context cues is like trying to solve a word puzzle. You need to look at many different pieces and make educated guesses about how they fit together. Then you continue reading and try to confirm your hypothesis. Context is tricky and you'll need to consider several strategies:

DOUBLE-COMMA CLUE: Sometimes definitions for new words are set off by double commas. Look for these clues in the text.

PART OF SPEECH: Sometimes the part of speech gives you a hint that helps.
- Is the word a noun? Sometimes you can tell by the article (*a, an, the*).
- Is the word an adjective—does it describe a noun? If so, look for more information that will help you figure out what the word might be describing.
- Is the word a verb—an action word? Does it tell you what someone is doing or how something is happening?
- Is the word an adverb—describes a verb? What type of action or thing does it describe? (Hint: adverbs often end in *ly*.)
- Do you have enough information to make an educated guess? If not, look for more clues.

LOOK FOR LISTS: Often an unknown word is part of a list of similar things.
MONITOR THE MOOD: Does the text describe feelings that give you clues about the word?

READ ON: Read the rest of the paragraph. Is there any other information in the text that helps you figure out the word's meaning?

DON'T GIVE UP! Context clues don't always work.

RETURN TO THE PROBLEM-SOLVING CUE CARD: Once you have an idea of what the word means, return to the problem-solving cue card
- MIX THE STRATEGIES.
  - Use more than one clarifying strategy to figure out a word.
- MONITOR AGAIN AND MOVE ON.
  - Double check: does it make sense?
  - When you know enough about the word to understand the text, continue reading.
  - If you can't figure out the word, put a Post-it on the page and look it up later if you need to know the exact meaning.

Figure 5.6   Nourishing Vocabulary Context Cue Card

The cue *part of speech* prompts students to consider parts of speech in the problem-solving process. Students must learn to identify clues in the sentence that signal the presence of specific types of words. For example, when students identify the article *the* in a sentence, they know that the next word must be a noun. This limits the range of possible word meaning to people, places, or things. When there is an unknown word between the article and the noun, they can infer that the word is an adjective. Use of the part of speech context cue is very helpful to students in determining approximate word meaning.

The cue *look for lists of things* helps students identify an unknown word that is presented as part of a group of like items. For example, a description of a sunset might include the words *yellow, orange, pink,* and *crimson,* an unknown word. Students can quickly determine that the word *crimson* is part of a list of colors that describe the sunset. The exact meaning of the word is usually unnecessary for comprehension of the text.

Novels often contain mood cues that provide hints about word meaning and support comprehension of the text. Mood cues are descriptive words and phrases that provide the reader with valuable insight. Mood cues suggest emotions such as joy, sorrow, fear, or despair that often hint at the meaning of an unknown word. For example, figuring out the meaning of the word *dilapidated* is facilitated by mood cues that describe the scene as dreary, hopeless, and situated in a run-down neighborhood.

If initial efforts to construct word meaning do not work, students are prompted to read the rest of the paragraph. Often context cues can be found a little farther from the target word. The following example demonstrates context cues that are located in the same paragraph as the target word *triceratops*. "The triceratops was hungry. He was searching for food and trying to avoid enemies. Although his three horns made him look very fierce, this dinosaur was usually quite gentle."

The last cue, *don't give up*, is very important to emphasize with students. Using strategies to figure out word meaning takes effort and does not always work. Students need a great deal of encouragement and practice to develop proficient context strategy skills. Teachers can help students develop strategic skills, by modeling the use of context cues with sentences such as those in the following examples.

"Get back!" he shouted *bellicosely*. (mood cue)

The *octogenarian*, an eighty-year-old man, was my favorite relative. (double-comma cue)

After striking out and losing the big game, Casey burst into tears and his teammates walked *morosely* off the field. (mood cue, part of speech cue)

The smoothie contained bananas, peaches, strawberries, and *guavas*. (list cue)

It was a *splendid* day to enjoy a walk in the park. (mood)

Mr. Jones did not want to hire an *unreliable* employee. (part of speech cue, mix word parts cue)

Birds *twittered*, bees buzzed, and ducks quacked. (list cue)

The king's *malevolence* terrified his subjects. (mood cue)

Motivating students to learn vocabulary is the first step in the problem-solving process. When teachers provide a clear rationale for devoting time and effort to vocabulary acquisition, students are more likely to develop the skill and will to become independent word learners. The following example is a motivation-building introduction to a lesson on prefixes:

"Today we're going to work on a group of negative prefixes that will help you understand a lot of new words. When you learn that *il-, im-, ir-, dis-,* and *un-* all mean *not*, you will be able to figure out the meaning of almost half of all of the English words in your school books that have prefixes. That's a lot of words! Learning these prefixes is really going to help you understand more words, so you'll read better and you'll do better in school."

Monitor

Students need to learn self-monitoring skills to become aware of unknown words encountered during reading. Although some students naturally self-monitor, others will not. Students become more metacognitively aware when self-monitoring, like other problem-solving skills, is explicitly taught. The teacher writes a short text containing pseudowords on the overhead and asks the students to read the passage silently (see box).

A Night of Terror

Lisa tiptoed into the baby's room and turned out the light. Just as she was about to leave the room she saw the zordecay.

Mr. Blake: Take a look at this text (puts a transparency on the overhead).

David: What's a *zordecay?*

Mr. Blake: It's a pseudoword—a made-up word. What happened when you were reading and you came to the word?

David: I stopped reading because I didn't know what *zordecay* meant.

Mr. Blake: Great! That's exactly what good readers do. They are constantly monitoring comprehension and they stop when something doesn't make sense. First you tried memory, but of course, you couldn't remember a made-up word. Did anyone figure it out anyhow?

Lisa: Yeah! A zordecay's something really scary.

Mr. Blake: How do you know?

Lisa: Well, the title is "A Night of Terror," so you know something scary is going to happen in the story.

Mr. Blake: Excellent! I want you to stay alert and look for unfamiliar words every time you read. Now let's review the problem-solving strategies we've been working on. Which strategy did Lisa use to figure out the word *zordecay?*

John: Context?

Mr. Blake: That's right! What kind of context was helpful here? Was it an appositive?

Ashley: No. I think it's description or mood, maybe. It's a scary story.

Mr. Blake: Excellent! The title gives you a description of the mood—fear—that you can use to make sense of the unknown word. If this were a real story we would continue reading to find out more about the zordecay.

Manage the Problem

The students in the previous vignette were exposed to several problem-solving strategies during the course of the lesson. Mr. Blake posed a problem— a pseudoword in the text—and helped the students identify the problem-solving strategies that they used to make sense of the word. He pointed out to the students that the first strategy most people try is memory; they try to remember if they have seen or heard the word before. This strategy develops students' lexical access, helping them retrieve partially known words from memory. Mr. Blake asked the students to think about other strategies that might help and the students identified text features (the title of the story) and context (mood) as useful problem-solving strategies. It is important to provide students with plenty of direct instruction in learning to monitor comprehension and regulate problem-solving strategies. Simple teacher-created texts such as "A Night of Terror" help students master these complex skills.

Once the students have been exposed to each strategy on the problem-solving cue card, it is important for them to transfer their problem-solving skills to natural texts. In the following vignette, a fifth-grade teacher provides direct instruction in figuring out the meaning of words in a social studies text. He also incorporates word family instruction into the lesson, pointing out morphological features and providing meaningful exposure to extended vocabulary words.

Mr. Salim:	Let's look at the word *prospered* in the first paragraph.
	"The Puritans worked hard and prospered in the new colony." That's a hard word that many of you marked with red dots on the word knowledge chart. How could you figure out what the word means?
Sam:	I think I remember hearing the word before. I think it's something good.
Mr. Salim:	Okay! That's a start! The first strategy most people use is memory. If that doesn't work, then we have to try something else. Which strategy do you think might help with this word?
Sam:	Context?
Mr. Salim:	Yes, context might help here. The book says that the Puritans worked hard. What happens when you work hard at something?
Deborah:	You get an A?
Mr. Salim:	That's the right idea! When you work hard at something, hopefully, you do well. So, the Puritans worked hard and they were successful.
Mika:	You mean they had a lot of money?
Mr. Salim:	You're right! Prospering usually refers to making money. So, now that you know the meaning of *prosper,* what do you think that *prosperous* means?

Mika: To be rich?

Mr. Salim: Yes, someone who is prosperous is wealthy. *Prosper* and *prosperous* belong to the same word family and have similar meanings. I want you to look closely at the words on the vocabulary list. Do you notice other words that are related?

Children: *worship-worshippers, economy-economic, Puritan-purify*

Mr. Salim: Great! These words belong to the same word families. This makes your problem-solving job a lot easier. Once you know the meaning of one word you can figure out the meaning of all of the related words.

Farah: What about *obedience* and *disobedience*—are they in the same family?

Mr. Salim: That's a good question! You can see they share the same base word, *obey.* But disobedience has a prefix, *dis-,* that means *not.* Prefixes are really tricky! They change the meaning of the word. Because of the negative prefix, *disobedience* means the opposite of *obedience,* so it is actually part of a different, but related word family. Groups of words with different prefixes are sort of like cousins; they are not immediate family, but they're still related. Does that make sense? (Children nod.) Okay! Do you think that knowing the prefix helps you figure out the meaning of the word?

Michael: Yeah! I know obedience means doing what you're told. So, I can figure out that disobedience is the opposite, like not doing what you're supposed to do.

Mr. Salim: Excellent! Now, let's think of some other related words. Michael, you are a very obedient boy.

Michael: Yeah, I'm obedient, but my dog, Max is really disobedient.

Mr. Salim: Are you teaching him to obey you?

Michael: Yeah, we start obedience school next week.

Note that Mr. Salim has designed a vocabulary list for the social studies unit that includes a number of word families that are found in the text. Word selection includes *worship-worshippers, economy-economic, Puritan-purify, prosper-prosperous,* and *obedience-disobedience.* The teacher extends the students' vocabulary learning by using word family members such as *prosperity, obey, disobey, pure,* and *purity* in classroom discourse. Instruction based on word families is highly effective in accelerating students' vocabulary acquisition. Rather than learning a list of unrelated words, students learn word families comprised of several related words. Additionally, the teacher draws students' attention to affixes and roots, with the intent of developing their morphological awareness, the ability to notice word parts.

It is important to explicitly teach morphological awareness by demonstrating how affixes, base words, inflected endings, and roots are combined to form words. In the early stages of instruction, it is easier to take words apart than to put them together. The teacher writes a word such as *unfriendly* on the board. He invites the students to point out the word parts, underlining the base word *friend* and circling the prefix *un* and the suffix *ly*. He explains the meaning of each word part with the students and discusses how the words parts contribute to the overall meaning of the word. The teacher provides several more examples for the students to break apart and discuss (*preview, reformation, undeniable, disagreement, uncomfortable*). In the early stages of instruction it is easier for students to work with base words (complete words) rather than Greek or Latin roots they may not fully understand.

Once the students have learned to break apart multisyllabic words with affixes, they are ready to transfer this knowledge to words found in texts. The following activity is designed to provide practice in morphological awareness. The teacher asks the students to follow along as she reads a text aloud. Then she asks the students to identify the words parts that they know (see Figure 5.7).

Finding Word Parts

- Find the words that have affixes, base words, or roots that you know.
- Underline each root or base word.
- Circle the prefix or suffix.
- Think about the meaning.

Long ago, California was a beautiful wilderness. Unlike today, there were no houses or cities and no means of transportation. The only people who lived in California were Native Americans who disagreed with the idea that land could be owned. They were respectful of nature and believed that the land belonged to everyone.

California was inhabited by many wild animals. Grizzly bears roamed freely in the mountainous areas. Great herds of deer and elk roamed undisturbed by people. European explorers discovered California and soon settlers arrived to colonize the territory. More and more people migrated to this wonderful location and soon California was transformed into the place we know today.

Prefixes	Suffixes	Base Words With Affixes	Roots With Affixes
un	ful	beauty	port
trans	tion	wild	form
dis	ly	like	
in	ous	agree	
	er(s)	respect	
	ize	habit	
	ed	free	
	ness	mountain	
		disturb	
		colony	
		wonder	
		locate	

Figure 5.7   Word Part Chart (partial list)

The students complete the activity working in pairs. When they are done, the teacher gathers the class again and invites students to identify base words, roots, and affixes on the overhead.

As they gain proficiency at identifying word parts, students increase their word learning proficiency. Word knowledge can be further extended through the construction of root word webs, such as in the following example, which is based on the Latin root *port* (Figure 5.8). The activity begins with brainstorming lists of prefixes and suffixes that can be added to the root. Students enjoy working in pairs or table groups competing to make a web with the most derived words.

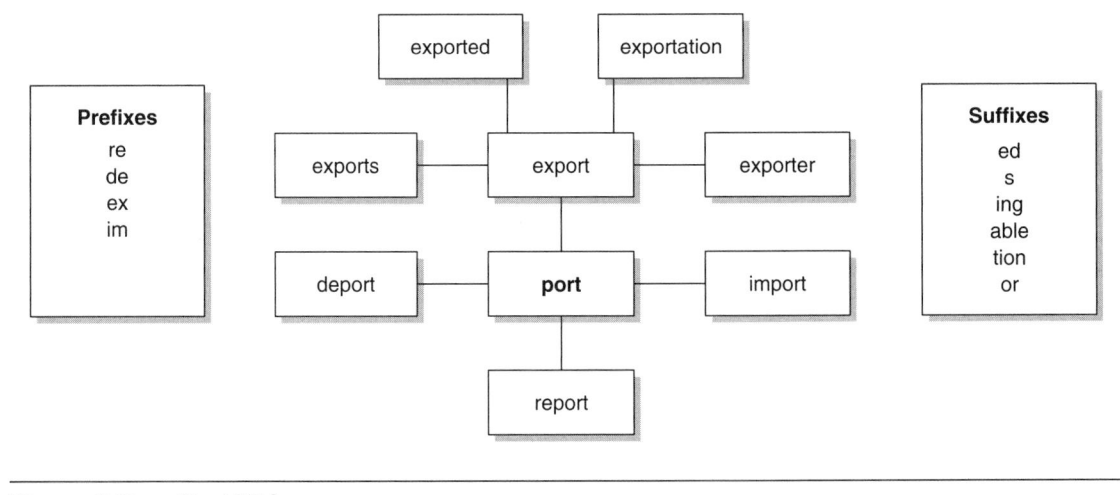

Figure 5.8   Root Web

Another method that helps develop morphological awareness is an open word sort. In this activity the students work together categorizing words in whatever way they wish. When they have finished the activity, each group shares its word sorting decision with the rest of the class. Students may choose to sort the words by prefixes, suffixes, roots, or parts of speech. The activity is helpful in sensitizing students to morphological features in words. The following is a set of words based on the roots *cred, spec, jud, port, ject,* and *form*:

credible, judicial, dejected, speculate, export, project, respect, expect, objection, adjudicate, report, inform, portable, incredulous, injection, transportation, expectation, respectable, judicious, information, reject, formative, objective, deformed, perspective, judge, import, incredible, reformation, speculation, transformation, speculative, performance, deportation, credulous, importance

Figures 5.9, 5.10, and 5.11 present possible sorting decisions that student might make.

cred	jud	spec	port	ject	form
credible incredulous incredible credulous	judicial adjudicate judicious judge	speculate respect expect expectation respectable perspective speculation speculative	export report portable transportation import deportation importance	dejected injection rejection objection project objective	inform information formative deformed reformation transformation performance

Figure 5.9   Root Word Sort

in/im	re	trans	ex	ob	de
incredulous incredible injection inform information informative import importance	respect respectable report rejection reformation	transportation transformation	expect expectation export	objection objective	deportation dejected deformed

Figure 5.10   Prefix Sort

ous	ion	ible/able	ative	ance	ial
credulous incredulous judicious	expectation speculation transportation deportation dejection injection objection information transportation	credible incredible respectable portable	informative objective speculative perspective	performance importance	judicial

Figure 5.11   Suffix Sort

It is important to plan activities that develop morphological awareness in all subject areas. This is particularly useful to older students, because approximately 60 percent of the words they encounter in texts can be analyzed and understood given knowledge of word parts (Nagy & Anderson, 1984).

The Spelling-Meaning Connection

As students enter the upper elementary grades, vocabulary and spelling instruction converge in terms of morphology. Students learn to identify word parts (affixes and Greek and Latin roots) and gradually master the spelling patterns that characterize the derivational relations stage of spelling development. Effective spelling instruction for upper elementary students teaches spelling and vocabulary simultaneously, emphasizing the spelling-meaning connection (Bear, Invernizzi, Templeton, & Johnston, 2007). We suggest that teachers integrate the activities in this chapter with the derivational relations spelling activities such as those found in both *Words Their Way: Word Study for Phonics, Vocabulary, and Spelling Instruction* (Bear, Invernizzi, Templeton, & Johnston, 2007) and *Words Their Way: Word Sorts for Derivational Relations Spellers* (Templeton, Johnston, Bear, & Invernizzi, 2006).

Another important task for upper-grade students is learning English grammar. The following activity helps students learn to identify adjectives and adverbs while building word family knowledge.

- Select a group of suffixes used to describe something:
    - □ *-ly, -ous, -ful, -less*
- Provide examples of how the suffix *-ous* changes the noun *danger* into an adjective and the suffix *-ly* changes it into an adverb:
    - □ Danger is a risky situation (noun).
    - □ Something dangerous causes a risky situation (adjective).
    - □ You behave dangerously when you do something that causes the risk (adverb).

Ask students to work with the chart in Figure 5.12 using suffixes *-ly, -ous, -ful,* and *-less.* Generate sentences with the words.

Base Word, Noun	Describing Word, Adjective	Describing Word, Adverb
danger	dangerous	dangerously
mystery	mysterious	mysteriously
envy	envious	enviously
hope	hopeful, hopeless	hopefully, hopelessly
respect	respectful	respectfully
beauty	beautiful	beautifully

Figure 5.12   Adjective-Adverb Sort

Once students have become familiar with suffixes that signal parts of speech, they can use the information strategically to make sense of unfamiliar words encountered during reading. In the following vignette, the teacher mixes the problem-solving strategies, using affixes and parts of speech to figure out word meaning.

Mix the Strategies

Ms. Fleming: Let's look at the sentence and try to figure out the word *enviously.* Mike stared at his friend's new iPod enviously. If you didn't know the word *enviously,* how could you figure it out? Can you tell which part of speech *enviously* is?

Judith:	Yeah—I know the ending means it describes the verb.
Ms. Fleming:	Right! We know from the *ly* that the word *enviously* is an adverb. That means it describes the verb stared. How would you look at someone's new iPod?
Natasha:	I'd be jealous!
Ms. Fleming:	So, *enviously* means the same thing as *jealously?* Does that make sense? (Students nod.) Yes, you're right. *Enviously* describes the jealous way that Mike stared at the iPod. Let's think of some more adverbs that describe ways that you might look at something.
Noah:	*Sadly, angrily* . . .
Tanya:	*Happily,* if it was mine!
Dave:	Yeah, *excitedly, delightedly!*
Ms. Fleming:	Good examples of adverbs, everyone! So, be sure to pay attention to the suffix *-ly* when you are trying to figure out new words. This suffix tells you that the word is an adverb that describes the verb in the sentence.

Monitor Again and Move On

Over the course of the school year, students practice each strategy on the problem-solving cue card and context cue card. It is important to point out to students that strategies do not always work and that good readers must be persistent in using a variety of clarifying strategies. Students must learn to continuously monitor their own comprehension of words, asking themselves, "Does this make sense?"

In the following vignette, Ms. Fleming asks the students to underline affixes in the text and to figure out what the words mean. She notices several errors in the students' papers.

Ms. Fleming:	I noticed that several of you underlined the *re* in the word *rented.* Do you think that this makes sense?
Sean:	Yeah, you said that *re-* is a prefix that means *again.* So, I underlined it.
Ms. Fleming:	Sean, look at the word rented carefully. If *re-* is a prefix, the base word is *nt.* Does that make sense?
Sean:	I guess not.
Ms. Fleming:	I can see that this is confusing, but you have to remember to double check and ask yourself—does it make sense? If not, you have to try your problem-solving strategies again.

Students need to learn that problem-solving strategies are heuristics, not formulas. They do not always work. That is why it is so important for students to know how to use multiple strategies and self-checking mechanisms. Learning to regulate the use of clarifying strategies takes a lot of practice. Teachers help students acquire self-regulating skills by providing ample opportunities for them to grapple with challenging words in texts and to discuss the clarifying process with the class. Gradually clarifying strategies and metacognitive skills are internalized. With practice, students become efficient word learners, and their ability to acquire vocabulary from texts accelerates.

WORD CONSCIOUSNESS

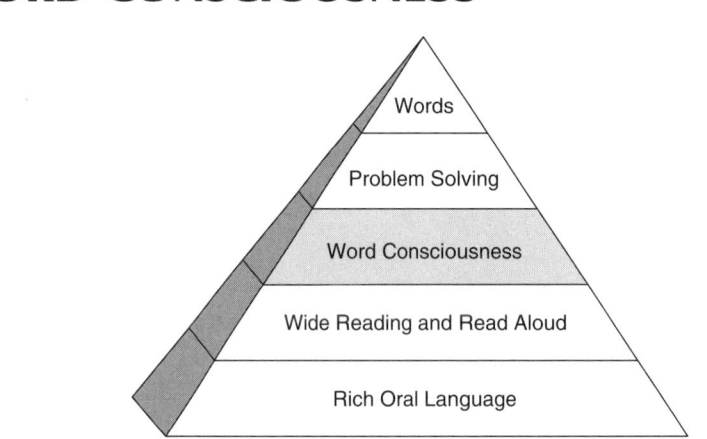

Figure 5.13

Word consciousness is a key factor in a well-balanced and effective vocabulary development program. Teachers develop word consciousness by encouraging playful interactions with words and providing students with an increasingly sophisticated understanding of how words work. One facet of word consciousness that is explicitly taught to upper elementary students is the organization of conceptually related words in knowledge structures known as schemata. Researchers believe that good readers rely on schemata to integrate newly learned content with prior knowledge stored in long-term memory (Ausubel, 1963, 1978; Kintsch, 1998; Kintsch & van Dijk, 1978).

As learners encounter new vocabulary, not only do they need to store words efficiently, they also need to create neural traces to access words needed for receptive (listening and reading) and expressive (speaking and writing) tasks. An important goal of vocabulary instruction is to help students construct schemata—that is, knowledge structures, filled with related words—for a wide range of topics.

We begin with a simple task: write down all of the words that you can think of relating to the word *park* in the box below.

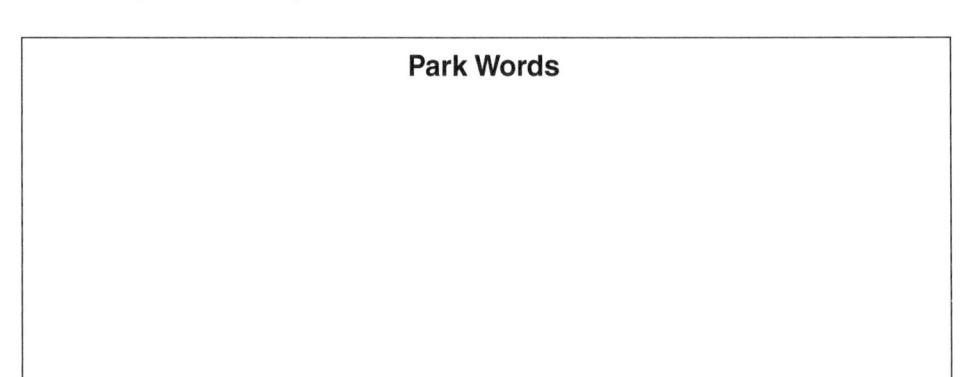

Figure 5.14 Park Words

If you are like most people, you will immediately think of words such as *grass, swings, slides, picnic tables, fields, pool, children, families,* and so on. People describe this process as a visualizing activity. You visualize a typical park in your mind and write words that represent every item that you see in the mental picture. Note that nearly all of the words that you generate are nouns.

Now try this: write down all of the words that you can think of relating to the word *law.*

Law Words

Figure 5.15   Law Words

You may have generated words such as *courthouse, judge, defendant, lawyer, trial, punishment,* and *jail.* Unless you are a lawyer, it was probably a lot more difficult for you to construct a mental image. Generating words was substantially more difficult, due to the abstractness of the concept *law* as opposed to the more concrete concept *park.* Additionally, accessing words associated with *law* is more difficult because the relationship between these words is more tenuous for most people.

So, what are the implications for vocabulary instruction? The first lesson is that schema-building instruction should start with a concept that is concrete and familiar, such as *park,* and then move to the more complex concepts found in grade-level texts. The following vignette illustrates the instructional sequence for schema-building that a fifth-grade teacher uses in a science unit on the weather.

The teacher begins with a simple task designed to familiarize the students with schemata and the process of semantic webbing. She asks the students to write all of the words that they can think of related to *park.* After they have done so, the teacher leads a discussion about the process. The following dialog demonstrates the beginning stages of word schema instruction.

Ms. Finnegan: Okay, is everyone finished writing words related to *park?* (Students nod.) How many words did you write? (Students count the words and raise their hands to share the number.) Fifty-six, sixty-nine, seventy-one. Wow! Sarah wrote seventy-four words—that's a lot! How did you think of so many words?

Sarah: Well, I thought about the park where I play soccer. Then I wrote all the words about the park.

Ms. Finnegan: You thought of a lot of words. Why do you think you could do this so quickly?

Sarah: Because I know a lot about the park. I'm there almost every day, for soccer practice.

Ms. Finnegan: Hmm. The reason you could come up with park words so quickly is that you already know a lot about parks. You could picture the park in your mind and write down all of the things you see. How many of you pictured Deerhill Park (a local park, not far from the school) in your minds? (Most of the students raise their hands.) Now look closely at your paper. Is there any pattern as to how you wrote down words? Are they in a particular order?

Sarah: Well, I wrote all the words about soccer first—*field, grass, goal, coach, kids, mom, dad, baby* . . .

Ms. Finnegan: Okay, this is really important. Sarah wrote down words in categories. How could we describe these categories?

Mike: Soccer stuff and then families.

Ms. Finnegan: Good! Those categories make sense (draws on the whiteboard).

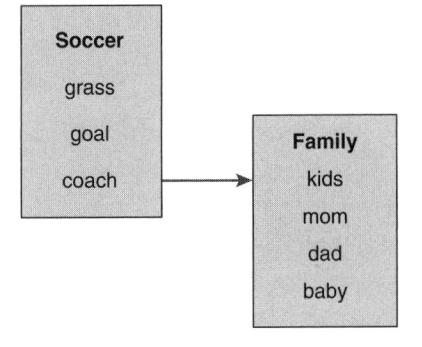

Figure 5.16 Sarah's Schema

Ms. Finnegan: Imagine that you are looking at knowledge structures in Sarah's mind (see Figure 5.16). Can you see how the words are organized and how she moved from one set of words into another? First she thought of words related to soccer: *field, grass, goal, and coach.* Then she thought of kids, because coaches coach kids. The word *kids* led her to think of another category, family members, that would include the words *mom, dad,* and *baby.*

Did anyone else write words in some kind of category? (Students nod.) The reason you did this is that your mind sorts information and stores related words together in your memory— kind of like a tree with lots of branches. As you learn new information, you store groups of words and related ideas in your memory. (Teacher draws a tree.) It's a lot easier to remember new words when you have a branch that connects the new word to words you already know. When you need information or words, you can retrieve the whole tree—it's called a schema.

The teacher and students work together, listing words on the board, identifying "big ideas" (sports, families, and nature) and sorting the words into categories, corresponding to the ideas. Then the teacher models the construction of a semantic web, explaining that it will help make the students' thinking visible. She explains that a semantic web is used to organize related words and concepts. Once the web is constructed, she tells the students, it can be transferred into memory and recalled as needed for a variety of learning and communication tasks.

Once the students have grasped the concept of sorting words and creating semantic webs, the teacher explains how to apply their newly learned skills with more abstract concepts, such as those found in the science textbook. The students in this fifth-grade class have just started a science unit on the weather. The teacher develops a series of vocabulary-enriched lessons. She begins by showing a number of pictures that demonstrate the effects of severe storms: New Orleans following Hurricane Katrina, towns destroyed by tornadoes, and people coping with blizzards. Students share examples of severe weather they have experienced. The teacher writes the topic *weather* on the board and circles it. She reminds the students that they already know a lot about the weather and the words we use to discuss it. She asks them to write down the important words that are used in discussing the weather. The students volunteer weather words and the teacher lists them on the board: *hot, cold, warm, dry, wet, windy, cloudy, rainy, sunny, storm, hurricane, tornado, thunderstorm, lightning, thunder, temperature . . .*

The teacher explains the need to organize all of the words so that they are easier to remember. She asks the students to think of subtopics—important categories that relate to the weather—and helps the students generate words and phrases such as *types of weather* and *storms.* The teacher writes each subtopic and links it to the topic, weather. She discusses each word on the list, helps the students decide where it goes, crosses it off the list, and links it to the appropriate subtopic. A web of words and concepts related to the weather is constructed (see Figure 5.17). The students complete their own webs and keep them in their binders for the duration of the weather unit.

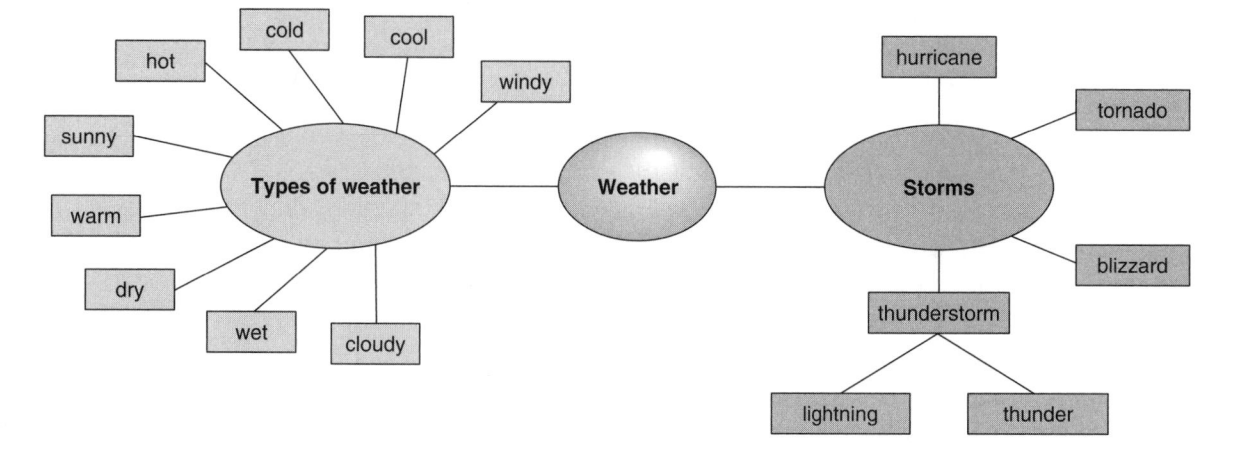

Figure 5.17   Semantic Web: First Weather Web

In subsequent lessons the teacher relates new concepts and words to the weather web. She adds new subtopics on causes of weather and another subtopic on measuring the weather and related details for each subtopic. She explains to the students that they will add new words such as *storm surge* and *flood* to the category *hurricane* under the subtopic *storms.* She also promises to add a separate category *Katrina* to organize all of the information the students will learn about that deadly hurricane. The teacher increases the visual power of the web with the use of color. She uses a different color marker for each subcategory. She reviews the web daily, suggesting that the students do the same: "Close your eyes and picture the web floating up into your memory." She reminds them that they can retrieve the weather schema anytime they need a word or concept.

The unit continues and the teacher adds new categories for causes and measurement. The students have become comfortable with sorting and webbing procedures and complete many of the activities individually or with a partner. The weather web now looks like this.

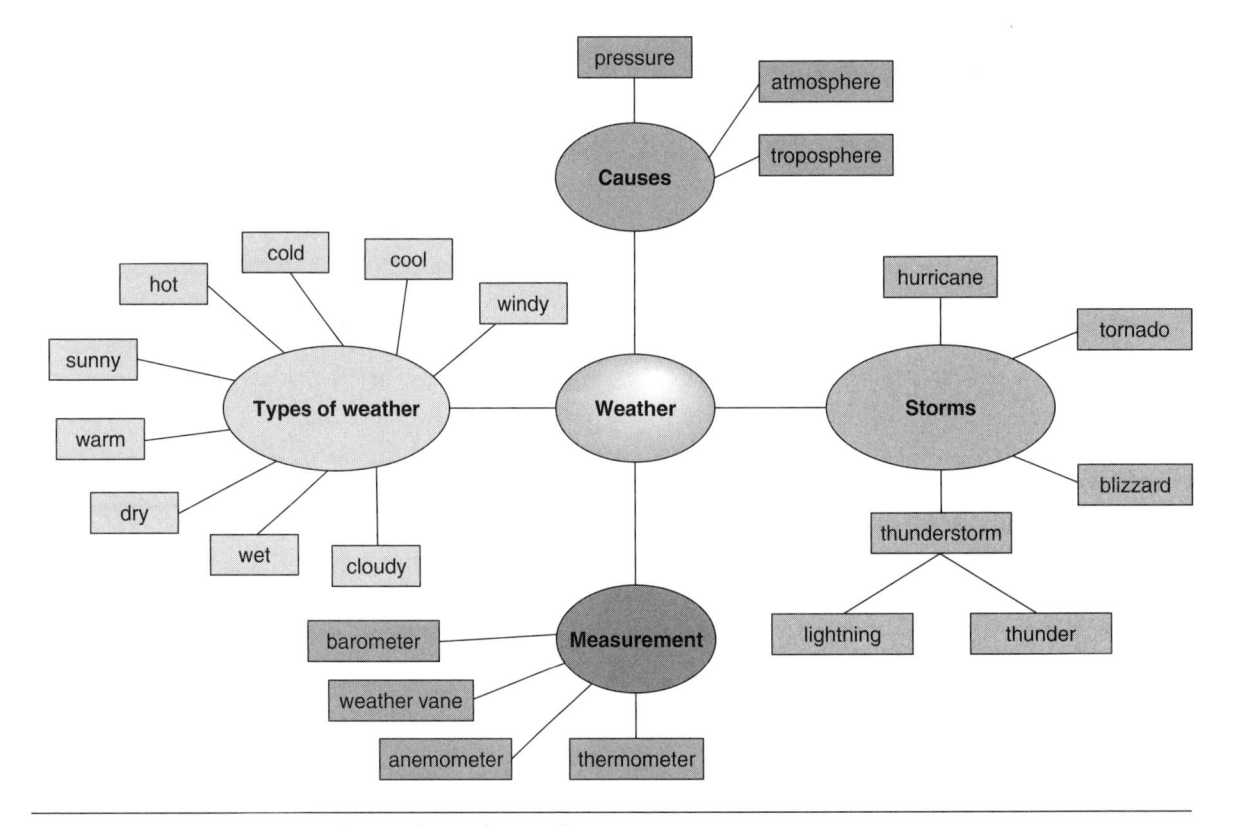

Figure 5.18   Semantic Web: Final Weather Web

As the children continue reading and discussing science content, they add new words to the webs. Words that are conceptually related are added, as are words that belong to the same word families. The web grows larger and more complex. Each time a new word is added, the teacher and students discuss the relevant schema. Periodically, the teacher asks the students to visualize the web, taking a mental snapshot. She also encourages the students to use the new words in classroom discourse and in their writing. Gradually the weather schema is internalized and the words are readily available for receptive and expressive use.

Teaching Students to Use the Dictionary

When children ask for help with unknown words, the most common response is often, "Go look it up!" This directive is more likely to cause frustration than vocabulary learning, unless it is accompanied by explicit instruction in dictionary skills. Before telling students to look it up, teachers need to consider the challenges inherent in using a dictionary. Even when dictionary skills have been carefully taught, students may still find the definitions they find there frustrating. Researchers have found that dictionary definitions, even those written for children, are difficult for children to understand without a great deal of adult support (McKeown, 1993; Miller & Gildea, 1987; Scott & Nagy, 1997). In addition, students often choose only a fragment of a definition as the entire meaning of a word and have difficulty with multiple word meanings. Dictionaries often rephrase the target word (for example, *reputable: someone of high repute*) or use complex vocabulary and syntax in definitions (McKeown, 1993).

With all of the problems associated with dictionary use, why don't we simply forget about the dictionary and teach children to use clarifying strategies such as context clues and structural analysis instead? The answer is that it is important to teach both clarifying strategies and dictionary use. Strategies work best during independent reading when searching through the dictionary would interfere with, rather than enhance comprehension. But clarifying strategies don't always work, and children are left unable to construct word meaning. The dictionary can help, of course, particularly to identify concrete nouns or to inform the reader of gradations of meaning. It is a wonderful tool, a vast repository of knowledge for those who know how to use it well. Rather than dismissing the dictionary from the curriculum, we should explicitly teach children how to use it proficiently. The protocol in Figure 5.19 can be used as a basis of dictionary instruction.

The teacher begins by teaching children how to alphabetize words and to locate words on an alphabetical list. This instruction begins in the primary grades and continues throughout elementary school with lists of increasingly challenging words. Children are taught to become word detectives and search for first-letter, second-letter, and subsequent letter-clues to word location.

The next step focuses on word family instruction, an important part of a vocabulary development program. Researchers estimate that children can understand up to 60 percent of the words they encounter in texts by using word parts (Nagy & Anderson, 1984). When children learn to identify base words and related words with inflected endings and suffixes, their vocabulary increases and they develop skills that can be applied to dictionary work.

Dictionary Instructional Protocol

Protocol for instruction: Explicitly teach each of the skills listed below.

- Step 1: Teach alphabetizing skills.
  - Teach children to alphabetize increasingly complex sets of words.
  - Demonstrate how dictionaries work, pointing out words at the top of the page that give clues to word location.
  - Teach children to find words based on first-letter, second-letter, and subsequent-letter clues.
  - Encourage children to be word detectives by providing them with increasingly challenging words to look up in the dictionary.

- Step 2: Teach inference skills.
  - Teach children how word families work.
  - Provide practice identifying base words and related words with inflected endings (ed, s, ing), and suffixes.
  - Teach children to group related words into word families.
  - Provide practice with word webs.
  - Teach children how parts of speech affect word meaning.
  - Teach children how to infer word meaning and transfer meaning from one word-learning task to another.

- Step 3: Teach definitional skills.
  - Demonstrate how to select an appropriate definition for a word when several definitions are provided.
  - Teach children how to look up a related word when it is used in a definition.
  - Teach children to state the definition in their own words.

- Step 4: Teach self-checking skills.
  - Teach children to self-monitor comprehension of words.
  - Teach children to replace the unknown word with a synonym to make sure that the definition makes sense.

Figure 5.19   Dictionary Instructional Protocol

Source: Adapted from Lubliner, S. (2005a). Go look it up: Dictionary instruction revisited. *The California Reader, 38*, (4).

Teachers reinforce word family skills by teaching children to group related words into word webs and identify members of word families in texts. A particular emphasis is placed on teaching children to draw inferences regarding word meaning, explicitly teaching them to transfer meaning between words that belong to the same word family.

Once children have learned to locate words in the dictionary and use related words to infer meaning, they are ready to grapple with dictionary definitions. Teachers explicitly teach children how to select an appropriate definition (when more than one is provided) and to rephrase that information in their own words. The teacher then demonstrates how to replace the target word with a synonym as a self-checking mechanism to make sure that the definition makes sense.

The following vignette takes place in a fifth-grade classroom. The teacher guides the students as they attempt to use the glossary (a textbook dictionary) to make sense of difficult words encountered in the fifth-grade social studies textbook.

Mrs. Yamimoto: (Reads) "Many former slaves and their supporters in the northern states joined forces to abolish slavery." Hmm . . . *abolish* is a hard word. Context clues aren't very helpful here and we can't tell what the word means by looking at the word parts. Let's look this word up in the glossary and see if that helps.

Mike: It's not there. Is *abolitionist* in the same family?

Mrs. Yamimoto: Good! You noticed that *abolish* is missing and found another word in the same word family. Let's look at the definition of *abolitionist* and see if we can infer the meaning of *abolish*. (Reads the definition of *abolitionist* from the glossary.) "A person who tries to outlaw or do away with slavery." Okay, that helps! The word *abolitionist* is a noun—a person who outlaws slavery. *Abolish* is a verb. It means to outlaw or do away with something, in this case, slavery. Let's try the synonym *do away with* in the sentence: "Many former slaves and their supporters in the northern states worked together to do away with slavery." Now, check it out! Does it make sense? (Children nod.) Okay, let's go on.

(Lubliner, 2005a, p. 27)

Proficient dictionary use entails the internalization of an array of complex skills, a process that takes a great deal of time and patient instruction. Young children are introduced to the dictionary and are taught prerequisite skills through teacher-directed reading activities. As students move into the upper grades, teacher scaffolding fades. Students internalize dictionary skills, allowing them to use the dictionary independently and proficiently to manage their own word learning.

Dictionary work is only one facet of a nourishing vocabulary program. A combination of instructional methods, including dictionary work, is likely to produce the best results, particularly when instruction includes repeated exposure and meaningful use of new vocabulary (Nagy, 1988). The activity we call "digging into the dictionary" helps students use the dictionary to clarify words with multiple meanings. The teacher models the activity with the word *right*, demonstrating how to generate sentences that reflect different word meanings. The teacher then points out the definitions and asks the students to match the definitions to the words in the sentences. The students work in pairs, generating sentences for the additional words and using the dictionary to complete the worksheet.

Digging Into the Dictionary

Name: _____

Some words are tricky and have more than one meaning. Think about the meaning of the word *right*. Look in the box below for sentences with the word *right* used in different ways. Fill in the dictionary definition that makes sense in each sentence. The first one is done for you as an example.

Definitions: (1) Correct, (2) Opportunity that is guaranteed, (3) A direction

Sentence: Turn right at the first stoplight.

Definition: a direction

Sentence: You have the right to remain silent.

Definition: opportunity that is guaranteed

Sentence: The teacher said that the answer is right.

Definition: correct

Now it's your turn!

Write sentences, using the word in different ways.

Look up the word in the dictionary and write a definition that matches the way the word is used in each sentence.

Draft
Sentence:
Definition:
Sentence:
Definition:
Sentence:
Definition:

Staple
Sentence:
Definition:
Sentence:
Definition:
Sentence:
Definition:

Block
Sentence:
Definition:
Sentence:
Definition:
Sentence:
Definition:

Wide Reading and Read Aloud

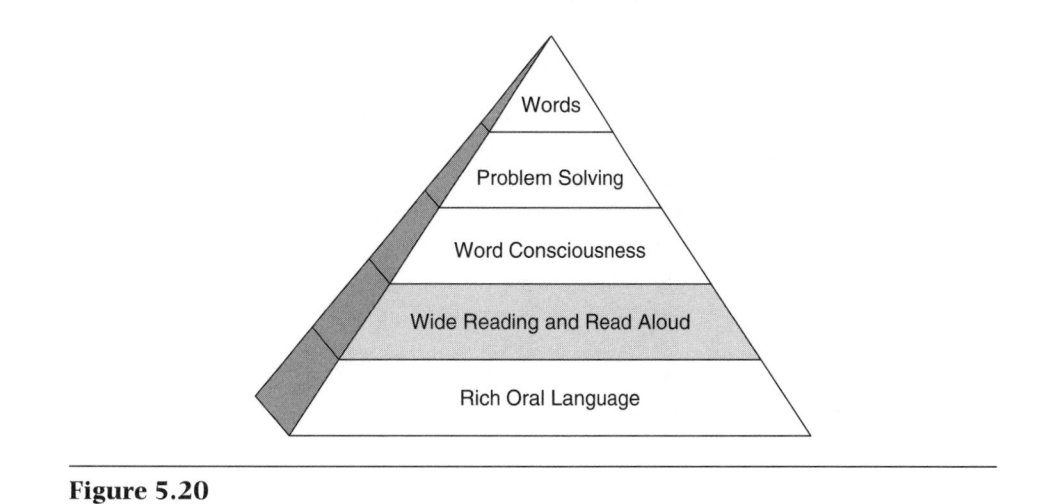

Figure 5.20

Researchers estimate that children routinely learn between 2,000 and 3,000 words per year, a staggering number, particularly in light of the fact that only 300 to 400 words are generally taught each year through direct instruction (Anglin, 1993; Nagy, Anderson, & Herman, 1986; Stahl & Nagy, 2006). Most vocabulary growth results from independent reading rather than classroom instruction. Adding twenty minutes per day of reading is likely to increase children's vocabulary by 2,000 words over the course of a year (Stahl & Nagy, 2006). The problem, however, is that many children lack the skill and the motivation to read widely. Without broad exposure to books, their vocabulary growth stagnates. The solution to this problem is to read aloud.

Teachers and parents often stop reading aloud when children enter the upper elementary grades and learn to read independently. This is a huge mistake that teachers must avoid. Until seventh grade or so, most children acquire more vocabulary from listening than reading. Struggling readers need read aloud much more than their higher achieving peers. Without the exposure to rich vocabulary that read aloud provides, struggling readers will fall farther and farther behind.

The following example highlights the value of reading aloud to upper elementary students. A fifth-grade teacher reads aloud *The Thirteenth Floor: A Ghost Story* (Fleischman, 1995), as a daily accompaniment to the social studies unit on the American colonies. This highly engaging story of a boy who is transported back in time to the period of the New England witch trials supplies students with a great deal of background information about the New England colonies, while exposing them to a vast number of rich vocabulary words. A single page of the book (page 35) includes the following words that are useful for children to learn: *prowling, lantern, mock, notion, vaguely, inform, gallows, piracy, courteous, ancestor, lunatic, muttered, regard, profession, flashing.* Many of the words are repeated in subsequent pages and chapters, providing multiple exposures and increasing the chance that word learning will occur. Reading aloud a chapter of a children's novel such as *The Thirteenth Floor: A Ghost Story* on a daily basis provides children with exposure to fifty or more rich vocabulary words per day. Researchers estimate that children learn approximately 5–7 percent of unknown words that are encountered once during reading or listening

(Nagy, 1985, 1988; Stahl & Nagy, 2006; Swanborn & de Glopper, 1999), so daily read aloud is an extremely fruitful and enjoyable method of accelerating vocabulary growth. In fact, reading aloud a chapter of *The Thirteenth Floor: A Ghost Story*, or chapters from other comparable trade books, may result in vocabulary growth of twelve or more words per week (5 percent of 250 new words encountered in an average chapter) depending on the children's prior vocabulary knowledge. There is simply no instructional method with the potential of producing as much vocabulary growth as daily read aloud.

To maximize the benefit of read aloud, teachers can prepare by highlighting key vocabulary and identifying important concepts in the text for the development of word schema. Preparations also include noting words that can be used in classroom discourse. Figure 5.21 shows a lesson plan for reading aloud Chapter 5 of *The Thirteenth Floor: A Ghost Story*. (A read-aloud lesson plan template is provided in Appendix B.)

Lesson Date: ____   Read-Aloud Text: *The Thirteenth Floor: A Ghost Story*   Chapter: 5

Author: Sid Fleischman   Genre: Historical Fiction   Subject Area: Social Studies

WORDS	*lantern, screeching, gazing, aboard, approaching, plundering, on the verge, hovering, stowaway, braced, bow, disbelief, scoffed, hull, darting, glimpse, squinted, gravel, eternity, careen, parchment, scrawny, rascal, prowling, mock, boldly, notion, vaguely, inform, gallows, piracy, courteous, ancestor, lunatic, muttered, regard, profession, flashing, dismissed, bred, shrugged, anxious, heaving, scholar, fantastical, rubbish, babbling, plunder, to fancy, marvelous, afloat, cutthroats, beached, privateer, galley, mast*
SCHEMA	Ship: *hull, bow, mast, galley, lantern, aboard, afloat, beached, braced, careen, heaving* Pirates: *piracy, plunder/plundering, cutthroats, privateer, gallows* Stowaway: *scrawny rascal, anxious, scholar* Ways of speaking: *screeching, scoffed, mock, inform, muttered, babbling* Ways of moving: *darting, prowling, hovering, shrugged*
INSTRUCTIONAL SEQUENCE	BEFORE READING • Review chapter and highlight challenging words in the text • Identify key concepts and words related to schemata • Invite students to summarize previous day's reading before beginning new chapter • Remind students to listen to the language and be aware of new words during the read aloud DURING READING • Read expressively, emphasize context when reading challenging words • Minimize interruptions during reading AFTER READING • Discuss key important concepts such as the pirate ship, using vocabulary from the story • Post words related to schemata on the word wall (ship, pirates, stowaway, ways of speaking, ways of moving) • Use rich oral language from story in classroom discourse

Figure 5.21   Read-Aloud Lesson Plan   *(Continued)*

(Continued)

RICH ORAL LANGUAGE	Show a picture of a seventeenth-century ship, discuss words that describe the ship and life aboard the ship
	Talk about the captain and his men from Buddy's perspective
	Discuss the stowaway (Buddy) from the perspective of the pirates
	Playful use of such language throughout the day can enhance word awareness; For instance you can use words from the chapter in conversation:
	• What scrawny rascal is prowling outside the door? • You mock me, kind sir. • Behold yonder scholars poring over their books. • Courteous children don't hover around my desk. • What a marvelous idea!

Figure 5.21   Read-Aloud Lesson Plan

Rich Oral Language

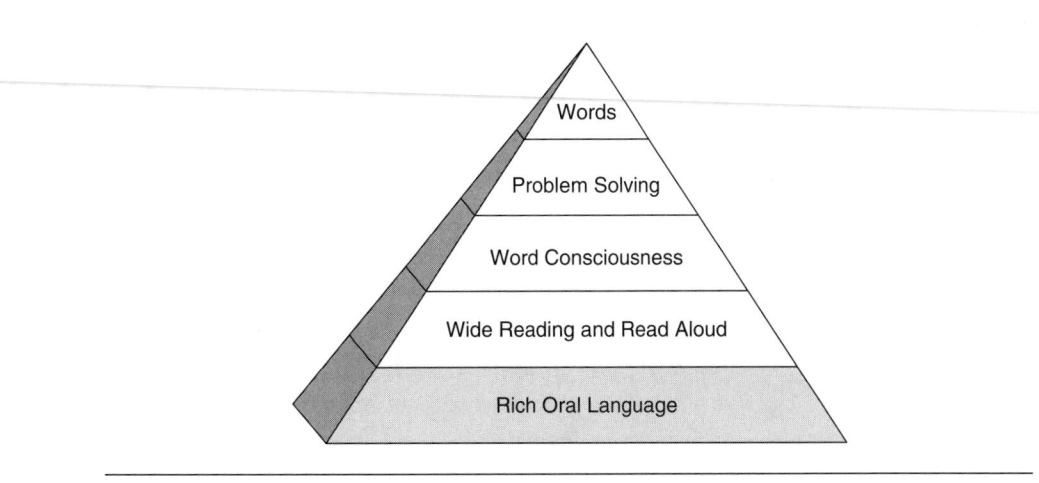

Figure 5.22

Rich oral language (ROL) is the foundation and the most important component of the vocabulary curriculum. It is not a discrete topic or skill, but rather a framework that pervades every aspect of classroom life. Examples of ROL can be found throughout this book in vignettes that illustrate the rich vocabulary used in discussions about every conceivable topic. A classroom that is filled with ROL is a lively, interactive environment, where children learn content through exposure to mature language and vocabulary. The ROL environment described in this book contrasts sharply with that of the many classrooms where teachers speak to children in simple child-friendly language.

Although it makes sense to avoid overwhelming students with a plethora of incomprehensible words, teachers can modify their discourse to help children understand rich vocabulary. As we discussed in Chapter 4, it is important to provide comprehensible input to scaffold children's understanding of new words. This can take the form of pictures, maps, charts, realia, and gestures. The following examples demonstrate the difference between normal classroom discourse and that designed to accelerate vocabulary acquisition. Both examples are introductory comments by a fifth-grade teacher just before reading a passage about the middle colonies of the Eastern seaboard in the social studies textbook. The first example illustrates impoverished discourse. Instruction provides no exposure to new vocabulary and does little to activate background knowledge that will support comprehension. The second example demonstrates ROL methods, with preteaching of key vocabulary through oral language. The teacher provides comprehensible input (a picture on the over-head) and structured discourse, exposing the children to vocabulary and concepts that they will encounter in the textbook. He embeds context in his discussion, occasionally rephrasing the more difficult words, such as *navigable.*

The teacher says...

Impoverished discourse: "Today we're going to read about the middle colonies. The colonists settled in New York and Pennsylvania because these places were easy to get to and the land was good for farming. Please open your books and follow along as I read."

ROL discourse: "Today we're going to read about the middle colonies. Take a look at this picture of a colony located on the Delaware River in Pennsylvania (points to a picture on the overhead). Notice the laborers loading goods onto large ships at the dock. You can tell from the size of the shipping vessels (points to ships) that the river was navigable—it was deep and wide enough for large ships. The colonists knew that being able to transport goods by river was important to their economy. They could import supplies—bring in the things they needed. They could also export goods they produced, selling them in other places. Look closely at the picture (points to the picture). You can see fields filled with grain in the background. The colonists chose a place with fertile soil, so that they could grow crops to feed their families and to export for cash. Please open your books and follow along as I read."

Semantic Word Walls

Word walls are familiar items in many elementary school classrooms. They are, however, often used exclusively for decoding and spelling instruction. Semantic word walls are used to display vocabulary words that the students are learning. Use of semantic word walls can enrich classroom discourse at all grade levels.

Instruction that incorporates rich oral language is tremendously valuable to students, particularly struggling readers; however, it requires practice. We suggest that teachers develop scripts that include key concepts and vocabulary in the early stages of instruction. Gradually, teachers internalize discourse patterns, allowing ROL to be implemented without extensive scripting. Even after a great deal of practice, it is easy to revert to old habits, using simple words that students already know. To increase the use of rich vocabulary in classroom discourse, we suggest that teachers post word lists and daily vocabulary objectives on the classroom wall. This reminds the teacher to incorporate vocabulary into instruction and can encourage children to use new words in oral and written discourse.

Figure 5.23 is an example of a fourth-grade semantic word wall. Words from reading, math, social studies, and science are color coded and displayed alphabetically. Figure 5:24 includes examples of teacher discourse based on the word wall.

Subjects: Red—Social Studies (Chapter 2, Lesson 1), Blue—Reading/Language Arts (Theme 1), Green—Science (Lesson 2), Orange—Math (Chapter 2)

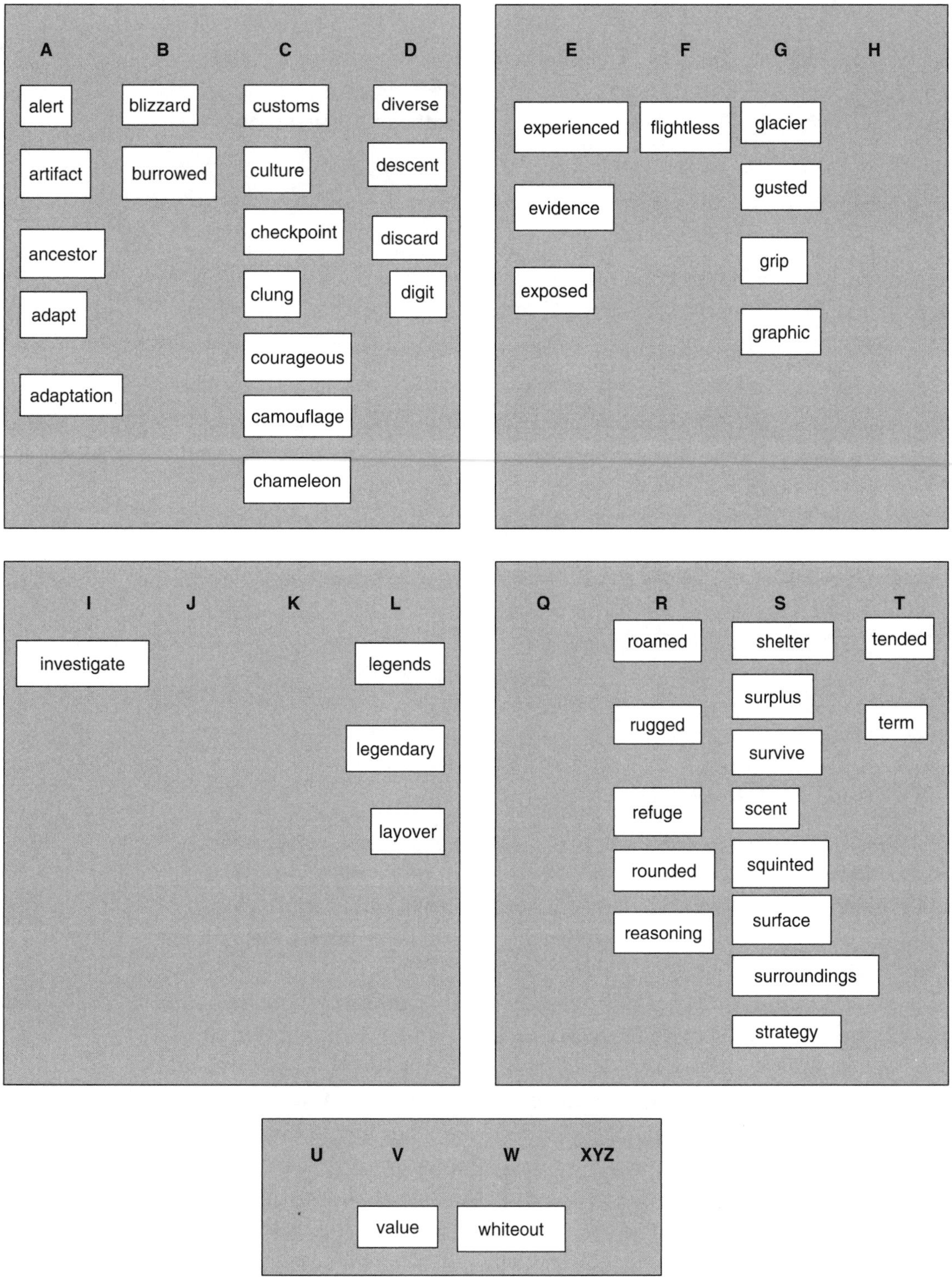

A	B	C	D
alert	blizzard	customs	diverse
artifact	burrowed	culture	descent
ancestor		checkpoint	discard
adapt		clung	digit
adaptation		courageous	
		camouflage	
		chameleon	

E	F	G	H
experienced	flightless	glacier	
evidence		gusted	
exposed		grip	
		graphic	

I	J	K	L
investigate			legends
			legendary
			layover

Q	R	S	T
	roamed	shelter	tended
	rugged	surplus	term
		survive	
	refuge	scent	
	rounded	squinted	
	reasoning	surface	
		surroundings	
		strategy	

U	V	W	XYZ
	value	whiteout	

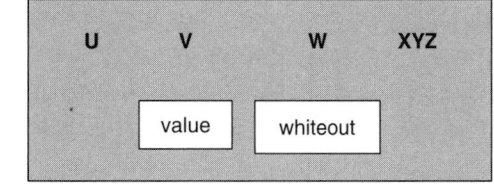

Figure 5.23 Upper Elementary Semantic Word Wall

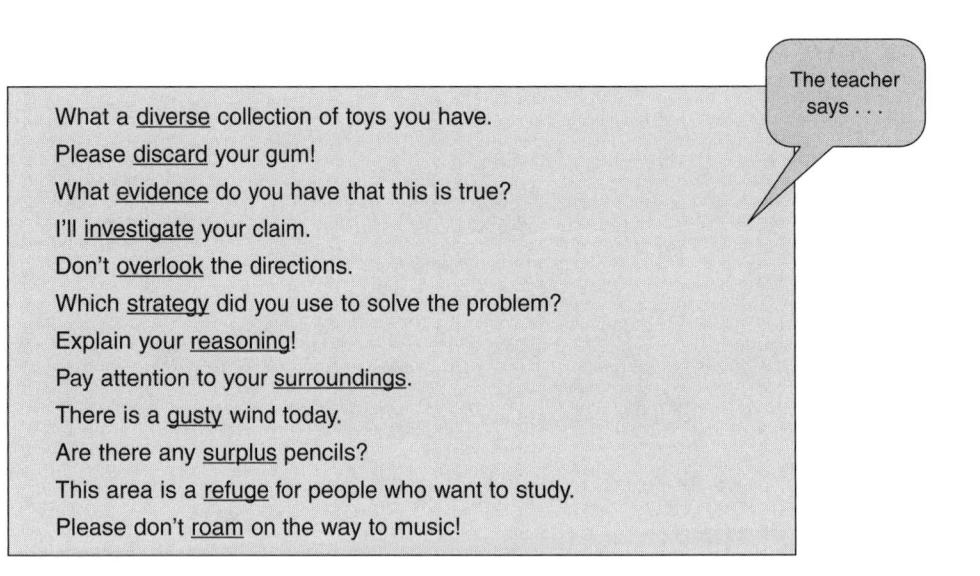

Figure 5.24   Word Wall Teacher Discourse

Children With Special Needs and English Learners

Nourishing vocabulary instruction provides an ideal framework for supporting children with special needs and English learners (see Figures 5.23 and sidebar). The focus on rich oral language encourages teachers to convey content in an oral context, providing access to the core curriculum to children who are unable to read well enough to acquire vocabulary and content through independent reading. English learners' vocabulary acquisition is accelerated with a comprehensive approach to instruction. Teachers provide mini-lessons focused on simple vocabulary and cognates (Chapter 6 includes more details regarding cognate instruction for Spanish-speaking students) and support comprehension of texts and classroom discourse with gestures, pictures, and realia.

> **ELL Strategies**
>
> - Use pictures, gestures, and realia to ensure comprehensible input.
> - Preteach vocabulary.
> - Preview texts in native language.
> - Provide mini-lessons in basic vocabulary and cognates.

Supporting Children With Special Needs

- Provide access to content and vocabulary in an oral context.
- Teach strategies in an oral context that can be transferred to reading at a later time when decoding skills develop.
- Emphasize word consciousness.

Resource Specialists

- Work closely with resource specialists to provide seamless vocabulary and content instruction.

Parents

- Send home texts or books on tape/CD to be read before they are introduced in class.
- Provide suggestions for developing vocabulary and content knowledge through read aloud.

Figure 5.25   Supporting Children With Special Needs

Putting it All Together

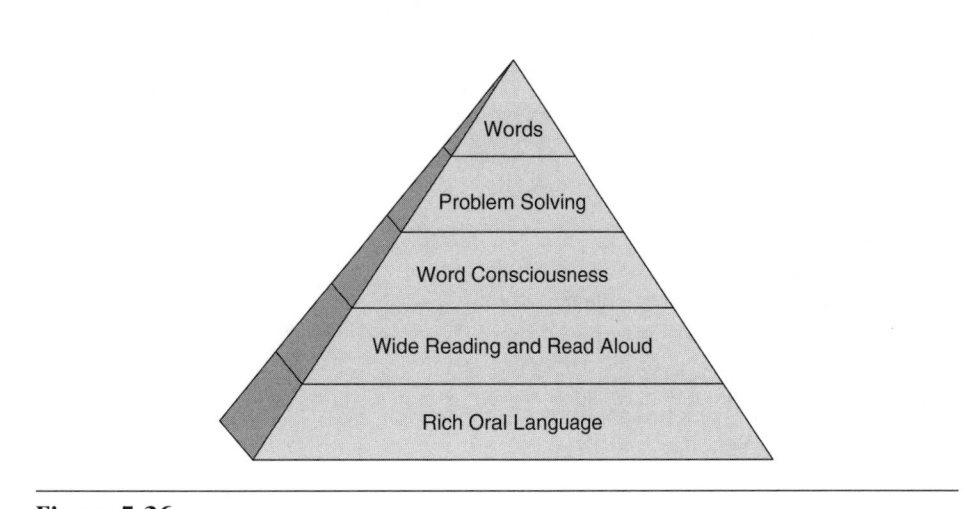

Figure 5.26

When teachers put together all of the methods described in this chapter, they provide upper elementary students with a nourishing and well-balanced vocabulary program. Planning begins with the development of a planning matrix containing content and vocabulary objectives in each subject area (reading–language arts, social studies, math, and science). Once the objectives have been identified, specific instructional methods and activities are selected and daily lesson plans developed, using the nourishing vocabulary menu. The following examples demonstrate the process that a teacher might follow in putting together vocabulary and content instruction for a fifth-grade class.

Step 1: Planning Matrix

The fifth-grade planning matrix presented in Figure 5.31 provides a framework for several days of vocabulary-enriched instruction. The teacher has developed content and vocabulary objectives in each content area. It is important to explain why the word *samovar* (a Russian teapot with a spigot) is included on the core vocabulary list for reading/language arts. Normally, this would be designated as a rare word, not worth the investment of instruction time. It appears repeatedly, however, and is of great significance in the story, *The Night Journey* (Lasky, 1981). It is therefore included in the core vocabulary list for this lesson. *Samovar* is an example of an unknown label for a variation of a known concept. An easy way to introduce this word is with a picture and a short explanation.

The planning matrix demonstrates the effectiveness of teaching vocabulary across the curriculum. The fifth-grade students are exposed to fourteen words during reading and the language arts, sixteen words in social studies, thirteen words in math, and thirteen words in science. This vocabulary-enriched approach provides children with exposure to fifty-six new vocabulary words, versus the fourteen that are taught when vocabulary instruction is limited to reading and the language arts. Although children may not actually learn fifty-six words in a given day, incorporating the newly taught vocabulary into multiple lessons and using the words frequently in classroom discourse will provide the multiple exposures to many that will enhance learning. Spending additional time teaching words that are particularly important to a particular unit of study, using a variety of methods, deepens understanding of word meaning. Over time, explicit instruction and repeated exposure to new words across the curriculum will result in an acceleration of vocabulary acquisition.

California Standards			
Reading and language arts content objectives:	*Social studies content objectives:*	*Math content objectives:*	*Science content objectives:*
Identify key problems in the plot of the story "The Night Journey" (Open Court anthology) *Reading 3.2	Describe cause and effects of Puritan settlement in the New England *History– Social Science 5.4, Reading 2.3	Understand and compute volume and area of simple objects *Measurement & Geometry 1.0	Students will identify the organs involved in the circulatory system and describe how they work *Life Sciences 2b
Vocabulary objectives:	*Vocabulary objectives:*	*Vocabulary objectives:*	*Vocabulary objectives:*
Demonstrate comprehension of core vocabulary words: *samovar, rebuilt, exclaimed, hesitation, apprehension, antique, initial, astonishment, disgusted, ignorance, luminous, consequently, recoiled, rearranged*	Demonstrate comprehension of core vocabulary words: *Puritan, purify, worship, worshippers, separatist, economic, economy, prosper, prosperous, plentiful, dissent, dissenters, obedience, disobedience, reconstruct, construct, construction*	Demonstrate comprehension of core vocabulary words: *parallelogram, quadrilateral, formula, estimate, compute, procedure, construct, two-dimensional, three-dimensional, perimeter, area, volume, visualize*	Demonstrate comprehension of core vocabulary words: *circulatory system, circulate, chambers, valves, veins, arteries, capillaries, eliminate, elimination, intake, expel, inhale, carbon dioxide, oxygen*
	Word structure: prefixes (*re-, dis-, in-, ex-*), suffixes (*-ly, -ist, -ful, -er, -ion, -ory*), word families		

Figure 5.27   Planning Matrix

Step 2: Select Methods and Activities From the Nourishing Vocabulary Menu

Once teachers have developed a planning matrix, vocabulary instruction can be embedded in lessons in each subject area. The nourishing vocabulary menu (page 25) provides a list of instructional activities.

Step 3: Vocabulary-Enriched Lesson Plan

The vocabulary-enriched lesson plan presented in Figure 5.32 is designed to help teachers plan vocabulary-enriched instruction. The teacher begins by scanning the text and identifying and listing key vocabulary words. She then assesses the students' level of vocabulary knowledge (use stoplight vocabulary or the stoplight chart) to determine which words need to be explicitly taught (red-light words). The next task is to identify important concepts and the vocabulary needed to discuss the concepts (schema). After that, the teacher plans the instructional sequence, identifying content and vocabulary instructional activities that will be conducted before, during, and after reading the text. The rich oral language box is designed to help teachers plan text discussion and classroom discourse that provide students with broad vocabulary exposure. Finally, the assessment box allows teachers to plan methods for evaluating students' progress in content and vocabulary.

When teachers provide upper elementary students with comprehensive vocabulary-enriched instruction, they will be prepared for the challenging texts they will encounter in middle school and high school.

Vocabulary-Enriched Lesson Plan

Lesson Date: _____ Subject: _____ Text: _____ Chapter: _____

Content standards and objectives: Describe positive and negative attributes of Puritan society in the New England colonies

Vocabulary objectives: Students will learn core and extended vocabulary words, word families (*purify, worship, economy, prosper, dissent, obey, construct*) and will use words in speaking and writing.

WORDS	Assess students' vocabulary knowledge (stoplight chart). Identify word families. Develop core and extended vocabulary list: *Puritan, purify, worship, worshippers, separatist, economic, economy, prosper, prosperous, plentiful, dissent, dissenters, obedience, disobedience, construct, construction.*
INSTRUCTIONAL SEQUENCE	Vocabulary, content
BEFORE READING	Vocabulary words: Preteach red-light words: *economy, dissent*. Vocabulary word consciousness: Build word schema: word families (*purify, worship, economy, prosper, dissent, obey, construct*), develop semantic webs Content: Introduce content activate prior knowledge: Look at chapter title, headings and pictures to predict topics in chapter, make connections to read aloud *The Thirteenth Floor: A Ghost Story*.
DURING READING	Vocabulary problem solving: Read text aloud while students follow along in their books. Guide students in clarifying vocabulary words encountered in text, emphasize word families, review meaning of affixes that appear in text. Content: Monitor comprehension, discuss key concepts using vocabulary words.
AFTER READING	Content: Develop a t-chart with positive and negative attributes of Puritan society. Ask students to develop and present an argument encouraging settlers to come or not to come live in a Puritan colony. Vocabulary: Encourage students to use vocabulary in oral arguments. Connection to Writing: Students write an essay discussing the positive and negative attributes of Puritan society.
RICH ORAL LANGUAGE	Vocabulary-content: Discuss the text, Use words in classroom discourse. Example: I expect everyone to obey the rules—no dissent is permitted!
ASSESSMENT	Vocabulary-content: Grade essays, evaluating content and quality of writing including use of at least ten vocabulary words.

Figure 5.28   Vocabulary-Enriched Lesson Plan

Planning Instruction for Secondary Students

6

Vocabulary Component	Page Number	Instructional Activity	Description
Words	80	Choosing words to teach	Word selection guidelines for secondary teachers
Words: Instructional activities	85–86	Setting/plot organizer	Used to examine plot features through vocabulary
	89–91	SAT word sorts	Used to categorize words according to a particular semantic relationship
	96	Feature analysis	Matrix used to review vocabulary and content
	103	Semantic web	Graphic organizer for words related by meaning
	104	Compare and contrast organizer	Used to compare and contrast through vocabulary
Problem solving: Selfmonitoring	82	Stoplight vocabulary Word knowledge chart	Methods to help students evaluate their own level of word knowledge
Problem solving: Clarifying strategies	93 94	Problem-solving cue card Context cue card	Guides students' efforts to use clarifying strategies to figure out word meaning
Problem solving: Word parts	100 105	Root and affix chart Prefix and suffix chart	Variety of instructional activities designed to build morphological awareness and knowledge of word parts
Problem solving: Context	94	Context cue card	Guides students' efforts to use context cues to figure out word meaning
Word consciousness	84–86	Text-based dialog	Building word consciousness through dialog regarding unique use of words in text
Wide reading and read aloud			Students are encouraged to read widely outside of class

Figure 6.1   Planning Instruction for Secondary Students

(Continued)

(Continued)

Vocabulary Component	Page Number	Instructional Activity	Description
Rich oral language	87	Text-based dialog Semantic word wall	Students engaged in text-based dialog Words posted on a word wall to encourage use in classroom discourse
Putting it all together: Planning	83 95 & 97 100	Unit plan and lesson plan: *The Scarlet Letter* Unit plan and lesson plan: Science News and Views cross-curricular lesson plan	Address multiple components of the vocabulary pyramid Planning vocabulary-enriched science lessons Planning integrated vocabulary-enriched instruction

Figure 6.1   Planning Instruction for Secondary Students

High school ushers in new challenges in terms of the conceptual and linguistic demands that texts pose. Students read novels that include an immense number of rare words, encounter archaic forms of English, and study textbooks filled with highly technical vocabulary. Students who enter high school with an impoverished vocabulary are at a huge disadvantage in mastering content. What should be done to help high school students who depend on schools for literacy? Teachers understand that many students are unable to comprehend their textbooks. Nonetheless, time for instruction is limited and there is pressure to cover a great deal of content. Teachers worry that allotting time to vocabulary instruction may interfere with the mandated curriculum.

This chapter is designed to help assuage these concerns. Vocabulary instruction is presented as an integral part of the curriculum, rather than a separate topic. Methods of vocabulary instruction are provided that can be embedded in lesson plans in each content area. As instruction is broadened to include math, science, history, and other subjects, students' understanding of the material will improve and their overall academic achievement will therefore be strengthened. A comprehensive approach to secondary-level vocabulary instruction is most effective when it has the support and participation of every teacher at a school.

CHOOSING WORDS TO TEACH

Once teachers have made the decision to participate in a comprehensive vocabulary development program, they are confronted with important instructional decisions: Which words should be taught? What is the best way to teach vocabulary? How much time should be devoted to vocabulary instruction? We will address these questions briefly and then share lesson plans and classroom vignettes that demonstrate effective instructional practices in several content areas. The following are general guidelines that may be useful to teachers in making instructional decisions.

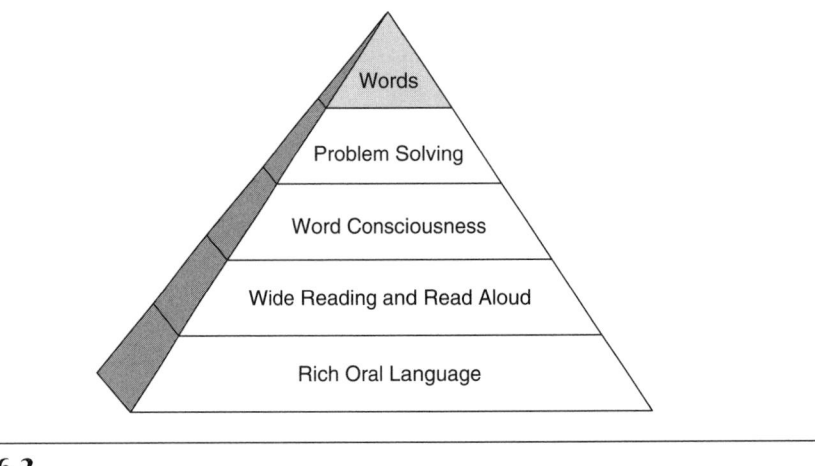

Figure 6.2

Which words should be taught?

- *Words that appear in novels and textbooks that the students read:* Context supports word learning and provides an authentic purpose for word learning.
- *Words that are important for comprehension:* When there are too many words to teach, select those that are most important to comprehension of the text.
- *Words that are worth learning:* Select core vocabulary words that the students are likely to encounter again.
- *Words that students do not already know:* Use a metacognitive device such as a word knowledge chart (Lubliner, 2005b) to determine which words the students do not already know.
- *Related words that are easy to learn:* Identify words from the same word family that extend vocabulary learning. Create an extended vocabulary list of related words (such as *elegant, elegance, elegantly*).

Vocabulary Instruction in the English Class

High school English teachers are responsible for teaching students a vast array of literary skills, including reading comprehension, literary analysis, composition, grammar, and vocabulary. Ideally, multiple methods of instruction are included in English lessons, enabling students to acquire vocabulary as they read literature and engage in speaking and writing activities during the course of daily instruction. Proficiency in one area helps to build skills in another because the language arts are closely interconnected. We will begin by examining vocabulary-enriched lessons in a literature-based unit.

LITERATURE-BASED INSTRUCTION

Students are introduced to great works of fiction in their English classes that present huge challenges in terms of vocabulary. The following vignette demonstrates how a high school English teacher embeds vocabulary instruction into his lessons.

Mr. Hall is preparing to teach Nathaniel Hawthorne's novel *The Scarlet Letter* to his eleventh-grade English classes. He realizes that the book was written in an archaic form of English and includes many difficult words and concepts that will be unfamiliar to his students. He plans carefully for instruction, focusing on challenging vocabulary words that his students need to learn. Mr. Hall compiles a list of words from the first two chapters and then uses a word knowledge chart to identify the words that the students do not already know. He lists words that he thinks may be difficult for the students on a piece of chart paper, posted on an easel facing the wall. The students are asked to place a tally mark in the column signifying their level of word knowledge, next to each word listed on the chart. The red column is used for words the students have never heard before; the yellow indicates partial word knowledge; and the green indicates that the word is known well and can be used independently. The teacher scans the chart paper for words that will be the focus of explicit vocabulary instruction. An excerpt of the word knowledge chart that Mr. Hall uses is presented in Figure 6.3.

	RED-LIGHT WORD ⬤ I've never seen this word before	YELLOW-LIGHT WORD ◯ I've seen this word before and have an idea of what it means	GREEN-LIGHT WORD ⬤ I know this word well and can use it in a sentence
elegance	‖	‖‖	ЖЖ ЖЖ ЖЖ ЖЖ ЖЖ ЖЖ ЖЖ
throng	ЖЖ ЖЖ ЖЖ ЖЖ ЖЖ ЖЖ	‖‖	‖
edifice	ЖЖ ЖЖ ЖЖ ЖЖ ЖЖ ЖЖ	ЖЖ ‖‖	‖
utopia	ЖЖ ЖЖ ЖЖ ЖЖ ЖЖ		‖
dignity	‖		ЖЖ ЖЖ ЖЖ ЖЖ ЖЖ ЖЖ ЖЖ

Figure 6.3   Word Knowledge Chart: *The Scarlet Letter*

The word knowledge chart (Lubliner, 2005b) demonstrates that most students already know words such as *elegance* and *dignity*. These words are therefore eliminated.

Mr. Hall scans the chart and identifies red-light words—words that most students do not already know and creates a core vocabulary list. He develops a unit plan including content and vocabulary objectives, based on the core vocabulary list. He plans vocabulary-enriched instruction including reading and writing activities and carefully scripts classroom discourse. He also plans to incorporate mini-lessons on metacognitive skills and clarifying strategies in the unit, and will also teach green-light words to the two English learners in his class in a mini-lesson. Figure 6.4 presents an excerpt of the unit plan for the first two chapters of *The Scarlet Letter*. A copy of the unit plan is provided in Appendix B.

Once he has completed the unit plan, Mr. Hall develops individual lesson plans. Figure 6.5 presents the introductory lesson plan, which uses vocabulary found in Chapters 1 and 2 of *The Scarlet Letter* to drive instruction. A copy of the vocabulary-enriched lesson plan is provided in Appendix B.

Subject: <u>English</u>   Grade: <u> 11 </u>   Text: <u>The Scarlet Letter</u>   Chapter: <u>1–2</u>   Dates: <u>_____</u>

Objectives and Assessment	Core Vocabulary Words	Extended Vocabulary Words	Instructional Methods	Classroom Discourse	Problem-Solving Instruction
Content objectives: Students will demonstrate understanding of the setting and the time frame and make inference about plot, students will compare and contrast views of Hester Vocabulary objectives: Students will use vocabulary from text to convey understanding of setting, characters Assessment: Graphic organizer, summary	throng edifice utopia ponderous portal inauspicious illustrious culprit indubitably scourged demeanor venerable infamy impropriety magistrate abashed evanescent ignominy visage flagrant	thronged edify utopian ponder auspicious scourge venerate infamous propriety unabashed ignominious grim-visaged unkindly-visaged flagrantly	Identify key words describing setting, characters, time frame, & plot, using graphic organizer Write summary of Chapters 1 and 2 using key vocabulary Web word families Venn diagram comparing different views of Hester, using key vocabulary	Do you think that the Puritans created a utopian society? What do you think the edifice looked like? Can you describe an auspicious/ inauspicious occasion in your life? Please do not throng around my desk. Please move away from the portal.	Meta-cogntive skills: self-monitoring Strategies: Context clues Structural analysis

Figure 6.4   Unit Plan: *The Scarlet Letter*, Chapters 1–2

Vocabulary-Enriched Lesson Plan

Lesson Date: _____Text: _____ Chapter: _____

Standards and objectives: Key Concepts, Skills: California English/Language Arts Standards 3.6, 3.7, 3.11 Students will demonstrate understanding of the setting, the time frame, characters, and make inferences about plot of the novel.

Content and vocabulary objectives: Students read the first chapter of the *The Scarlet Letter* and identify vocabulary words that describe setting, time frame, characters, and plot using a graphic organizer. Students make inferences about the story based on the graphic organizer.

Core vocabulary: throng, edifice, utopia, ponderous, portal, inauspicious, illustrious, culprit, indubitably, scourged, demeanor, venerable, infamy, impropriety, magistrate, abashed, evanescent, ignominy, visage, flagrant

Introduction: Discuss the first chapter of the novel *The Scarlet Letter* and ask students what made it difficult to read.

Figure 6.5   Vocabulary-Enriched Lesson Plan   *(Continued)*

(Continued)

> **Content and Vocabulary: Instructional Sequence**
>
> _Direct vocabulary instruction:_ Teacher discusses the importance of vocabulary in understanding the novel, explains and models the use of graphic organizer.
>
> _Student activities:_ Students work in pairs, completing a graphic organizer and selecting words that describe setting, time period, characters, and plot.
>
> _Use of words in classroom discourse:_ The students share the words they have identified on their graphic organizer and make inferences about the setting, time period, characters, and plot, students discuss the character of Hester using core vocabulary such as _hussy, malefactress, elegant, dignified._
>
> _Problem solving:_ The teacher asks the students how they identified the key words, points out the importance of context clues.
>
> _Homework:_ Students read Chapter 2 and write an imaginary journal entry, taking one character's perspective, of events in first two chapters. Use core vocabulary from the novel.
>
> _Assessment:_ Students' perspective journal entries are assessed for content and the use of core vocabulary. However, students are not penalized for trying to use a word, and using it incorrectly. We want to encourage them to experiment with language and see this as an opportunity to teach how words go together. If students are penalized, they will only use familiar words and miss this opportunity to learn.

Figure 6.5   Vocabulary-Enriched Lesson Plan

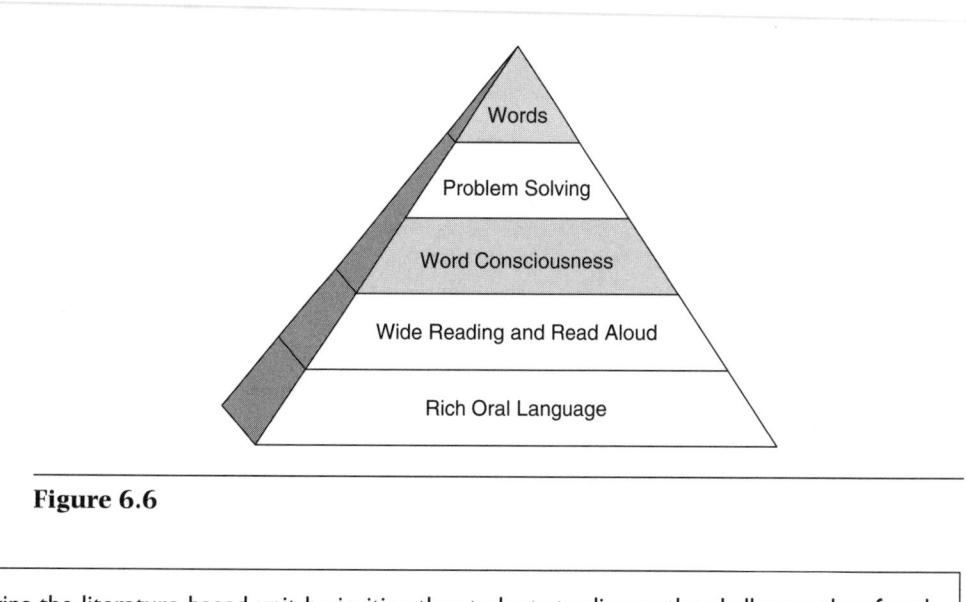

Figure 6.6

> Mr. Hall begins the literature-based unit by inviting the students to discuss the challenges they faced in reading the first chapter of _The Scarlet Letter._ He attempts to draw them into the novel by focusing on Hawthorne's use of vocabulary—building word consciousness related to the first chapter of _The Scarlet Letter._
>
> Mr. Hall: Good morning! Please take out your books and let's get started! Do any of you have any comments about the first chapter of _The Scarlet Letter_ you read for today? (Calls on Michelle.)
>
> Michelle: It had so many weird words and things. I didn't get it at all.

Mr. Hall:	Yes, Hawthorne uses a lot of difficult words. Did anyone notice anything else? (Calls on Jason.)
Jason:	It's not the way people talk. Like who says "sad-coloured garments?" Why doesn't this guy just say what he means?
Mr. Hall:	Right! It's not the way we talk today. The language is archaic, an older form of English. Some of the words are spelled differently too, like *coloured*. But I think you can figure out what Hawthorne is trying to tell us.
Amir:	I think he's trying to say that the people weren't too happy.
Mr. Hall:	Good! "Sad-coloured garments" doesn't mean they were wearing dark clothes. The first scene is painting a gloomy picture of life in this town.
Sarah:	This is going to be really depressing!
Mr. Hall:	No, it will be great! Try to approach the book with an open mind. Now, you've already noticed the challenging vocabulary and unusual way that words are used in this novel. We're going to find words and phrases that help us figure out the setting (where the story took place), the time frame (when the story took place), the characters (who the story was about), and the plot (what happens in the story). Take a look at this graphic organizer (passes out graphic organizer in Figure 6.7 and places a transparency on the overhead). Let's fill out the first column together. Your job is to find words and phrases that tell us about the setting.

Setting–Time Frame–Characters–Plot Organizer			
Setting	*Time Frame*	*Characters*	*Plot*
Words & Phrases	Words & Phrases	Words & Phrases	Words & Phrases
Inference:	Inference:	Inference:	Inference:

Figure 6.7   Blank STCP Organizer

Dan:	You mean like *wooden edifice*? Is that a setting?
Mr. Hall:	Exactly! The wooden edifice describes the building where the first scene takes place.
Miguel:	Oh yeah! It's like *edificio* in Spanish. That means *building*.
Mr. Hall:	Excelente! Great use of cognates, Miguel! You noticed that *edifice* and *edificio* are the same in Spanish and English (writes *wooden edifice* on the transparency). What other words describe the setting?

(Continued)

(Continued)

Ashley:	How about *new colony?*
Mr. Hall:	Yes, that also tells us about the setting of the story. It takes place in a wooden edifice in a new colony . . .

Mr. Hall encourages the students to identify key words and phrases from the text and uses the words multiple times in his discourse. This provides the students with repeated exposures to new vocabulary and the opportunity to observe how the words are used in conversation as well as in the text. It is also important to note Miguel's awareness of cognates (*edifice-edificio*), demonstrating that he has internalized the instruction that Mr. Hall provided to his Spanish-speaking students earlier in the year. This instruction has developed students' morphological awareness—the ability to notice word parts, enabling them to use cognate information to make meaning of new vocabulary.

Mr. Hall writes the students' suggestions on the graphic organizer on the overhead transparency and reminds them to fill in their own graphic organizers at the same time. Once the students have identified all of the words and phrases that convey information about the setting, Mr. Hall asks them to make an inference about the setting of the story. The students suggest that the story takes place in front of the jail, in a new Puritan colony in New England. Mr. Hall then asks the students to continue working with a partner, identifying words and phrases from Chapter 1 that describe the time frame, characters, and plot of the story. Mr. Hall reminds the students to read the second chapter for homework, keeping the graphic organizer in mind.

The next day, the class completes the STCP graphic organizer, discussing the key vocabulary and making inferences about the time frame, characters, and plot of the novel. Figure 6.8 shows is the completed graphic organizer for the first two chapters of *The Scarlet Letter.*

Setting	Time Frame	Characters	Plot
wooden edifice, Boston, New England, vicinity of Cornhill, Isaac Johnson's lot, King's Chapel, wooden jail, New World, market-place, Prison Lane	steeple-crowned hats, new colony, wheel track of the street, Puritans	Puritans, inhabitants of Boston: grim rigidity, bearded physiognomies, stern-browed men, unkindly visaged women: hard-featured dame, iron-visaged old dame Hester Prynne: malefactress, brazen hussy, naughty baggage, dignity, elegance, beautiful, ladylike, delicate, evanescent, indescribable grace, misfortune, ignominy, culprit, antique, gentility, infant misshapen Scholar: well-stricken in years, penetrating power	awful business, token of her shame, fantastic flourishes of gold thread-Scarlet Letter, iniquity is dragged out in the sunshine, place appointed for her punishment, scaffold, pillory, taint of deepest sin, infant she had born
Inference: The story takes place in Boston colony	Inference: The story takes place in the 1600s	Inference: The story will be about Puritans, Hester, her baby, and the scholar	Inference: The plot is about Hester's shame; She is an unwed mother.

Figure 6.8   STCP Organizer: *The Scarlet Letter*, Chapters 1–2

The following vignette takes place on the second day of the unit, as the students discuss the characters column of the graphic organizer, focusing on Hester Prynne.

Mr. Hall:	So what do we know about this character, Hester Prynne?
Doug:	It's like he [Hawthorne] can't make up his mind. He calls her words like *hussy* and then he says she's beautiful and ladylike.
Sandi:	What's a hussy?
Doug:	Isn't it like a slut or something?
Mr. Hall:	Yes, that's right. Here's another interesting word: *malefactress*. What do you think that means?
Juana:	I know it's something bad. There's the root *mal* inside the word.
Avi:	Yeah, and there are other parts we know too. *Fac* is like in the word *factory*—where they make things and the -*tress* ending is like *waitress*—a woman who waits on tables. So, my guess is that *malfactress* means a woman who makes badness, like an evildoer.
Mr. Hall:	Great! You both did an outstanding job of using word parts to figure out the meaning of the word. Now look at this! According to the book, Hester is a brazen hussy, a malefactress, and a beautiful, delicate, elegant, dignified lady. How do you make sense of these contradictions?
Colin:	It's all about your point of view. The Puritans thought Hester was a slut because they were really narrow-minded. But Hawthorne is saying that she was really a beautiful, dignified woman.
Mr. Hall:	You're right! Hawthorne is showing us totally different views of the same character, using words to paint pictures in our minds.

Note that Mr. Hall extends the students' vocabulary knowledge by using related words (members of the same word families) in his discourse. For example, the students have listed the words *elegance* and *dignity* to describe Hester. Mr. Hall extends the vocabulary, describing Hester as *elegant* and *dignified*. Once he has selected core vocabulary words from the novel (high-utility words the students do not already know), he places the words onto a semantic word wall (Figure 6.9) so that he will remember to incorporate the words into classroom discourse. Each day Mr. Hall glances up at the word wall and makes an effort to incorporate core and extended vocabulary into the class discussion. As the students move through subsequent chapters, Mr. Hall continues to identify core vocabulary and adds words to the word wall. The semantic word wall in Figure 6.9 includes vocabulary words encountered during the first two chapters of the novel.

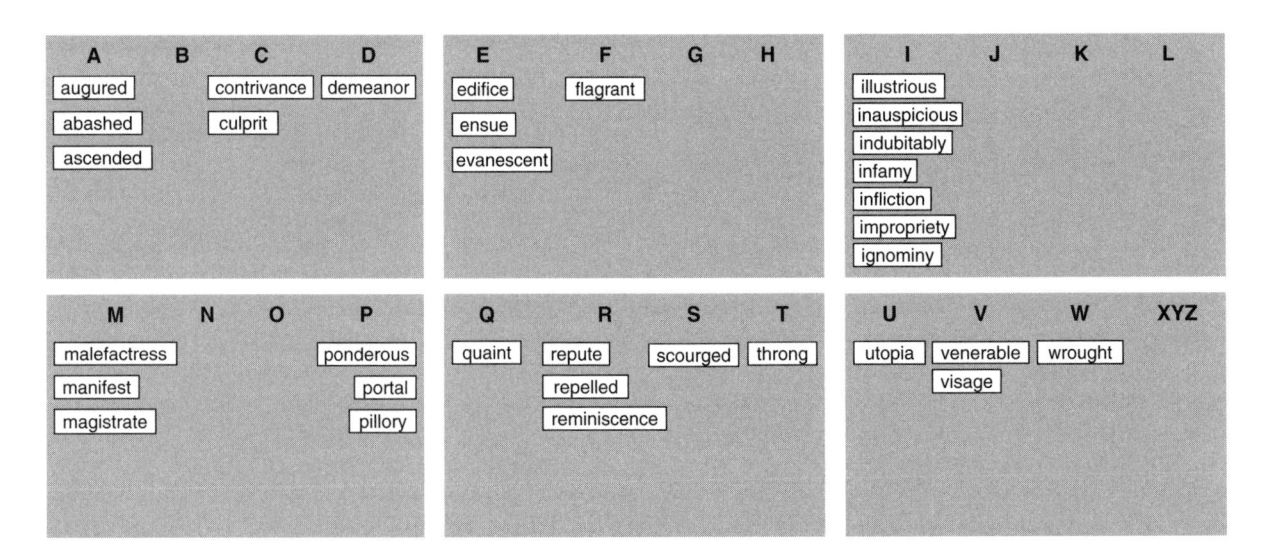

Figure 6.9   Word Wall: *The Scarlet Letter*, Chapters 1–2

TEACHING SAT WORDS

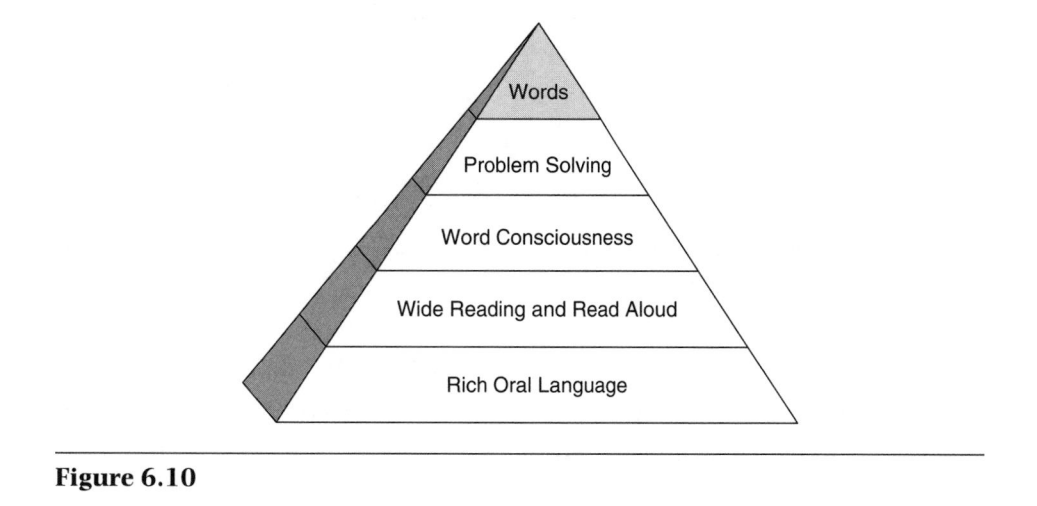

Figure 6.10

High school English teachers often have the responsibility of teaching students vocabulary likely to be found on the SAT test. Rather than giving students lists of words to memorize and quickly forget, it is important to provide activities that maximize retention of newly learned words. The key principles of effective instruction are *meaningful use* and *repeated exposure*. Figure 6.11 shows a set of SAT words (taken from 5000 Free SAT Words at www.freevocabulary.com) and activities that incorporate principles of meaningful use and repeated exposure into instruction.

SAT Words: Behavior, Management, and Classroom Activities					
admonish	flagrant	invective	repository	remiss	tactics
aggravate	fortitude	irate/ire	onus	reproof	tantamount
appall	guile	jubilation laud	persevere	repudiate	temerity
boisterous	harangue	lenient	proficiency	requisite	tenacious
brandish	imminent	levity	prohibition	rescind	tendency
buffoon	impertinence	limitation	proscribe	revoke	tirade
chastise	impropriety	livid	puerile	sanctimonious	tolerate
compulsory	inadvisable	loquacious	punctilious	scrupulous	transcend
defiant	incite	magnanimous	quandary	skeptics	transgress
deportment	inept	miscreant	reassure	slothful	travesty
deprecate	infamous	mitigate	recur	somniferous	truculence
deterrent	ingenious	mollify	refute	somnolent	umbrage
disparage	iniquity	munificence	reiterate	spontaneous	unique
edify	instigate	necessitate	relent	stratagem	vindicate
effrontery	insurrection	notorious		stupendous	vociferous
egregious	reprimand	obviate		subterfuge	
exemplary		odious		surmise	
repudiate					

Figure 6.11   Selected SAT Words

SAT Vocabulary: Guidelines for Instruction

- *Word selection*: Choose words that are semantically related so that they can be grouped for vocabulary development activities and used in classroom discourse. The words on the sample list (Figure 6.6) were chosen because they relate to the topics of behavior, management, and classroom activities.
- *Word sorting*: Ask students to sort the words into semantically related categories.
- *Closed sorts*: Teachers generate the categories and students select the words.
- *Open sorts*: The students were given a list of SAT words to sort. The boxes below (figures 6.12 and 6.13) demonstrate sorting decisions made by the students.
- *Extended vocabulary*: Identify extended vocabulary words from SAT words
- *Synonyms and antonyms*: Identify relationships between selected SAT words.
- *Similar words*: Ask students to distinguish between similar words on the SAT list. Discuss how the following sets of words are similar and different:
  - *admonish, chastise, reproach*
  - *vociferous, boisterous, loquacious*
- *Semantic word wall*: Post SAT words on a word wall, use them in classroom discourse, and encourage students to use them in writing and speaking.

Speech	Behavior
admonish	aggravate
deprecate	appall
disparage	incite
edify	instigate
harangue	relent
reprimand	revoke
laud	surmise
mollify	tolerate
reassure	transgress
reprimand	
repudiate	

Figure 6.12   Words That Describe Speech and Behavior

Negative	Positive
admonish	laud
deprecate	mitigate
disparage	mollify
haranguer	reassure
eprimand	tolerate
repudiate	

Figure 6.13   Negative and Positive Words

- *Humor*: Use SAT words humorously in classroom discourse and encourage students to do the same.

Teacher examples

- Students who have the *effrontery* to behave like *buffoons* will be *chastised!*
- I hope that this *admonishment* will *obviate* the need for future *tirades*.
- I do not mean to *disparage* students whose conduct has been *exemplary*. I *laud* your *fortitude* and apologize for *haranguing* you!

○ Let me *reiterate* the point: *transgressions* of the rules will not be *tolerated!*

○ Who is the *miscreant* responsible for this mess?

Student examples

○ That was an *odious* assignment.

○ Please *relent* and give us more time to finish this assignment.

○ Isn't our *deportment exemplary* today?

Sort the following SAT verbs into categories. Explain why.	
admonish	mitigate
aggravate	mollify
appall	reassure
chastise	relent
deprecate	reprimand
disparage	repudiate
edify	revoke
harangue	surmise
incite	tolerate
instigate	transgress
laud	

Figure 6.14 SAT Words: Open Sort

SAT Verbs	*Extended Words*
aggravate	aggravation
chastise	chastisement
edify	edification
harangue	harangue (noun)
incite	incitement
mitigate	mitigation
persevere	perseverance
reassure	reassurance, assure,
relent	assurance
reprimand	relenting, unrelenting
repudiate	reprimand (noun)
revoke	repudiation
tolerate	revocation, invoke,
transgress	invocation
	toleration, tolerance,
	intolerant, intolerance
	transgression, regress,
	regression

Figure 6.15 SAT Verbs and Extended Words

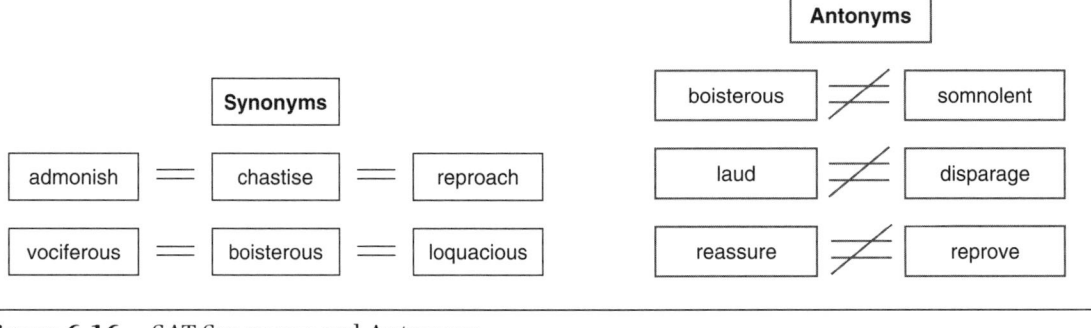

Figure 6.16   SAT Synonyms and Antonyms

PROBLEM-SOLVING SKILLS

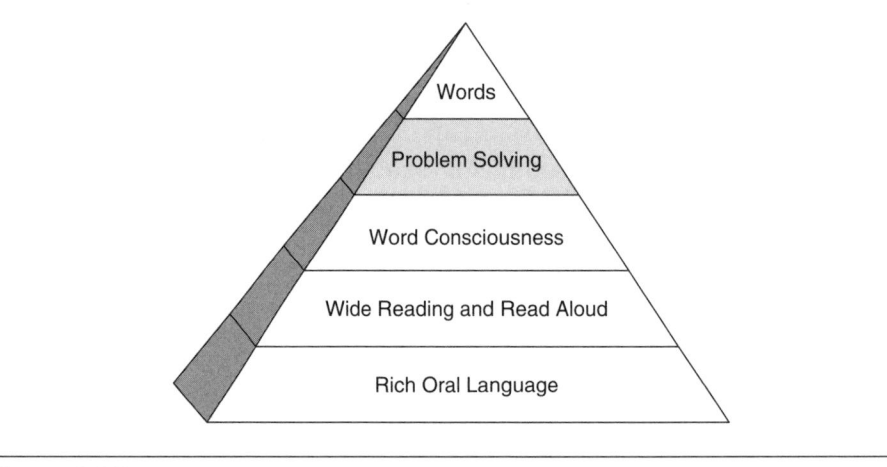

Figure 6.17

Problem-solving skill instruction is vital to any comprehensive vocabulary development program. Students are taught metacognitive skills such as self-monitoring and self-regulation and the use of effective clarifying strategies to make sense of unknown words they encounter during reading. Teachers develop students' metacognitive skills by using devices such as the stoplight vocabulary chart and stoplight vocabulary to help students learn to monitor their levels of word knowledge. Students are frequently prompted to identify words that they don't know in text and are taught to use effective clarifying strategies to figure out word meaning.

The problem-solving cue card (Figure 6.18) is used as the basis of clarifying strategy and metacognitive skill instruction. Teachers begin by introducing and explicitly teaching each strategy. Modeling is provided with specially constructed texts, followed by guided practice and instruction designed to help students transfer strategic skills to natural texts.

The strategies in the first group are listed under the category *monitor* and are designed to build metacognitive skills. Students are prompted to "Think about the meaning of words as you read" and "Notice when you don't understand a word so that you can fix the problem." Self-monitoring is often a problem for struggling students who are unable to identify most of the words that they do not know. When students are given explicit instruction and plenty of practice monitoring their comprehension of words and texts, their ability to self-monitor improves substantially (Lubliner & Smetana, 2005).

The second group of strategies is categorized as *manage the problem*. This set includes *memory*, which is designed to encourage students' lexical access as they reach purposefully into memory for partially learned words. *Try topic cues* prompts students to review their knowledge of the topic and consider the unknown word in relationship to that knowledge structure. For example, students faced with the unknown word *debilitating* can use what they already know about serious diseases and information provided in the article to infer the meaning of the word.

Try word parts is a strategy based on morphology. Students are prompted to use knowledge of prefixes, suffixes, base words, and roots to construct word meaning. Students must have developed morphological awareness (the ability to notice word parts) and knowledge of high-frequency affixes and roots in order to use this strategy effectively.

Try text clues directs students' attention to text features that contribute to the construction of word meaning. For example, textbook authors routinely use chapter titles, section titles, boldface print, and highlighting to indicate significant concepts discussed in the text. When students pay attention to text features, they are often able to discern the meaning of unknown words in relationship to the topic.

The final management strategy, *try context*, is complex. We have therefore developed an additional cue card to use during instruction (page 94).

Once students have learned each of the management strategies, instruction shifts to effective strategy implementation. *Mix the strategies* reminds students that strategies often work better in tandem than in isolation and encourages them to use more than one strategy to figure out word meaning. For example, morphological analysis might provide partial word knowledge; however combining morphology with context increases the likelihood that the construction of meaning will make sense.

Finally students are encouraged to *monitor again and move on*. They double check word meaning and make sure that they understand the text well enough to continue reading. If they are unable to figure out the meaning of an unknown word, students are prompted to put a Post-it in the text and look up the word later if they need to know the exact meaning (Lubliner, 2005b).

A Focus on Context: The Nourishing Vocabulary Context Cue Card

Using context cues to construct meaning of unknown words is one of the hallmarks of a proficient reader. However, context is tricky and doesn't always work. The nourishing vocabulary context cue card (Figure 6.19) is designed to help students learn to use a range of context substrategies effectively. We suggest that context be taught as form of hypothesis testing. Students begin by considering the unknown word in the text and generate a hypothesis regarding word meaning. They try context cues and check to see whether the hypothesized meaning

---

NOURISHING VOCABULARY PROBLEM-SOLVING CUE CARD

MONITOR
- Think about the meaning of words as you read.
- Notice when you don't understand a word so that you can fix the problem.

MANAGE THE PROBLEM
Choose a problem-solving approach: Read the sentence and think about the unfamiliar word. Which of these clarifying strategies might help?

- TRY <u>MEMORY</u>: Have you ever seen or heard the word before? How was it used?
- TRY <u>TOPIC CUES</u>: What do you know about the topic that helps you figure out the word?
- TRY <u>WORD PARTS</u>: Use your knowledge of prefixes, suffixes, base words, or roots to help you fix the problem.
- TRY <u>TEXT CLUES</u>: If you are reading a textbook, use chapter titles, subtitles, headings, and bold-face print to get information that might help you understand the word. Remember that key words are often defined in the text.
- TRY <u>CONTEXT</u>: See context cue cards.

MIX THE STRATEGIES
- Use more than one clarifying strategy to figure out a word.
- Always come back to context. Make sure that the meaning of the word makes sense in the sentence.

MONITOR AGAIN AND MOVE ON
- Double check: does it make sense?
- When you know enough about the word to understand the text, continue reading.
- If you can't figure out the word, put a Post-it on the page and look it up later if you need to know the exact meaning.

Figure 6.18 Nourishing Vocabulary Problem-Solving Cue Card

makes sense so that the hypothesis can be confirmed or rejected. Let's take a closer look at each type of context cue!

Students find context cues easiest to use when information is located in close proximity to the target word. Learning to check for double-comma cues (appositives) is a quick and easy strategy that students master readily. The following is an example of a double-comma cue: "The Puritans decided that the malefactress, an evil woman, was responsible." Note that the definition of malefactress is provided in the same sentence, set off by double commas.

The cue *part of speech* prompts students to consider parts of speech in the problem-solving process. Students must learn to identify clues in the sentence that signal the presence of specific types of words. For example, when students identify the article *the* in a sentence, they know that the next word must be a noun. This limits the range of possible word meaning to people, places, or things. When there is an unknown word between the article and the noun, they can infer that the word is an adjective. Use of the part of speech context cue is very helpful to students in determining approximate word meaning.

The cue *look for lists of things* helps students identify an unknown word that is presented as part of a group of like items. For example, Edgar Allen Poe describes the raven as a "grim, ungainly, ghastly, gaunt and ominous bird of yore" (Poe, 2002). Students do not need to understand the exact meaning of the word *ominous* to understand the poem. Knowing that it is one of five words that describe the fearsome raven is enough to support comprehension of the poem.

Novels often contain mood cues that provide hints about word meaning and support comprehension of the text. Mood cues are descriptive words and phrases that provide the reader with valuable insight. Mood cues suggest emotions such as joy, sorrow, fear, or despair that often hint at the meaning of an unknown word. For example, figuring out the meaning of the word *bleak* is facilitated by Poe's mood cues that describe the scene as a dark and dreary night.

If initial efforts to construct word meaning do not work, students are prompted to read the rest of the paragraph or section. Often context cues can be found farther from the target word. The following example demonstrates context cues that are a bit harder to find. The word *ebony* is used to describe the bird in the eighth stanza of "The Raven." It is only in the seventeenth stanza that Poe mentions the bird's black plume, providing a definition of ebony (black).

The last cue, *don't give up*, is very important to emphasize with students. Using strategies to figure out word meaning takes effort and does not always work. Students need a great deal of encouragement and practice to develop proficient context strategy skills.

Nourishing Vocabulary
Context Cue Card

Looking at context cues is like trying to solve a word puzzle. You need to look at many different pieces and make educated guesses about how they fit together. Then you continue reading and try to confirm your hypothesis. Context is tricky and you'll need to consider several strategies:

DOUBLE-COMMA CLUE: Sometimes definitions for new words are set off by double commas. Look for these clues in the text

PART OF SPEECH: Sometimes the part of speech gives you a hint that helps

- Is the word a noun? Sometimes you can tell by the article (*a, an, the*)
- Is the word an adjective—does it describe a noun? If so, look for more information that will help you figure out what the word might be describing.
- Is the word a verb—an action word? Does it tell you what someone is doing or how something is happening?
- Is the word an adverb—describes a verb? What type of action or thing does it describe? (Hint: adverbs often end in *ly*).
- Do you have enough information to make an educated guess? If not, look for more clues.

LOOK FOR LISTS: Often an unknown word is part of a list of similar things.

MONITOR THE MOOD: does the text describe feelings that give you clues about the word?

READ ON: Read the rest of the paragraph. Is there any other information in the text that helps you figure out the word's meaning?

DON'T GIVE UP! Context clues don't always work.

RETURN TO THE PROBLEM-SOLVING CUE CARD: Once you have an idea of what the word means, return to the problem-solving cue card.

- MIX THE STRATEGIES.
  - ○ Use more than one clarifying strategy to figure out a word.
- MONITOR AGAIN AND MOVE ON
  - ○ Double check: Does it make sense?
  - ○ When you know enough about the word to understand the text, continue reading
  - ○ If you can't figure out the word, put a Post-it on the page and look it up later if you need to know the exact meaning

---

Figure 6.19   Nourishing Vocabulary Context Cue Card

Vocabulary Instruction in the Content Areas

Math, science, history, and other teachers are primarily responsible for teaching the content specific to their disciplines. However, content area instruction cannot be divorced from vocabulary that is used to label concepts and discuss the relationship between concepts and other information. Students often struggle in high school math, science, and history classes due in part to their inability to comprehend textbooks. Textbooks used at the secondary level are densely packed with information and extremely challenging vocabulary. When teachers provide vocabulary-enriched instruction, they help students acquire the skills they need to comprehend their textbooks and succeed in content area classes.

The same general guidelines for vocabulary instruction that were provided for English classes work well for content area teachers. We also suggest following the same planning process, beginning with a unit plan. The content area teacher identifies the objectives and standards that will be covered in an instructional unit. He examines the textbook chapters the students will be reading and identifies a list of challenging vocabulary. Using the stoplight chart (Chapter 8), the teacher then eliminates the green-light words, which the students already know. The core vocabulary list is thus comprised primarily of red light-words, which the students need to learn. The teacher also identifies extended vocabulary words that belong to the same word family to include in classroom discourse. Instructional methods are selected with an emphasis on integrating vocabulary and content into every lesson. Figure 6.20 presents an example of a high school biology unit on kingdoms of life.

Subject: _Biology_   Grade: _9th/10th_   Text: _Biology_   Chapter: _4-6_   Dates: _11/4–11/18_

Objectives and Assessment	Core Vocabulary	Extended Vocabulary	Instructional Methods	Classroom Discourse	Strategy and Metacognitive Skills Instruction
Content objectives: Students identify characteristics and member organisms belonging to five kingdoms of life _Vocabulary objectives:_ Students identify words representing characteristics on a feature analysis	_heterotropic immobile multicellular unicellular eubacteria cyanobacteria motile protozoa aquatic autotropic monera protista fungi plantae animalia cilia eukaryotic flagella archaebacteria_	_heterozygous mobile, mobility, immobility cell bacteria, bacterial fungus, fungal_	Read chapters and answer questions, Identify affixes and roots in words Sort words by kingdom of life, Fill out feature analysis review of unit	I'd like you to remain immobile in your seats during class. You are a multicellular organism. We are members of the animalia kingdom. Think of some examples of words with the prefix, _hetero._	Students recognize prefixes: _hetero, im, multi, aqua, auto_ in words and use knowledge of prefixes to construct word meaning

Figure 6.20   Unit Plan: Science

Students encounter many words in the content areas that include affixes and roots, providing teachers with ample opportunities to teach structural analysis as a clarifying strategy. Math and science textbooks, in particular, use many words formed from Greek and Latin affixes and roots. Lists of common roots and affixes are readily available online. However, asking students to memorize long lists of roots and affixes rarely results in long-term learning. Instruction is most effective when it is closely tied to the texts that students are reading. For example, when students open their biology books, it is a good time to teach them that the word *biology* is comprised of two Greek roots: *bio* (life) and *ology* (the study of). When the students read about unicellular and multicellular organisms, it is helpful to teach them the Latin roots *multi* (many) and *uni* (one). As students read their textbooks, they encounter these words numerous times, facilitating retention of affix, root, and overall word meaning.

Multiple exposures to roots and affixes are important, but students also need to develop morphological awareness—the ability to notice word parts—in order to benefit from strategy instruction. Morphological awareness can be developed through thoughtful instruction and a great deal of practice. Teachers point out affixes and roots as they appear in texts and prompt students to use information strategically to construct word meaning. The teacher can teach students to use word structure in a variety of ways.

- *Develop morphological awareness:* Ask students to underline or highlight words containing a set of roots and affixes that have been discussed in class (*biography, geology*).
- *Use word parts to construct meaning:* Ask students to figure out the meaning of words containing the same roots that have been recently taught. For example, for biography, *bio* means life and *graph* means something written, so a biography is something written about someone's life.
- *Play with morphology:* In groups, have students create new, possible words that don't exist in formal English, such as *surfology—the study of surfing*, using the morphological units introduced. They then trade their words with other groups, who have to guess the meanings developed by the first group. Each correct guess yields a point for the creating group and the guessing group, and each morpheme can only be used once. The group with the most points wins the game.

Although this type of instruction takes a bit of extra time in the content area classroom, it is well worth it. As students acquire morphological awareness and learn to recognize familiar affixes and roots, they develop the ability to figure out the meaning of unfamiliar words and learn vocabulary independently as they read.

The following high school biology lesson demonstrates the advantage of combining content and vocabulary instruction into a single lesson. The teacher uses a semantic feature analysis to review key concepts in a unit on classification of living organisms. A semantic feature analysis form and lesson plan are presented in Figures 6.21 and 6.22.

	heterotropic	immobile	multicellular	motile	aquatic	autotrophic
monera						
protista						
fungi						
plantae						
animalia						

Figure 6.21   Semantic Feature Analysis

Vocabulary-Enriched Lesson Plan: Science

Lesson Date: November 17 Text: Biology
Chapter: 3–5

Standards and objectives: Students will review key concepts in Chapters 3-5 to prepare for the unit test. Students will correctly identify characteristics of each kingdom of living organisms using a feature analysis.

Content and vocabulary objectives: Students will correctly identify vocabulary words that describe characteristics of each kingdom of living organisms using a feature analysis.

Students will identify meaning of the prefixes *hetero, im, multi, uni, eu, cyano, aqua, auto, prot,* and *archae*.

Core vocabulary: heterotropic, immobile, multicellular, unicellular, eubacteria, cyanobacteria, motile, protozoa, aquatic, autotropic, monera, protista, fungi, plantae, animalia, cilia, eukaryotic, flagella, archaebacteria.

Prefixes		
im	not	(Latin)
multi	many	(Latin)
uni	one	(Latin)
eu	good	(Greek)
cyano	blue	(Greek)
aqua	water	(Latin)
auto	self	(Greek)
prot	first	(Greek)
archae	ancient	(Greek)

Introduction: Students will write down as many things as they can remember about each kingdom of life without looking at the book.

Content and Vocabulary: Instructional Sequence

1. *Direct vocabulary instruction*: The teacher reviews each kingdom of life with the students and models filling the first column of the feature analysis.

2. *Student Activities*

   Feature analysis: The students work in pairs placing a check for each word that is an appropriate descriptor for the kingdoms of life listed on the vertical axis.

   Prefix work: The students list at least three words with the following prefixes and figure out what the words mean: *hetero, im, multi, aqua,* and *auto*.

Figure 6.22   Vocabulary-Enriched Lesson Plan: Science   *(Continued)*

(Continued)

---

3. *Use of words in classroom discourse*: The teacher and students discuss the kingdoms of life using core and extended vocabulary.

4. *Problem-solving skill*: Students practice structural analysis, identifying and attempting to figure out the meaning of words with prefixes *hetero, im, multi, aqua, auto*.

5. *Homework:* Study for unit test.

6. *Assessment:* Feature analysis, scores on unit test

Figure 6.22   Vocabulary-Enriched Lesson Plan: Science

Cross-Curricular Lessons

Newspaper articles are ideal for teaching clarifying strategies and metacognitive skills, due to the fact that articles tend to be short, highinterest, and filled with rich vocabulary used repeatedly. The following cross-curricular lesson is based on a newspaper article about terrorism, published in the *San Francisco Chronicle*, and the problem-solving cue card.

The following vignette describes the *News and Views* lesson that takes place in Mrs. Levin's ninth-grade English class.

Mrs. Levin teaches ninth-grade English and is chair of the English department. She works closely with her colleagues in the history department and tries to coordinate instruction between the two disciplines whenever possible. Mrs. Levin plans to teach her students how to use word structure as a clarifying strategy and has chosen a newspaper article about al Qaeda as a basis of instruction. The students are discussing the Middle East in their world history classes, so Mrs. Levin knows that the students will have background knowledge that will help support their comprehension of the article. She has already spent time teaching each of the clarifying strategies to the students based on the problem-solving cue card. Copies have been given to the students and posted on the classroom wall. Her colleagues in the history department have promised to encourage students to use the same strategies while reading the history textbook.

In this cross-curricular lesson titled *News and Views*, Mrs. Levin focuses on the development of clarifying strategies and metacognitive skills. She teaches the students to monitor comprehension of words and select appropriate clarifying strategies, such as structure and context, to make sense of challenging words found in the article. Mrs. Levin has developed a root and affix chart with Greek and Latin affixes and roots found in the article, based on the website *Dictionary of Latin and Greek Words* (www.wordinfo.info). An excerpt from the newspaper article, instructional materials, and a complete lesson plan for *News and Views* are presented in Figures 6.24 through 6.27. Copies are provided in Appendix B.

By Jonathan Curiel
Chronicle Staff Writer

Stripped of its pre-Sept. 11 base in Afghanistan, al Qaeda has found a way to stay in business by establishing small, decentralized training camps in countries where large 0 numbers of people are sympathetic to its goals, analysts say.

At the same time, the terrorist organization has settled on a strategy of small- and medium-scale attacks that can still cause serious death and destruction, as happened in Monday's coordinated bombings in Saudi Arabia that killed 34 people.

"Al Qaeda can't do operations on the scale of Sept. 11 anymore, but they're able to do operations like this one and the ones (last year) in Bali and Mombassa (Kenya)," said Rohan Cunaratna, author of "Inside Al Qaeda: Global Network of Terror."

Though authorities have, over the past few months, made a number of arrests of prominent al Qaeda leaders in Pakistan, the United States must concentrate now on countries in other regions if it wants to combat Osama bin Laden, according to Gunaratna and other terrorism experts.

"You must imagine that the organization is like a bee hive," Gunaratna said. "When a hive is attacked, the bees disperse. That's exactly what happened. Al Qaeda is decentralized, They're looking for new theaters for safe haven."

In addition to Saudi Arabia, such havens are being established in Muslim countries like Bangladesh and Indonesia,

said Zachary Abuza, a political science professor at Boston's Simmons College and an expert on al Qaeda's operations in Southeast Asia.

Abuza said the organization has at least 15 small camps in Bangladesh where it trains recruits to bomb buildings and carry out other terrorist acts.

"They have small camps all over the place," said Abuza, whose book, "Militant Islam in Southeast Asia," will be published this summer. "In Southeast Asia, I can name about 10 (al Qaeda) operatives who are still at large."

Abuza says al Qaeda's pattern of going after "soft" targets—like the bombing last year in Bali that killed scores of people and hurt the island's economy—are the organization's priority.

"Go back to bin laden's statement in October of 2002, when he said he will strike at 'the nodes of your economy,'" Abuza said. "That was right before the French oil tanker was struck in Yemen, and then Bali (Indonesia) happened.

"He wasn't kidding. You have to take him at his word," said Abuza, who believes other popular Western tourist destinations in Asian countries, like Thailand, could be next.

"If you want to cripple an economy and go after a soft target, that would be a place to do it," Abuza said.

Peter Bergen, author of "Holy War Inc.: Inside the Secret World of Osama bin Laden," said al Qaeda has been able to maintain its strength because "it's an organization, but it's also an ideology that's the basis of tenets that are widely spread."

"We can expect plenty more of small operations similar to the ones we saw in Saudi Arabia in countries where they have a reservoir of support and where people are willing to martyr themselves," he said.

Analysts said Monday's bombing should be a wake-up call to U.S. officials who may have thought al Qaeda had been severely damaged in the 20 months since it orchestrated the attacks on New York and Washington—and that the deposing of Iraqi leader Saddam Hussein would discourage anti-American groups around the world.

"We're not going to remove them just by fighting wars," said Daniel Benjamin, a senior fellow at the Center for Strategic and International Studies and author of "The Age of Sacred Terror," a book that chronicles the rise of al Qaeda.

Michael Swetnam, a counter-terrorism specialist at the Washington-based Potomac Institute for Policy Studies and co-author of "Usama bin laden's al-Qaida: Profile of a Terrorist Network," said: "Remember, time is on their side. They aren't in any hurry to hit us. When we drop our guard, that's when they'll hit.

In the meantime, they'll hit us overseas. . . The war on terror is going to be measured in decades. Don't assume if you haven't heard about bin Laden in six to seven months that you can lower your guard. The moment you do that, you're going to get hit."

E-mail Jonathan Curiel at jcuriel@sfchronicle.com.

Figure 6.23   *Downsized al Qaeda*

Source: "Downsized al Qaeda settles for smaller terrorism targets" by Jonathan Curiel (Chronicle staff writer), p. 100. *San Francisco Chronicle,* 05/15/03.

News and Views

1. Look at the title of the article and think about the meaning.

2. Skim the article to get a sense of its meaning.

3. Find each word listed on your root and affix chart in the newspaper article and underline the root or affix.

4. Think about the meaning of each word that you have underlined based on the meaning of the root or affix and the context in which it is used.

5. Re-read the article, making sure to think about the overall meaning of the text.

6. Write a short summary including the important points in the article.

Figure 6.24   News and Views

Word in Text	Root/Affix	Meaning	Origin
established	sta	make firm	Greek
decentralized	de/centro	away from/center	Latin
sympathetic	sym/path	same/feelings	Greek
terrorist	terri/ist	fright/believer in	Latin
organization	organ(o)	structure with parts	Greek
strategy	strato	army	Greek
destruction	de/struct	away from/build	Latin
coordinated	co/ord	together/order	Latin
operations/			
operative	oper	work	Latin
global	glob	round ball	Latin

Figure 6.25   Root and Affix Chart

Vocabulary-Enriched Cross-Curricular Lesson Plan

Lesson Date: October 5   Text: Downsized al Qaeda Settles for Smaller Terrorism Targets Source: San Francisco Chronicle

CA reading and the language arts standards: 9/10th Grade: Vocabulary and Concept Development, Standard 1.2 - Use knowledge of Greek, Latin, and Anglo-Saxon roots and affixes to understand content area vocabulary

CA history and social science standards: 9/10th Grade: 10.10 Analyze Nation Building in the Contemporary Middle East, Important Trends and Whether They Appear to Serve the Cause of Individual Freedom and Democracy.

Content and vocabulary objectives: Students will develop morphological awareness—the ability to identify Greek and Latin roots and affixes in the newspaper article and will learn to self-regulate—use structure and context strategies to figure out the words and the overall meaning of the text.

Core vocabulary: established, decentralized, sympathetic, terrorist, organization, strategy, destruction, coordinated, operations-operative, global, authority

Extended vocabulary: establishment, centralize, decentralization, centralization, sympathy, organizational, reorganize, reorganization, destroy, destructive, coordination, authorization, reauthorize, reauthorization

Introduction: Ask students, "What do you do when you're reading and you come to a word that you don't understand?" Review strategies on the problem-solving cue card.

Figure 6.26   Vocabulary-Enriched Cross-Curricular Lesson Plan

---

Content and Vocabulary: Instructional Sequence

Clarifying strategy and metacognitive skill instruction: Pass out the newspaper article and the list of Greek and Latin affixes and roots. Model finding and underlining words with affixes and roots on the list. Model *try word parts*: use the root *sta* to make meaning of the word established. Use context and structure together to construct meaning. Demonstrate use of metacognitive skills to monitor comprehension and regulate strategy implementation.

Student activities: Transfer responsibility: Students work in pairs, finding the affixes and roots and clarifying the words using the structure and context strategies.

Use of words in classroom discourse: Discuss content of the article using core and extended vocabulary.

Homework: Students find another newspaper article on world events, underline challenging words, look up Greek and Latin word parts on the website, and figure out word meaning. Students generate a summary of the key points in the article.

Assessment: Students' worksheet and summary are graded for evidence of strategy use and comprehension of the article's content.

Figure 6.26   Vocabulary-Enriched Cross-Curricular Lesson Plan

---

Mrs. Levin:	Now that we've reviewed the strategies on the problem-solving cue card, I'd like to look more closely at the strategy *try word parts*. I've given you a short newspaper article about al Qaeda, which you can also see on the overhead. Please skim the article, so you have an idea of what it's about. . . . Okay, now I'm going to pass out a root and affix chart. Take a look! It has a list of challenging words from the article and the Greek or Latin affix or root of each word. We'll use this chart to try to figure out the meaning of the unfamiliar words in the article. Let's look at the first word on the list, *established*. (She underlines *established* on the overhead transparency.) As you can see from the chart, the root of established is *sta*, which means *make firm* in Latin. Can anyone tell me how we can use this information to make sense of the word *established?*
Stacey:	It means that al Qaeda was making firm camps. I mean that it was making them firmly, so they wouldn't disappear.
Mrs. Levin:	Good! So, we can use the root to make sense of the word. Notice that Stacey used another strategy to help construct meaning.
Stacey:	Context?
Mrs. Levin:	Exactly! That's why the cue card tells you to mix the strategies. Two strategies are much more powerful together than either strategy by itself. Each one adds important information that helps you make sense of the text.
Dan:	*Establish* is a pretty easy word. I didn't need to look at the root or context to know what it means.
Mrs. Levin:	True! Many of you already know these words. But I'd like you to learn the process of using word structure to make sense of unfamiliar words. Then when you get to really hard words you'll know what to do. Okay? Now, I'd like you to work with a partner and find each word on the list in the article. Use the affix or root to clarify the word and check context to be sure. When you're finished, I want each person to write a summary of the article. Does everyone know what to do? Okay, let's get to work.

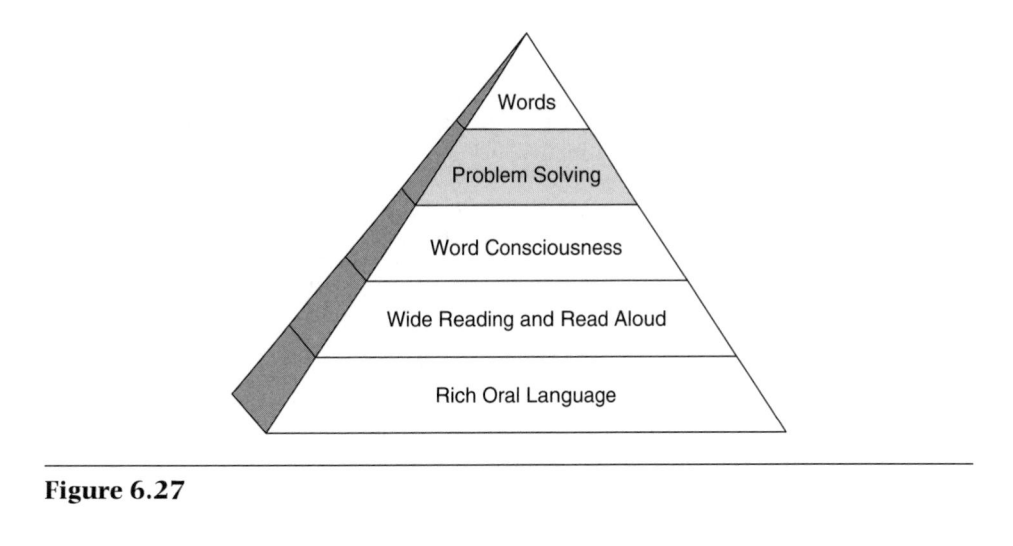

Figure 6.27

Mrs. Levin's lesson illustrates several important points about problem-solving instruction. First, students need to acquire metacognitive skills to monitor comprehension and to become aware of morphological features of words. They need to develop the ability to regulate clarifying strategies, knowing when a particular strategy or set of strategies is likely to be effective. It takes a great deal of practice to learn to use strategies flexibly and independently, so that strategic knowledge supports comprehension. As Mrs. Levin points out to her students, it is a good idea for students to practice using strategies with relatively easy words, then transfer strategic knowledge to more challenging words and texts. Note that Mrs. Levin quickly transfers responsibility for strategy implementation to the students. She does not demand they memorize long lists of affixes and roots, but instead provides them with the information they need to make sense of vocabulary found in the particular article they are reading. Over time, students acquire morphological awareness, noticing and making use of high-frequency word parts that they have learned from repeated meaningful exposures during reading.

Many of the words found in newspaper articles and history textbooks are included on the academic word list (Coxhead, 2000), which is available online at www.uefap.com/vocab/select/awl.htm. The list is comprised of 570 high-frequency word families and related words such as *establish, disestablish, disestablished, disestablishes, disestablishing, disestablishment, established, establishes, establishing, establishment, establishments.* Secondary students with well-developed vocabularies will already know most of the words on the academic word list, but teachers may need to teach many of these high-frequency word families to students who depend on schools for literacy.

The following cross-curricular lessons combine content from three subject areas, English, social studies, and science. The lessons are based on a *National Geographic* article titled "Leprosy Was Spread by Colonialism, Slave Trade," by Stefan Lovgren (May 12, 2005). The following is an excerpt of the article.

It is an infectious disease that dates back at least to biblical times, yet leprosy has puzzled scientists since the identification, in 1873, of the bacterium that causes it.

Known for its disfiguring skin lesions and potentially debilitating nerve damage, leprosy, or Hansen's disease, is a very difficult disease to transmit. It also has a long incubation period, making it hard for a doctor to determine where a leprosy patient contracted the disease.

But now a team of French scientists has discovered how the disease evolved and how it was spread across the continents by human migrations . . .

Researchers also found that leprosy probably originated in East Africa and not India, as previously thought. The disease was brought eastward and westward by colonialism and the slave trade, the scientists believe.

Source: Stefan Lovgren, 2005.

The first lesson is based on a semantic web, an activity that helps students organize information and encode it in knowledge structures called schemata (Figure 6.28). The teacher begins by asking students to identify big ideas in the article. The topics—*description, symptoms,* and *origin*—are listed on the semantic web. Then students identify words and phrases from the article that relate to each topic and add them to the semantic web. As each word or phrase is added, the students and teacher discuss the meaning. This activity builds vocabulary while helping students organize the information presented in the article. The use of a semantic web increases the likelihood that newly learned concepts and words will be retained in long-term memory.

Students examine a range of clarifying strategies based on the problem-solving cue card and the nourishing vocabulary context cue card. In addition to teaching students to use word parts in the *News and Views* lesson, the teacher guides the students in the use of other clarifying strategies as they read the leprosy text. The following strategies found on the nourishing vocabulary cue card

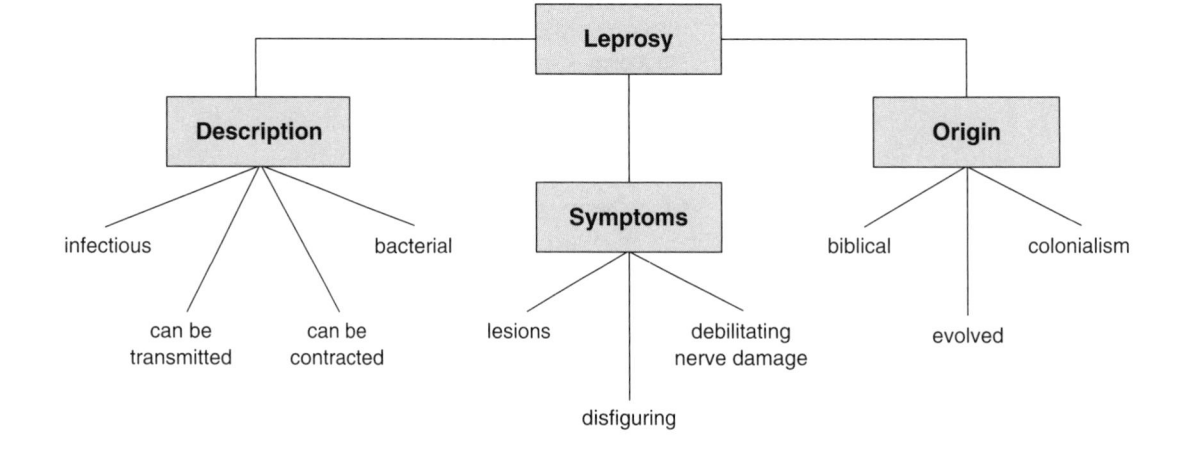

Figure 6.28　Semantic Web: Leprosy

are helpful in making sense of difficult words. She points out a variation of the double-comma clue (appositive) where the definition comes before the word *leprosy*. The parts of speech cue helps clarify the word *bacterium,* a noun that is the cause of the disease. The teacher returns to the problem-solving cue card to point out that the word *debilitating* can be understood in terms of what students already know about serious diseases.

A compare and contrast organizer provides a second lesson option, also embedding vocabulary into instruction (see Figures 6.29 through 6.32). Vocabulary words are categorized in terms of description of leprosy, how leprosy is similar to AIDS and how it is different from AIDS. The discussion of the article is based on the vocabulary listed on the graphic organizer. Note that this activity includes vocabulary and content from the leprosy article and another article, "Origins of HIV," that the students read in a previous lesson (Time Online, May 25, 2006, http://time.blogs.com/global_health/2006/05/originsofhiv.html).

Other instructional activities based on this article can also be used to teach content and vocabulary. For example, the article could be used to review affixes and to teach problem-solving strategies.

Description of the Topics			Similar	Different
Key words	lesions infectious debilitating disfiguring transmit incubation	originated biblical bacterium evolved colonialism	contracted stigmatized originated	progression lethal
Questions and answers	Can you describe leprosy? Leprosy is an *infectious* disease. It is not easy to *transmit.* It's a *debilitating* disease that causes nerve damage. Leprosy is also *disfiguring.* It causes *lesions*—sores—and damage that looks terrible. Leprosy has a long *incubation* period. That means that you have it for a long time before you get symptoms.	Where did leprosy *originate?* It *originated* in *biblical* times. Scientists discovered that a *bacterium* causes it. Leprosy started in Africa and was spread by slave trade and *colonialism.* Scientists think that leprosy *evolved* over a long time.	How is leprosy similar to AIDS? Leprosy and AIDS are both *infectious* diseases. Both diseases can be *debilitating.* Both diseases sometimes cause *lesions* that are *disfiguring.* People who have *contracted* leprosy and AIDS have often been *stigmatized.* Both diseases *originated* in Africa.	How is leprosy different from AIDS? Leprosy is caused by a *bacterium* but AIDS is caused by a virus. Leprosy was always *lethal* in *biblical* times, but it can be controlled by medicine today. Doctors can slow down the *progression* of AIDS, but it is still *lethal.*

Figure 6.29   Compare and Contrast Organizer: Leprosy and AIDS

Word	Prefix
contracted	con/com (together)
debilitating	de (away from)
disfiguring	dis (not)
infectious	in (put in)
incubation	in (put in)
progression	pro (forward)
transmit	trans (across)

Figure 6.30   Prefix Chart: Leprosy

Word	Sufffix
lesion, incubation, progression	ion (noun) state of
infectious	ious (full of) adj
stigmatize	ize (become like) verb
lethal, biblical	al (like) adj
orginate	ate (be associated with) verb
colonialism	ism (act or condition) noun

Figure 6.31   Suffix Chart: Leprosy

Putting It All Together: Instructional Guidelines

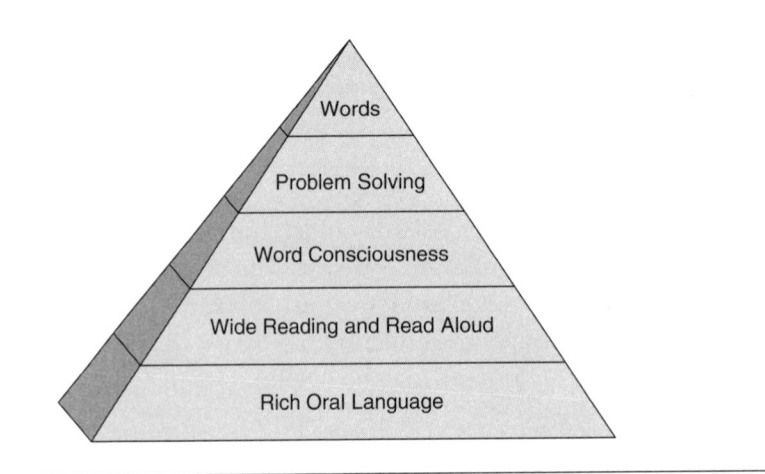

Figure 6.32

Providing secondary students with nourishing vocabulary instruction requires a paradigm shift for many teachers. Rather than viewing vocabulary as a separate topic in the curriculum (usually the responsibility of the English teacher), nourishing vocabulary teachers embed vocabulary into every facet of instruction. The following guidelines summarize the instructional methods included in this chapter.

Words

- Teach vocabulary every day in each subject area. Develop lesson plans that include vocabulary and content objectives for each lesson.
- Encourage active engagement on the part of the students in the word learning process. Active engagement promotes learning.

Problem Solving

- Explicitly teach clarifying strategies and metacognitive skills. The goal of instruction is to increase students' independent word learning proficiency

Word Consciousness

- Make word learning fun. Encourage student interest in words and motivation for word learning.
- Build word schemata. Develop deep conceptual knowledge and interconnected vocabulary words related to important topics in the curriculum.

Wide Reading and Read Aloud

- Encourage wide reading. Reading is the source of most vocabulary learning.

Rich Oral Language

- Immerse students in a word-rich environment. Post core vocabulary on a word wall to encourage use of new words.
- Use rich vocabulary yourself. Include core and extended vocabulary words in classroom discourse, providing multiple exposures to new words.
- Encourage the students to use rich vocabulary in speaking and writing. Develop expressive knowledge so that vocabulary can be used for a variety of literacy purposes.

Secondary teachers often ask how much time should be devoted to vocabulary instruction. There is no simple answer. The time allotted will vary depending on the amount of instructional time available to the teacher and the needs of the students. The suggestions that follow address the problem of limited time for vocabulary instruction and may be helpful.

- We suggest that mini-lessons (approximately ten minutes) be scheduled twice per week, providing explicit instruction in each component of the vocabulary program, including core and extended vocabulary words, affixes and roots, clarifying strategies, and metacognitive skills.

- Provide additional mini-lessons to students with special word learning needs such as ELL (mini-lessons on cognates and idioms) and students with limited vocabulary development (mini-lessons on words that other students already know; sidebars).
- Embed vocabulary in content instruction (increase vocabulary exposure without allotment of extra instructional time).
- Teach content and vocabulary simultaneously, whenever possible, compounding the time devoted to vocabulary instruction.
- Expose students to a maximum number of words in classroom discourse.
- Assign homework that includes a vocabulary component.

The methods described in this chapter provide a framework for providing vocabulary-enriched instruction to secondary students. These methods will be effective with most students, but students with severely underdeveloped vocabularies will need additional instruction if they are to keep up. Chapter 7 focuses on providing more intensive vocabulary support to students with special needs and English-language learners.

ELL Strategies

- Use pictures, gestures, and realia to ensure comprehensible input.
- Preteach vocabulary.
- Teach high-utility words.
- Preview texts in native language.
- Provide mini-lessons in basic vocabulary and cognates.

Supporting Students With Special Needs

- Provide access to content and vocabulary in an oral context
- Teach strategies in an oral context that can be transferred to reading at a later time when decoding skills develop
- Use reciprocal teaching methods to increase exposure to texts and oral vocabulary

Resource Specialists

- Work closely with resource specialists to provide seamless vocabulary and content instruction

Parents

- Send texts home to be read at home before they are introduced in class
- Provide suggestions for developing vocabulary and content knowledge through read aloud, books on tape/CD

Differentiating Instruction for English Learners and Students With Special Needs

7

Vocabulary Component	Page Number	Instructional Activity	Description
Words	112–116	2,000 most common word lists	2,000 most common word list, academic word list
	115	2,000 most common word sorts Text & word sort	Used to categorize words according to a particular semantic relationship *Grandfather's Visit* text and word sort
Problem solving: Self-monitoring	119–122	Cognate strategy	Introduction to cognate strategy
Problem solving: Clarifying strategies	121	Cognates: Teacher narrative	Instructional sequence for teaching Spanish-speaking students to use cognates
Problem solving: Word parts	117 118–119 123 123	Word family web Antonym chart, cloze Compound word chart Spanish prefixes	Instructional activities designed to build morphological awareness and knowledge of word parts
Problem solving: Context	117 118–119	Word frame Antonym list and cloze	Text with missing words, designed to increase students' skill at using context cues

Figure 7.1   Differentiating Instruction for English Learners and Students With Special Needs   *(Continued)*

(Continued)

Vocabulary Component	Page Number	Instructional Activity	Description
Word consciousness	124	Collocation frame	Text with missing words, designed to increase students' skill at using collocations: words that belong together
Wide reading and read aloud	126–128	Reciprocal teaching Books on tape/CD	Four comprehension strategies used in a text-based dialog
Rich oral language	128–129	Mini-lesson	Small-group oral discourse and explicit instruction in vocabulary or cognates
Putting it all together	129	Mini-lesson plan	Vocabulary mini-lesson format designed for ELL and students with special needs

Figure 7.1   Differentiating Instruction for English Learners and Students With Special Needs

ENGLISH LEARNERS

English-language learners (ELLs) are one of the fastest growing groups of students in our classrooms. These students face a huge vocabulary challenge when they enter American schools. Depending on the age of entry, ELLs may need to master tens of thousands of words to catch up with their English-speaking peers, as Figures 7.2 and 7.3 demonstrate.

Because English learners are often segregated in schools and communities where little English is spoken, they rely almost entirely on schools for vocabulary acquisition. Designing a complete instructional program for beginning English learners is beyond the scope of this book. A few general guidelines, however, are provided.

- Teach the most common academic vocabulary words first.
- Teach word families to extend vocabulary knowledge.
- Provide Spanish-speaking students with explicit cognate strategy instruction.
- Teach affixes and roots (Latin roots are particularly helpful to Spanish-speaking students).
- Read aloud high-interest, culturally relevant texts.
- Provide an environment filled with rich oral language and language support to ensure comprehension and vocabulary acquisition.

Vocabulary Gap Between English Language Learners (ELLs) and English-Only (EO) Students

- English-speaking children know approximately 5,000 words at the time of school entry (Nation, 2001).
- Average third graders know 10,000 words (Nagy et al., 1984, 1986).
- Average eighth graders know 25,000 words (Graves, 2004).
- Average high school graduates know between 40,000 (Nagy & Herman, 1985) and 75,000 words (Snow & Kim, 2007).
- The average EO student learns approximately 2,000 to 3,000 words per year (Anglin, 1993; Nagy 1985, 1988; Stahl & Nagy, 2006).

If an ELL enters school in fifth grade and is taught 500 words per year, the maximum number of words he or she will learn from this type of instruction by the end of twelfth grade is 4,000 words. These are crude estimates but the point is that there is a tremendous amount to learn, and an ever-increasing gap. To close such a gap, we need to accelerate word learning by English learners, teach strategies that generalize across words, and help ELLs develop vocabulary through as many sources as possible.

Figure 7.2   Vocabulary Gap

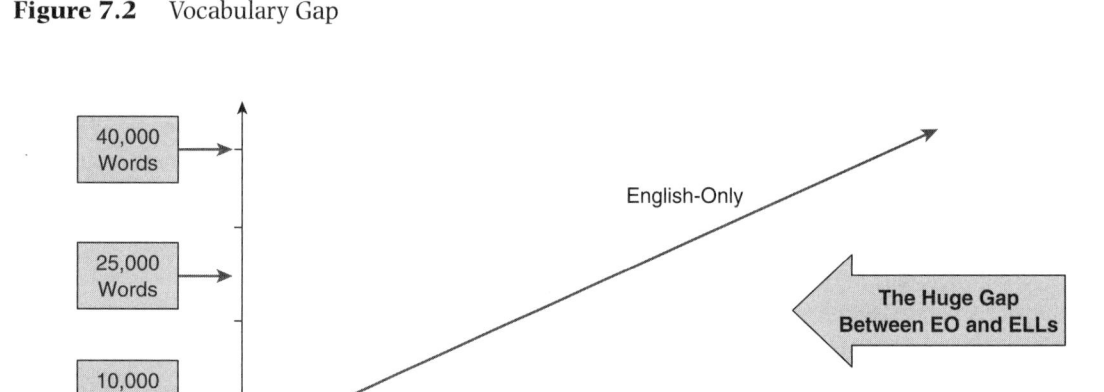

Figure 7.3   Vocabulary Gap Graph

Most Common Academic Vocabulary Words

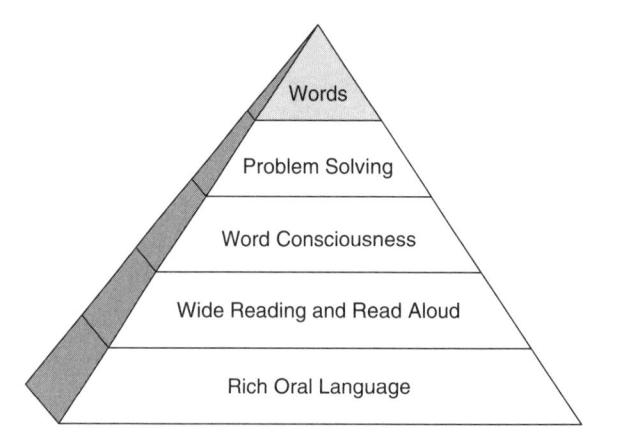

Figure 7.4

In discussing word selection earlier, we suggested that teachers avoid teaching the 2,000 most common words because most English-speaking students already know them. Words that occur frequently, however, are more useful than words that are very rare or uncommon. English learners may need a focus on high-utility words, at least initially, in a way that is not true for native speakers. Several researchers have tried to identify the set of most useful words for English learners. The general service list (West, 1953) selects the 2,000 most common words in academic texts, covering 80 percent or more of school texts from the 1940s and 1950s. Also included on the general service list are semantically related members of the same word families (for example, *accident, accidents, accidental, accidentally*) resulting in a total list of 3,500 high frequency words. A second resource worth examination is the academic word list (Coxhead, 2000), comprised of 570 word families (totaling 3,000 words) that appear frequently in academic texts. Lists of words that are specific to content areas including math, science, business, music, and health are also important resources for secondary English learners. These lists are available online at www.uefap.co.uk/vocab/select/select.htm. A third resource was developed by Paul Nation. This includes the 2,000 most common words, the 3,000 most common words, the 1,000 most common word families, the 2,000 most common word families, and the academic word list. All are organized in order of word frequency and include derived forms of the words. The Nation lists are available online at www.edict.com.hk/textanalyser/wordlists.htm.

We want to emphasize that vocabulary instruction is most effective when students are taught words they encounter in texts and use in meaningful oral and written communication. Word lists do not constitute a vocabulary curriculum. They can, however, be helpful in narrowing the vast number of words that English learners need to learn.

Word Groups From the 2,000 Most Common Word List

Teachers do not have time to explicitly teach 2,000 words to ELL, so it is important to make thoughtful word selection decisions. The following section includes sets of words drawn from the 2,000 most common word list, organized in an escalating pattern of complexity. It is important to remember that English learners readily learn new words in English that map onto concepts and concrete items they already know in another language. Common and familiar words such as the ones in Figure 7.5 are new labels for well-established word

Animals	*bear, bird, cat, dog, fish, horse*
Colors	*blue, color, gold, green, gray, red, white*
Family	*baby, brother, child, daughter, family, parent, sister, son, wife*
Food	*dinner, drink, egg, eat, food, fruit, glass, meal, milk, tea*
Home	*bed, bedroom, floor, garden, gate, home, house, kitchen, roof, room, table, window, yard*
Human body	*arm, back, body, blood, bone, brain, breath, disease, ear, eye, face, finger, foot, hair, hand, head, heart, human, knee, leg, lip, leg, mouth, nose, shoulder, skin, tooth*

Figure 7.5   Familiar Words

schemas and may require little or no explicit instruction. They are usually learned through basic interpersonal communication in a relatively short time (Cummins, 1994).

Other words might be somewhat familiar and pictures are very effective in conveying the meaning of concrete nouns. It is worthwhile, however, to use the stoplight method with such words so that instruction is targeted on words that students don't know. The conceptual word knowledge that students bring to a classroom in their native language can vary widely.

Word sorts can help students both solidify the vocabulary they have and learn new words. The word sorts in Figure 7.6 help students develop a concrete word vocabulary and learn to categorize things found mainly in cities or in nature. (Words may fit in more than one category.)

Things Found in a City	Things Found in Nature
bank, bridge, building, business, church, citizen, community, construction, court, customer, department, factory, hospital, hotel, market, museum, neighbor, office, park, restaurant, shop, store, street, theater, town, traffic	*field, flower, forest, ground, hill, island, land, leaf, mountain, plant, sea, sky, star, stone, sun, tree, weather, wind, wood*

Figure 7.6   Word Sort: High-Utility Words

Word sorts can be followed by cloze activities, designed to extend receptive word knowledge to the ability to use words in speaking and writing. Figure 7.7 includes things found in a city:

Mrs. Gomez took her class on a field trip to the _____ of history. The trip took a long time. They crossed a _____ over the river and passed the Catholic _____ on the corner of Main _____. There was a lot of _____ so the bus driver had to drive very slowly. They finally arrived at the beautiful new _____, where the museum was located. Next door to the museum was a nice _____ where the students had lunch.

   After a long day in the _____, the students were happy to return to their quiet town.

city, church, traffic, museum, street, restaurant, building, bridge

Figure 7.7   Cloze Activity Word Bank

Sorting words according to setting is valuable because it teaches the context for using the words as well as the meaning of them. Below is a set of school-related words. Figure 7.8 shows how a simple teacher-generated text, based on a list of forty-two school-related words, can be used to enhance word knowledge.

addition, administration, art, assembly, award, ball, band, behavior, block, board, book, box, boy, chair, chapter, character, class, club, college, computer, concentrate, concept, conclusion, curriculum, cut, debate, define, describe, design, desk, detail, discipline, discover, discuss, divide, division, draw, earth, economy, education, environment, equal, equipment, error, estimate, evidence, examination, example, excellent, exercise, experiment, explain, explore, fact, factor, fail, finish, football, game, goal, health, history, holiday, idea, illustrate, investigate, know, knowledge, language, learn, letter, library, line, list, listen, literature, lunch, map, measure, memory, mistake, music, number, paper, percent, play, proportion, public, pupil, question, read, report, research, school, science, secondary, skill, social, species, sport, story, student, study, sum, teacher, team, test, text, university, write

Figure 7.8   School-Related Words

To generate a text for word learning:

1. Look at a list of related words.

2. Think of a simple plot that could incorporate some of the words.

3. Write the scenario, using some words in the first draft.

4. Rewrite the story, expanding it to include more words from the list.

Word sorts are an effective method of grouping school-related words for instruction. Teachers select a limited number of words from the school-related word group and discuss the words in relation to a text. If no appropriate text is available, a simple teacher-generated text can be used. The following text is based on a list of forty-two school-related words.

Before introducing the text, "Grandfather's Visit," the teacher preteaches particularly abstract words such as *environment* and *investigate*. The teacher then reads the story aloud while the students follow along in their text. After reading, the teacher asks the students comprehension questions, requiring them to respond in full sentences. For example, the teacher asks the students to describe what Van is studying in each subject. Once students are familiar with the words in the text, the teacher provides a chart and asks the students to sort the words that belong in each category. The word sort in Figure 7.9 includes the forty-two school-related words that appear in "Grandfather's Visit." Note that an additional category, all subjects, has been added to incorporate words that relate broadly to education and are not limited to a particular subject.

Once the words have been sorted, the teacher invites the students to examine the list and discuss which words are missing. Students are asked to add words relevant to each subject and are prompted to consider why the school-related word list includes words such as *addition* and *division*, but not the words *subtraction* and *multiplication*. This discussion provides an interesting opportunity for the teacher to talk about word frequency. The teacher points out that high-frequency words often have multiple meanings. For example, *addition* refers to a specific math operation, but it is more commonly used in texts to signal something more. It is useful to provide examples of the word in a text, drawing the students' attention to the way the word is used:

- In addition to math homework, James had to read a chapter in English, and study for a science test.

Grandfather's Visit

Van's grandfather came from Vietnam to visit her family. Grandfather was a very educated man. He wanted to know all about her education. Van explained that pupils in elementary school learn most subjects in the same class. A single teacher is responsible for the pupils' education. Van's grandfather was very interested in math and science. He wanted to know when students learned skills such as addition and division. He wanted to know what proportion of the day Van spent studying math. Van estimated that she spent one hour each day in math class. She showed Grandfather a recent math test. He looked at the number of errors and how the examination measured her knowledge of math. Van explained that the B+ grade was equal to 88 percent.

Then they discussed science. Van told Grandfather that she was studying the environment. She told him about endangered species and important things that people should do to protect the earth. Grandfather was interested in Van's science experiment. She was investigating how education helps people learn to recycle. Grandfather was happy that Van was so knowledgeable about science.

Van also told Grandfather about her other classes. She explained that she was studying American history this year in social studies. She told Grandfather that she had to write a report about the government and economy of the Jamestown colony. Grandfather had never heard of Jamestown. Van showed him a story about Jamestown and showed him where it was on the map. Van told Grandfather that she was also reading historical literature about American history.

Grandfather was surprised that Van had physical education classes every day. Van told Grandfather that exercise is very important for your health. Van explained that she likes sports so much that she plays on a soccer team. She told Grandfather that she scored the winning goal in the game last week. Grandfather offered to buy Van new soccer equipment. He promised to come to watch her play soccer next Saturday. Van was very happy that Grandfather came for a visit.

Math	Science	Social Studies	Reading	Physical Education	All Subjects
addition division equal error estimate measure number percent proportion	earth environment experiment health investigate species	economy government history map	literature story	equipment exercise game goal score sport team	class education examination knowledge library learn pupil read skills report student study test write

Figure 7.9   School-Related Word Sort

- The addition to the library made it easier to find books and articles.
- Marie liked her math class this year. Additionally, she discovered that she was good in math.

As an alternative you can ask groups of students to sort these words without providing category headings. Their task is to generate the headings as part of the word sort. The instructions for the word sort are that students can use up to five categories, with one to include words that don't fit. The value of this activity is that students have to think deeply about the words to find links between them. After they have decided on their categories, they explain the categories to the other members of the class. The exercise helps students realize that there are many ways to sort words and the type of links that can be found between words.

Developing Verb Knowledge

The 2,000 most common word list contains a large number of verbs that must be learned if ELLs are to become literate in English. The sheer number and variety of verbs can be overwhelming. The guiding principle is to group words for instruction based on the relationships of words to a theme. This will help ELL develop word schemata—knowledge structures that facilitate word learning and retention of newly learned content and vocabulary. The early stages of instruction focus on simple verbs connected to students' everyday experiences. For example, the teacher might begin with a group of verbs that relate to motion (*climb, jump, reach, run, shake, slip, stand, step, stop, throw, walk*) that can easily be pantomimed. Other categories can be generated such as words related to speaking (*announce, argue, call, cry, laugh, reply, say, shout, sing*) and feeling (*care, fear, hope, hurt, love, suffer, worry*). Once several categories of words have been presented, students can be given word sort activities to reinforce word learning.

The following sequence of instructional activities is designed to teach abstract verbs to ELLs, based on a simple text, *Monsters of the Deep* (Blake, 1996). The teacher begins by pointing out the word *imagine* in the text, and discusses its meaning. Students are actively engaged, providing examples of things that are imaginary. The teacher compliments the students' imaginative comments. Note that the word *imagine* and related words are used repeatedly in oral discourse.

Web the Word Family

Once the students are familiar with the meaning of the word, *imagine*, the teacher constructs a word web, demonstrating how words related to *imagine* have a similar meaning and how suffixes change parts of speech (see Figure 7.10).

The teacher helps Spanish-speaking students by pointing out that the word *imagine* (*imaginarse* in Spanish) is a cognate, a word that looks or sounds like a word in English and means the same thing. The construction of a word family web works much the same in Spanish as in English, though there are many

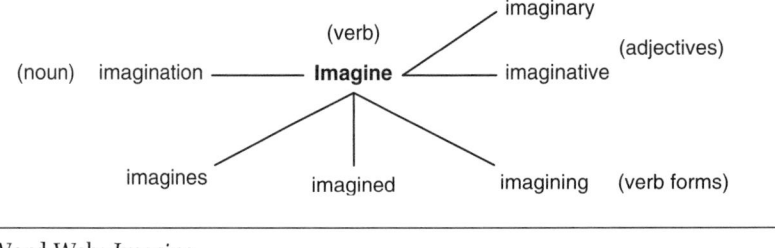

Figure 7.10   Word Web: *Imagine*

more verb forms in Spanish. Only the present tense of the verb *imaginarse* is included in this word family web (Figure 7.11).

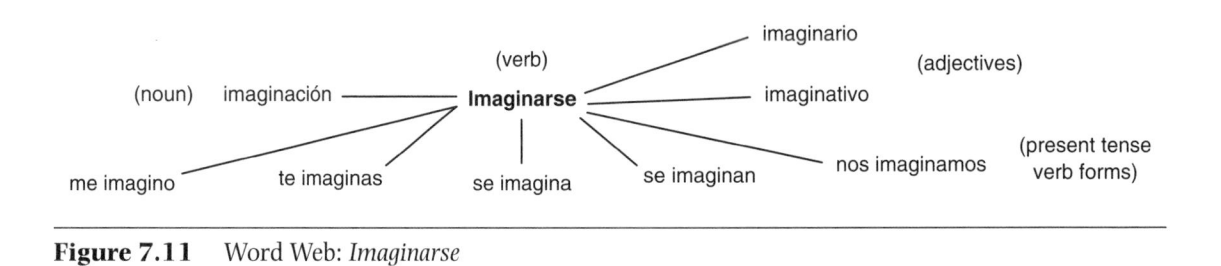

Figure 7.11   Word Web: *Imaginarse*

Word Frame

Students are often familiar with a word family such as that of *imagine,* but lack experience using various forms of the word in writing and speaking. The teacher introduces a word frame activity to help the students learn appropriate use of the adjective *imaginary.*

Here is an example of a word frame activity. The new word is *imaginary.*

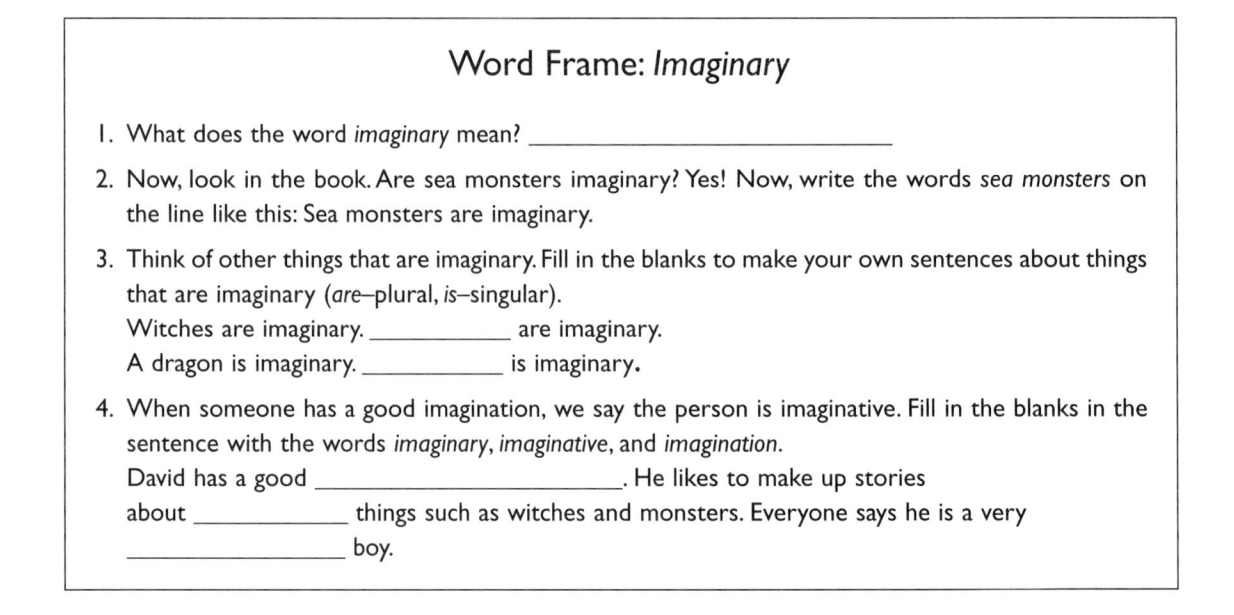

Cloze Activities

As the students' vocabulary develops, more complex cloze passages can be designed, with a broader range of target words, drawn from the 2,000 most common words. The cloze passage in Figure 7.12 is designed to provide students with practice using words from the *imagine* word family and a variety of other high-frequency words that are found in the text. Students can be prompted to use their word webs to help identify the correct forms of the verbs used in the cloze.

Chose words from the box below and put them in the correct spaces in the story.

Long ago, people wanted to _____ the world, but they were afraid of terrible monsters that lived in the sea. They _____ sea monsters were like huge snakes. They believed that ships _____ because sea monsters ate them. Brave _____ were not afraid. They traveled to far away places and some of them never _____ home again. Each winter storytellers came to the village and told _____ stories about sea monsters and the _____ of ships. When the children listened to the storytellers' tales, they _____ themselves as brave heroes. Each winter the children waited eagerly for the storytellers to _____ to the village.

imagined, imaginative, explore, explorers, disappeared, disappearance, returned, return

Figure 7.12   Cloze Word Bank

Antonyms

English includes a broad range of words, called antonyms, that express opposite meanings. Antonyms are used in oral and written expression and often appear in standardized tests. The following are common antonyms that English learners need to know.

Location	Verbs	Time	Description	Description
in-out	*come-go*	*before-after*	*pretty-ugly*	*cold-hot*
up-down	*open-close*	*early-late*	*fat-thin*	*narrow-wide*
forward-backward	*give-take*	*day-night*	*tall-short*	*little-big*
in front of-behind	*break-fix*	*beginning-end*	*good-bad*	*light-dark*
near-far	*sink-float*	*never-always*	*young-old*	*true-false*
over-under	*buy-sell*	*hello-goodbye*	*friend-enemy*	*shallow-deep*
inside-outside	*laugh-cry*		*son-daughter*	*best-worst*
above-below	*push-pull*		*father-mother*	*dirty-clean*
	lost-found		*interesting-boring*	*dry-wet*
			poor-rich	*tight-loose*
			happy-sad	*war-peace*
			quiet-noisy	*fast-slow*
			awake-asleep	*right-wrong*
			king-queen	*lucky-unlucky*
			healthy-sick	
			nice-mean	

Figure 7.13   Antonyms

Many antonyms can be taught using gestures and movement such as *up-down* or facial expressions such as *happy-sad*. Students in the early stages of learning English benefit from practice with antonyms, using oral language and sentence frames like the following:

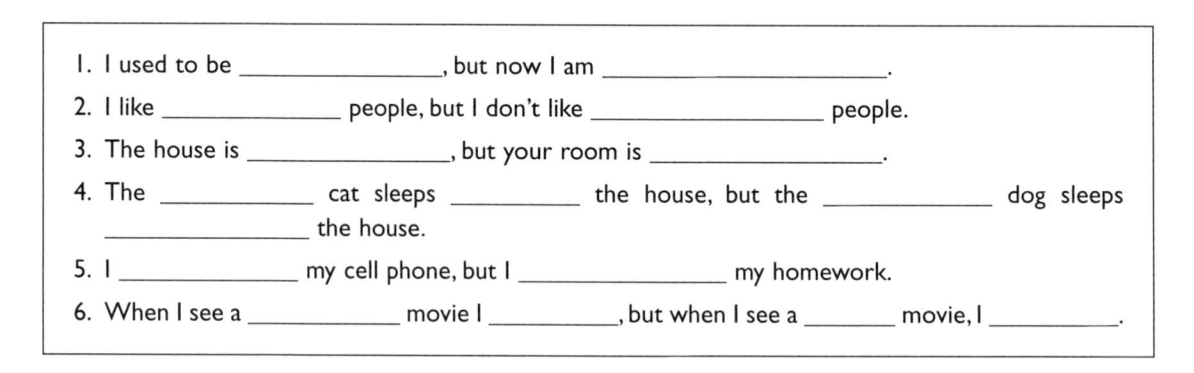

1. I used to be _____, but now I am _____.
2. I like _____ people, but I don't like _____ people.
3. The house is _____, but your room is _____.
4. The _____ cat sleeps _____ the house, but the _____ dog sleeps _____ the house.
5. I _____ my cell phone, but I _____ my homework.
6. When I see a _____ movie I _____, but when I see a _____ movie, I _____.

Building on this activity, you can discuss shades of meaning for other words you encounter (for a further description of this activity, see Scott, Skobel, & Wells, 2008). This is particularly useful for English-language learners because it helps them understand how word meanings are packaged in English. Many of these pairs of antonyms are points on a continuum of meaning. There are many such continuums in English as English tends to package the degree of intensity into individual word meanings. For instance, temperature and feelings have various degrees of intensity. Someone who is *furious* is more *angry* than someone who is *annoyed*. When you read aloud from books, you can identify, and help students collect, these shades of meaning for familiar words. One way to help make this concept concrete for ELLs is to have students line up along a continuum of meaning. Choose two familiar points on any continuum of meaning (such as, *angry-happy; cold-hot; soft-loud*). Pass out word cards with one word per card for the concept (such as *furious, annoyed, angry, mad, dismayed, livid*). Then, have students line up according to intensity across the room. Doing this activity creates a context in which students discuss and decide where their words fall in the line. For example, is someone who is *livid* more or less angry than someone who is *dismayed*?

Problem Solving: Cognates

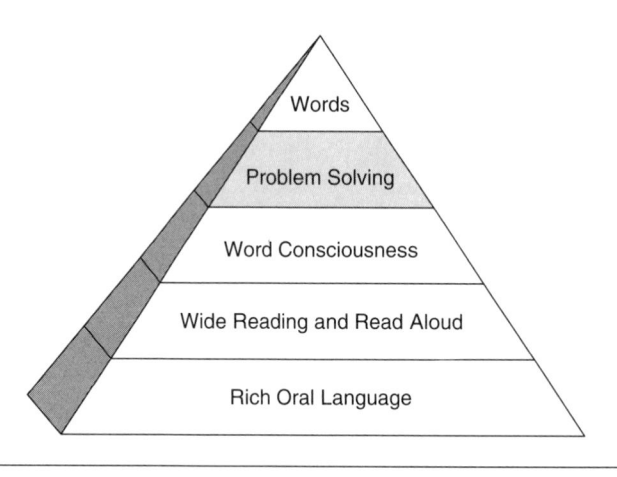

Figure 7.14

Teaching cognates, which are words that are similar in two languages, is one of the most fruitful methods of instruction for English learners who speak Spanish as their first language. Researchers estimate that English-Spanish cognates account for one-third of educated adult vocabulary (Nash, 1997) and 53.6 percent of English words are of Romance-language origin (Hammer, 1979). Cognates can provide a potent method of comprehending English vocabulary, but many Spanish-speaking students do not notice even the most transparent cognates they encounter in texts. When cognates are pointed out, these students have no idea how to use cognate clues to figure out the meaning of English words.

Several factors, including differences in pronunciation, differences in spelling, and lack of morphological awareness, may inhibit students' ability to use cognates.

Cognate instruction is most effective when it builds on students' oral language proficiency in Spanish. Recognition of cognates in English requires that students know the meaning of the corresponding word in Spanish. Students are likely to know many more words orally than they recognize in print, particularly if their native language literacy is limited. Spelling differences between English and Spanish often make it difficult for students to identify cognates. Spanish has a transparent orthography, meaning that there is a close mapping between sounds and letters. Words are generally spelled the way they sound. English, on the other hand, has an opaque orthography. There are twenty-six letters, approximately forty phonemes, and 250 spelling patterns. Spanish-speaking students may simply not recognize English words that correspond to Spanish words in their speaking vocabulary. Effective cognate instruction begins with a list of highly transparent cognates.

family—familia

adventure—aventura

animal—animal

history—historia

map—mapa

The teacher models looking carefully at the English word and pointing out similarities and differences in the way the Spanish and English words are written. He points to the cognates *family—familia* and asks, "What is the same and what is different?" He circles the letters *f, a, m, i,* and *l* in each word and underlines *y* in family and *ia* in familia. He invites students to come up to the board and follow the same process of identifying similarities and differences between the other cognate pairs. Then the teacher models saying the word aloud and points out similarities and differences when the Spanish and English words are spoken. Once students grasp this concept, you can move to transparent cognates with different spelling patterns:

The following are spelling differences that Spanish-speaking ELLs might recognize.

- *Ph* in English is spelled with an *f* in Spanish (*photography—fotografía*).
- English words spelled with a *y*-vowel, such as symbol, are spelled with an *i* in Spanish (*symbol—símbolo*).
- The English *psy* is *si* in Spanish (*psychological—sicológico*). Many useful cognate lists can be found online at www.cognates.org.

One of the most difficult tasks for English learners is to transfer the cognate strategy from lists of discrete words to words found in natural texts. This process is most likely to be successful if the teacher provides explicit instruction and a great deal of modeling. The following teacher narrative demonstrates the instructional process. Note that the teacher provides a rationale and explicit instruction with modeling, teaches the students how to transfer the strategy to the social studies book, guides practice, and gradually releases responsibility to the students. This sequence, modeled on effective practices in strategy instruction (Lubliner, 2001), is designed to help students internalize the cognate strategy so that they can use it independently while reading.

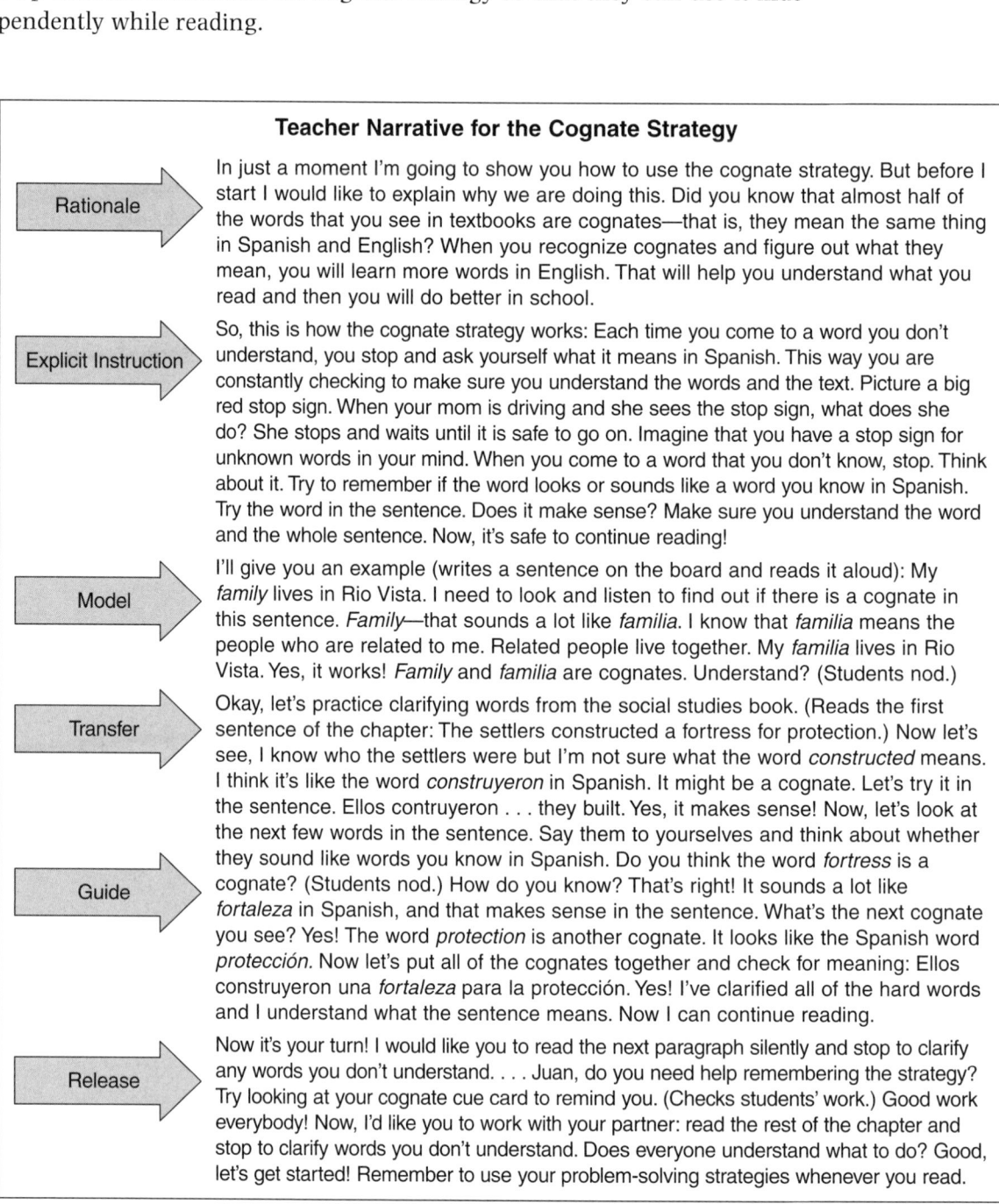

Teacher Narrative for the Cognate Strategy

Rationale

In just a moment I'm going to show you how to use the cognate strategy. But before I start I would like to explain why we are doing this. Did you know that almost half of the words that you see in textbooks are cognates—that is, they mean the same thing in Spanish and English? When you recognize cognates and figure out what they mean, you will learn more words in English. That will help you understand what you read and then you will do better in school.

Explicit Instruction

So, this is how the cognate strategy works: Each time you come to a word you don't understand, you stop and ask yourself what it means in Spanish. This way you are constantly checking to make sure you understand the words and the text. Picture a big red stop sign. When your mom is driving and she sees the stop sign, what does she do? She stops and waits until it is safe to go on. Imagine that you have a stop sign for unknown words in your mind. When you come to a word that you don't know, stop. Think about it. Try to remember if the word looks or sounds like a word you know in Spanish. Try the word in the sentence. Does it make sense? Make sure you understand the word and the whole sentence. Now, it's safe to continue reading!

Model

I'll give you an example (writes a sentence on the board and reads it aloud): My *family* lives in Rio Vista. I need to look and listen to find out if there is a cognate in this sentence. *Family*—that sounds a lot like *familia*. I know that *familia* means the people who are related to me. Related people live together. My *familia* lives in Rio Vista. Yes, it works! *Family* and *familia* are cognates. Understand? (Students nod.)

Transfer

Guide

Okay, let's practice clarifying words from the social studies book. (Reads the first sentence of the chapter: The settlers constructed a fortress for protection.) Now let's see, I know who the settlers were but I'm not sure what the word *constructed* means. I think it's like the word *construyeron* in Spanish. It might be a cognate. Let's try it in the sentence. Ellos contruyeron . . . they built. Yes, it makes sense! Now, let's look at the next few words in the sentence. Say them to yourselves and think about whether they sound like words you know in Spanish. Do you think the word *fortress* is a cognate? (Students nod.) How do you know? That's right! It sounds a lot like *fortaleza* in Spanish, and that makes sense in the sentence. What's the next cognate you see? Yes! The word *protection* is another cognate. It looks like the Spanish word *protección*. Now let's put all of the cognates together and check for meaning: Ellos construyeron una *fortaleza* para la protección. Yes! I've clarified all of the hard words and I understand what the sentence means. Now I can continue reading.

Release

Now it's your turn! I would like you to read the next paragraph silently and stop to clarify any words you don't understand. . . . Juan, do you need help remembering the strategy? Try looking at your cognate cue card to remind you. (Checks students' work.) Good work everybody! Now, I'd like you to work with your partner: read the rest of the chapter and stop to clarify words you don't understand. Does everyone understand what to do? Good, let's get started! Remember to use your problem-solving strategies whenever you read.

Figure 7.15 Teacher Narrative for Cognate Strategy

For students to benefit from cognate instruction they must have acquired morphological awareness, the ability to identify word parts. Morphological awareness entails the use of metacognitive skills and the ability to use information gleaned from cognates strategically to construct meaning. Lack of morphological awareness is often evident in students' inability to use English affixes, base words, and roots to figure out the meaning of new words encountered during reading. Shira first noticed this problem when working with a ninth-grade sheltered English class. All of the students in the class were intermediate to early advanced students who spoke Spanish as their first language. She was attempting to model comprehension strategies for their teacher, using a simplified newspaper article. The title of the article included the word *downsized.* She asked the students if they could figure out the meaning of the word *downsized.* When no one responded, she asked the students to look inside the large word for smaller words they already knew. The students looked puzzled. Only after Shira broke the word apart and showed the words *down* and *size* separately, were the students able to figure out the meaning of the larger word. This demonstrated a serious lack of morphological awareness. Without the ability to recognize word parts, the students were limited in their ability to learn new words from written texts.

Compound words are not easy because they don't necessarily follow the same pattern. A *garbageman* takes away garbage but a *mailman* brings the mail; a *snowman* is made of snow and a *fireman* puts out fires. A houseboat is a house that floats on the water and a spaceship is a vessel that rockets into space.

English-language learners need explicit instruction that helps students develop morphological awareness and helps them see how units of meaning can fit together. We begin with compound words comprised of smaller words that students already know. The activity in Figure 7.16 is based on a story about the underwater world. The teacher begins by pointing out a compound word, such as *underwater,* in the text. The students are explicitly taught how to break apart the compound word and identify the meaning of each separate word inside the compound word. Then the word meanings are combined and the compound word meaning constructed. Finally, students are encouraged to provide original sentences containing the compound word.

Once students are comfortable identifying and constructing meaning of compound words, instruction moves to affixes and base words. Suffixes are much easier to work with in the early stages of instruction, because they rarely change word meaning. If students know the verb *object* (disagree), it is not difficult for them to infer the meaning of related words such as objected, objecting, and objection. The parts of speech have changed but the meaning remains relatively stable. Prefixes, on the other hand, change word meaning. Therefore we conceptualize them as related but different word families. Students who know the word *object,* for example, may find it very difficult to infer the meaning of words such as *reject, project,* and *eject* without a great deal of instruction. Activities that engage students in locating suffixed words and identifying word meaning help build morphological awareness. The next step is to teach high-frequency prefixes and help students use prefixes to construct meaning. A small group of negative prefixes (*un-, il-, im-, in-, ir-,* and *dis-*) account for more than 40 percent of all words with prefixes in English school texts (White, Sowell, & Yanagihara, 1989). Cognates that

Compound Word Chart

Compound Word	First Word/ Meaning	Second Word/ Meaning	Compound Word Meaning	Example
underwater	under (below)	water (H₂0)	under the surface (top) of the water	There are many strange <u>underwater</u> creatures.
underground				
paperwork				
hammerhead				
spaceship				
overfishing				

Figure 7.16   Compound Word Chart

include negative prefixes are also high frequency in Spanish, so it is very helpful to teach them to Spanish-speaking students. Figures 7.17 and 7.18 include high-frequency cognates with negative prefixes.

English	English (il, im, in, un)	Spanish	Spanish (il, im, in)
legal	illegal	legal	ilegal
possible	impossible	possible	imposible
complete	incomplete	completo	incompleto
dependence	independence	dependencia	independencia
visible	invisible	visible	invisible
exact	inexact	exacto	inexacto
necessary	unnecessary	necesario	innecesario

Figure 7.17   Spanish Prefixes

English	English (dis)	Spanish	Spanish (des)
obey	disobey	obedecer	desobedecer
appear	disappear	aparecer	desaparecer
connect	disconnect	conectar	desconectar
cover	discover	cubrir	descubrir
obey	obey	obedecer	desobedecer

Figure 7.18   More Spanish Prefixes

WORD CONSCIOUSNESS: COLLOCATIONS

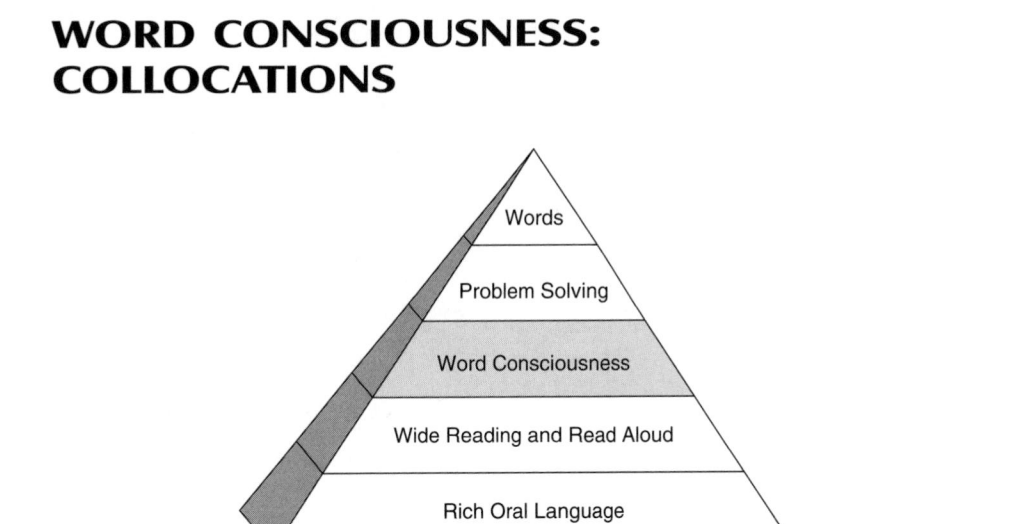

Figure 7.19

English learners acquire simple vocabulary and basic communicative skills relatively quickly, but they also need to develop word consciousness, a sense of how words work in English, to become fully proficient. One of the more challenging aspects of word consciousness is the mastery of collocations—words that belong together. Phrases such as *ride in a car* and *ride on a bus*, and *get out of a car* and *get off of a bus* are mystifying to English learners and require explicit instruction. The sentence frame in Figure 7.20 is an example of an activity designed to teach collocations that also reviews content from the story "Grandfather's Journey" (Say, 1993). The book, which is read aloud to the students, is filled with rich vocabulary and vivid images. The instructional activities that follow provide multiple exposures to new words and many opportunities to use the words in classroom discourse. The teacher begins with the collocation frame in Figure 7.20. A full-sized version of this activity is included in Appendix B.

Collocation Frame

Imagine that you were traveling with Grandfather on his journey. What stories would you tell?

- I longed for _____

- I was excited by _____

- I was amazed by _____

- I was bewildered by _____

- I marveled at _____

- I remembered _____

- I was reminded of _____

Figure 7.20   Collocation Frame

The sentence frame provides students with the opportunity to practice high-utility collocations and the vocabulary found in the story. Note that the activity is based on a story about a Japanese immigrant whose experiences of adjustment, loneliness, and loss are likely to be particularly relevant to immigrant students. The first-person structure of the activity allows the students to reflect on the text and their own immigrant experiences as they respond to the prompts. Follow-up activities include writing a story about your own journey or that of a family member. Students are encouraged to interview family members as they write their stories. The stories are shared with the class, providing additional opportunities for expressive language development. Writing is a wonderful way to help students learn idiosyncratic formations in English. We encourage students to write and to risk experimenting with word use. Then we can see collocation errors easily and use this teachable moment to inform the students that this is a good guess, but happens to not be the convention in English.

Abstract Words

Instruction in the location words can be made more concrete through activities that engage children in movement and speech. For example, the teacher puts a chair in the center of the room and provides each student with a different location card. Students are asked to place themselves in the correct location relative to the chair. Matt is behind the chair; Sarah is beneath the chair; Alma is next to the chair; Danny is on the chair; and so forth. As each child is called on, he or she must provide a sentence to explain his or her location. Matt states, "I am behind the chair."

The teacher moves Matt and asks the students where he is now. The children reply that Matt is "front the chair." The teacher smiles and repeats the response with the correction, "Matt is in front of the chair." She beckons to several children and places them in front of other objects in the classroom. The children practice the collocation *in front of* multiple times as they describe the location of their classmates. Actively engaging children in discussion and physically moving them around the room provide the practice they need to master abstract location words including collocations.

Rich Oral Language

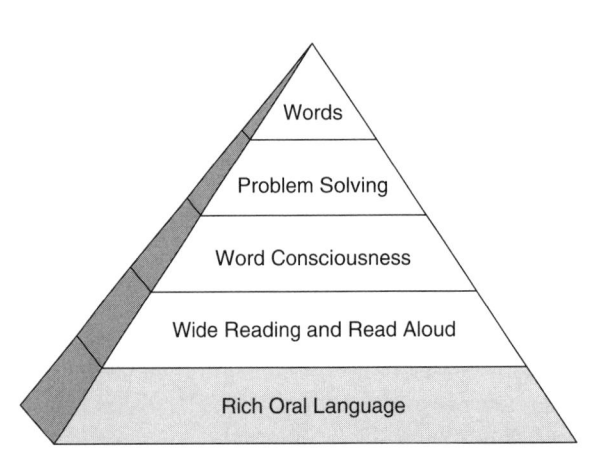

Figure 7.21

The materials that are used to teach beginning ELLs often focus on conversational vocabulary, leaving students unable to comprehend words found in texts. It is important to emphasize the difference in terms of vocabulary demands. Books contain far more challenging words than oral language. As Hayes and Ahrens (1988) point out, children's books contain 30.9 rare words per 1,000 in contrast to the 17.3 per 1,000 in the speech of college-educated adults. When teachers speak to students, particularly ELLs, they are likely to use even fewer rare words, limiting the opportunities for student to acquire new vocabulary from teacher discourse. We suggest that teachers make a concerted effort to change this pattern. Enriching classroom discourse is an important component of a balanced vocabulary program for ELLs, with the caveat that comprehensible input is provided. In other words, teachers do not simply use rich language that children cannot understand. They provide pictures, gestures, and realia to ensure that ELLs are able to comprehend their discourse.

Wide Reading and Read Aloud

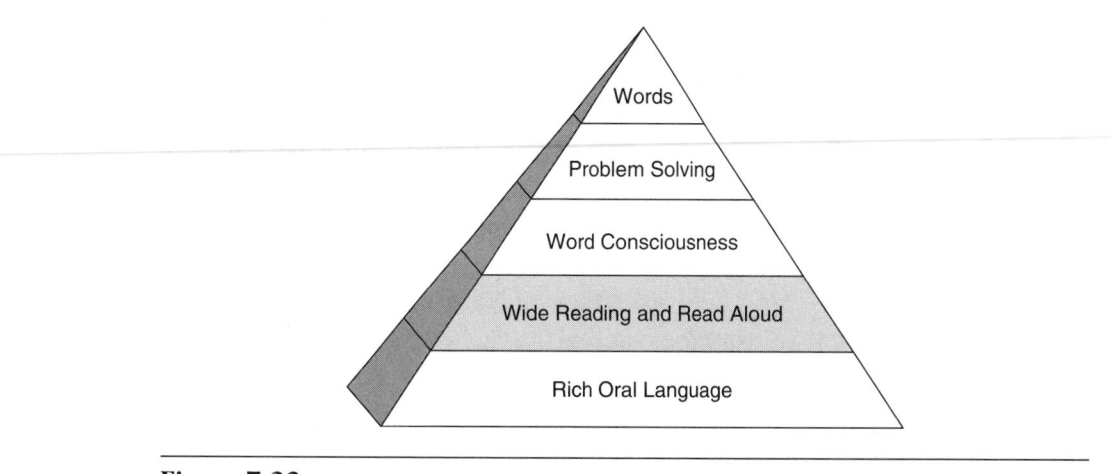

Figure 7.22

There simply are not enough hours in the school day to teach all of the words that English learners need to know. Reading aloud to students and motivating them to increase their independent reading are essential in order to provide exposure to a broad array of important English vocabulary. We suggest reading aloud poetry and high-interest stories on a daily basis to increase students' exposure to vocabulary.

Books on Tape/CD

Books on tape/CD are a very valuable resource for English learners. Texts can be translated in students' native languages. Listening to native language translations provides ELLs with a preview of content prior to reading and discussing the text in English with the rest of the class. Books on tape/CD help ELLs acquire conceptual understanding and word knowledge in their first language. This makes it much easier for them to learn new labels (words in English) for the concepts. If commercial CDs are not available in the range of languages that students speak, parents and other volunteers can be enlisted to help record texts, creating a master set of CDs corresponding to the books used in the classroom.

STUDENTS WITH SPECIAL NEEDS

Students with reading disabilities often lose ground in vocabulary because they do not read well enough to learn words from books. This problem can be avoided if teachers provide content and vocabulary in an oral context. Several methods can be used to facilitate oral exposure.

Books on Tape/CD

Books on tape/CD are also an excellent resource for students with limited reading skills. Parents and other volunteers can be enlisted to help record texts, creating a master set of CDs corresponding to the books used in the classroom. Students can listen to texts with headphones during class time and can also listen at home. Listening to books on tape/CD while following along with the written text makes the experience even more worthwhile. Students' decoding and reading fluency are strengthened as they are exposed to vocabulary and content. Once students have listened to texts in an oral context, they are more likely to benefit from reading and classroom discussion.

Read Aloud

Daily read aloud benefits all students in the class but is particularly important for students with reading disabilities. Oral language is the primary way these students can gain access to the language and vocabulary that are unique to books. Read aloud offers students the opportunity to become immersed in stories and exposed to content. It is also a highly motivating experience that can persuade students that learning to read is worth the effort.

Teachers often ask whether they should interrupt the read aloud to discuss key vocabulary and concepts. Although it is tempting to teach words that appear in read aloud texts, we suggest that you resist doing so. Breaking up a read aloud to discuss vocabulary diminishes the pleasure that students experience as they immerse themselves in the story. Asking students to define words, write summaries, think aloud, and other literacy tasks are fine when the goal is to dissect a text in the reading anthology. But read aloud is not necessarily the best time for this sort of instruction. Students acquire vocabulary from read aloud just by listening and enjoying the flow of language and the thoughts of the author.

However, read alouds can be used to model reading strategies and to acknowledge the eloquence of the author's choice of words. The key is to embed such instruction so that it doesn't interrupt the flow and pleasure of the reading. It is often better to read the section first, uninterrupted, and then go back to examine the examples of the author's craft or to summarize what they have just heard. This can be done with chart paper, adding challenging vocabulary words that appeared in the story, interesting word use to enhance description or mood, points that they want to remember, and predictions about what is to come. A volunteer from the class records these points on the chart paper. The next day, another student is chosen to summarize the previous day's recordings before the teacher begins to read aloud the next chapter. The chart paper often includes comments from students, such as "yes" next to a correct prediction, and definitions inserted after a challenging word has been discussed. This process allows the teacher to maximize the students' retention of vocabulary and content, without interrupting the flow of the story.

RECIPROCAL TEACHING

A large body of research demonstrates the effectiveness of teaching students, particularly struggling readers, to implement four powerful strategies in cooperative groups (Brown & Palincsar, 1985, 1986; Palincsar 1983, 1984, 1985, 1986; Palincsar & Brown, 1983, 1984). The reciprocal teaching strategies include questioning, clarifying, summarizing, and predicting. Students are placed into small heterogeneous groups and are taught to work together to construct meaning from the text. Each student takes a turn as the group leader, reading aloud a paragraph of text, asking main idea questions, clarifying difficult words, summarizing what has been read, and predicting what will come next. When the group leader is a student with a reading disability, he or she can request a pinch hitter to read the text aloud. Once the text has been read, the leader implements the four strategies and guides the discussion. The leader with a disability is usually fully capable of implementing the strategies and leading the text-based discussion. Reciprocal teaching has been found to be effective with a wide range of students including those with disabilities and English learners when it takes place in a dynamic oral context (Klinger & Vaughn, 1996).

Rosenshine and Meister (1996) conducted a review of the reciprocal teaching research and noted that students in the studies rarely used the clarifying strategy. Apparently, they had not been taught how to clarify words encountered in texts and found little value in this strategy. The problem-solving cue card with explicit instruction for clarifying may help. If students learn to implement the clarifying strategy well, it is likely that reciprocal teaching will be even more effective than previous studies have demonstrated. For a more detailed description of reciprocal teaching methods, see *A Practical Guide to Reciprocal Teaching* (Lubliner, 2001).

DIFFERENTIATING INSTRUCTION THROUGH MINI-LESSONS

Classrooms are busy places and students have widely varying levels of vocabulary development, language proficiency, and academic achievement. English learners and students with more limited academic vocabulary often need additional instruction to that the rest of the class receives. Mini-lessons can provide that additional boost. A mini-lesson is a short instructional sequence (approximately fifteen to twenty minutes) that focuses on a specific topic that a small group of students need to learn. Mini-lessons are particularly valuable for ELLs and students with special needs because they provide an opportunity for oral discourse in a smaller, more supportive context. Possible mini-lesson topics include cognates, clarifying strategies, metacognitive skills, and high-frequency vocabulary words that most of the other students already know, thereby preteaching vocabulary prior to reading a text.

The teacher identifies students with the same area of need, in terms of vocabulary. For example, a group of Spanish-speaking students might be targeted for a set of mini-lessons, based on the advantage that could be obtained by using cognates. This instruction would be of little use to the rest of the class given that they don't know Spanish words. Mini-lessons allow teachers to focus on specific student needs. The following guidelines may be useful in designing mini-lesson for ELLs and students with special needs. A full-sized version of the mini-lesson plan in Figure 7.23 is found in Appendix B.

Mini-Lesson Guidelines

- Select a group of students with the same area of need, in terms of vocabulary.
- Bring together the group while the rest of the class is occupied with independent reading or other activities.
- Explain the purpose of the mini-lesson or lessons.
- Provide explicit instruction.
- Help students transfer vocabulary knowledge or strategy to a text.
- Monitor student learning to determine if additional instruction is needed.

Mini-Lesson Plan

Students: _____

Shared area of need: _____

Mini-lesson objectives: _____

Text and materials: _____

Lesson sequence: _____

_____

_____

_____

_____

Assessment: _____

Follow-up: _____

_____

Figure 7.23 Mini-Lesson Plan

English learners and students with reading disabilities pose a significant challenge to teachers. How can students be taught enough vocabulary words quickly enough to catch up with their peers and succeed in school? The methods outlined in this chapter are designed to provide an enriched diet of vocabulary instruction to students who depend on schools for literacy. Teaching students high-utility words and academic vocabulary while immersing them in reading and rich oral language has the potential to improve student outcomes and narrow the vocabulary-related achievement gap.

Vocabulary Assessment and Evaluation 8

Target Skill	Page Number	Assessment Type	Description
words (receptive)	133	multiple choice	Students select the correct synonym to match the target word.
words (expressive)	134	fill-in-the-blank	Students fill in the blank with the correct definition.
words (context)	136	cloze	Students fill in the missing words in the text.
words (lexical access)	137	five-minute vocabulary test	Students are given five minutes to write down as many words as they can think of.
words	137	opposites test	Students fill in the opposite of each word, using the word bank.
metacognitive skills (self-monitoring)	138–139	metacognitive test	Students circle unknown words in a text and then take a multiple-choice test on the same words.
metacognitive skills	140	stoplight vocabulary test	Students rate level of word knowledge on stoplight vocabulary sheet and then fill in definitions of the same words on a fill-in-the-blank (constructed response) vocabulary test.
morphological awareness	142	morphological awareness test	Students identify designated word parts (prefixes, suffixes, roots or base words) in a text.
strategic skills	141	clarifying strategy self-report	Students respond to the prompt, "What do you do when you're reading and you come to a word

Figure 8.1 Vocabulary Assessment and Evaluation

(Continued)

(Continued)

Target Skill	Page Number	Assessment Type	Description
		clarifying strategy self-report	that you don't understand? If you don't have a dictionary how do you figure out what the word means?"
word schema	143	word web assessment	Students construct a word web demonstrating the relationship between a set of concepts.
word schema	144	word sort assessment	Students sort words into categories based on conceptual relationships.
word schema	145	word concept diagram	Students draw a diagram, label and explain concepts using target words.
word consciousness	147	rubric	Measures student interest and engagement with words.

Figure 8.1   Vocabulary Assessment and Evaluation

Assessment and evaluation are important components of a comprehensive vocabulary development program. Although the terms are often used interchangeably, educators have made a distinction between the two: assessment is seen as the process of gathering information or evidence, and evaluation involves using that information or evidence to make judgments. We assess our students continually in the ongoing observation of their work. Assessment occurs as we collect baseline data, find out what students know before instruction, and document student progress. A wide range of vocabulary assessments can be used to measure different aspects of vocabulary development. Evaluation happens when we use the information we have gathered through assessment to judge a student's work and to assign it a grade or a mark.

A major issue arises when we discuss vocabulary assessment—what is the purpose of the assessment? Sometimes, we want to know whether students have grasped the concepts and academic vocabulary we've taught. At other times, we want to know what strategies they're using, and which ones we need to re-teach. In addition, school districts and state departments of education often use vocabulary growth over time as a measure of growth in knowledge, school performance, and teacher performance.

The purpose of the assessment is complicated by issues related to the breadth of word knowledge (how many words does the student know) and the depth of word knowledge (how well does the student know particular words) (Nation, 2001).

Let's look first at the question of breadth. It is challenging to design high-quality vocabulary assessments given the huge number of words in the English language. Nagy and Anderson estimate that there are 88,500 distinct word families in printed school texts (1984).

Standardized vocabulary tests are generally used to look at the breadth of word knowledge in large populations. However, they are notoriously insensitive to instructional interventions, because the likelihood of a match between words taught and words assessed is quite low.

STANDARDIZED VOCABULARY TEST FORMATS

---

1. *Multiple-choice—isolation*: students select the correct synonym to match the target word.
   - Measures receptive word knowledge based on recognition of the correct response; format may favor test-wise students.
   - Example: Circle the definition that best describes the word *astonished*.

   A. angry
   B. sorry
   C. surprised
   D. happy

2. *Multiple-choice—in context*: students select the correct synonym to match the target word in the sentence.
   - Measures a combination of receptive word knowledge based on recognition of the correct response and the ability to make sense of words in context; format may favor test-wise students.
   - Example: Circle the definition that best describes the italicized word in the sentence.
   - The children were *astonished* to find a baby bird sitting in front of their classroom door.

   A. angry
   B. sorry
   C. surprised
   D. happy

Most large-scale standardized vocabulary tests are used primarily to produce a judgment regarding students' general capabilities and are in multiple-choice format. This form of testing is simple to score and generally has high psychometric levels of reliability (consistency) and validity (measures what it is intended to measure). However, numerous problems are associated with multiple-choice tests, including the selection of words and whether the words selected represent the material covered in the curriculum. Also, multiple-choice tests do not measure or account for many aspects of the complexity of word knowledge (Scott, Lubliner, & Hiebert, 2006).

Figuring out the meaning of a word in isolation is a difficult task that is even more difficult when a word has multiple meanings. Progressively, the trend has been to embed multiple-choice vocabulary items in contexts (Pearson, Hiebert, & Kamil, 2007). This practice may result in higher scores because of the cueing effects that the text has in terms of student memory (Nation, 2001; Watanabe, 1997). Multiple-choice tests measure receptive vocabulary knowledge and are useful in developing generalizations about vocabulary levels. Whether these generalizations are due to differences in background knowledge, specific knowledge for a given topic, test-taking strategies, general intelligence, or something else is not yet determined (Pearson, Hiebert, & Kamil, 2007).

To measure expressive vocabulary, or the ability to use a word correctly, we can use constructed response tests. These require students to supply a word or definition without a word bank. They measure expressive vocabulary knowledge, which is a much higher level than the receptive knowledge that multiple-choice tests measure. However, they are much more difficult to score, and thus are not often used for large-group assessment. The following are examples of constructed response tests.

---

1. *Fill-in-the-blank—words in isolation with word bank*: students select definitions from a list and fill in the blanks (more definitions than words reduce the likelihood of guessing).
   - Measures receptive word knowledge based on recognition of the correct response
   - Example: Select the best definition from the box and write it next to the correct word (not all words in the box are used).

   A. astonished _____

   B. thunderous _____

   C. motionless _____

   D. jolt _____

   > move sharply
   >
   > very loud
   >
   > without movement
   >
   > surprised
   >
   > furious
   >
   > very sure
   >
   > sorry

   Figure 8.2   Word Bank

2. *Fill-in-the-blank—words in isolation, constructed response*: students fill in the blank without a list of words to choose from. Scoring is based on a rubric such as the following: 1 point—a category to which the word belongs or an example of the word, 2 points—partial definition, 3 points—full definition.
   - Measures expressive word knowledge
   - Example: Write a definition for each of the following words.

   A. astonished _____

   B. thunderous _____

   C. motionless _____

   D. jolt _____

Classroom Vocabulary Assessment

It is important for teachers to monitor their students' vocabulary growth on a regular basis. Classroom assessment can measure knowledge of the words that have been taught in a particular grade level. Teachers select words to teach, following the guidelines in Chapters 4 (primary), 5 (upper elementary), or 6 (secondary) and develop assessments to track student progress. If same types of vocabulary tests are used after each instructional interval, test results can be compared and student progress evaluated. We suggest that teachers administer several vocabulary tests at each testing interval to provide a multi-faceted profile of students' vocabulary knowledge.

Figure 8.3 is a sample score sheet that a teacher might use to track students' progress in vocabulary assessment at the end of several units of instruction. If multiple methods of vocabulary assessment are used (as recommended), a separate scoring sheet is used for each test. Tests are administered at the end of each instructional unit and class averages are computed to measure progress. A blank scoring form is available in Appendix B.

Grade Level: 5th	Test: MC Unit 1		Test: MC Unit 2		Test: MC Unit 3		Test: MC Unit 4	
Student Name	Date	Score	Date	Score	Date	Score	Date	Score
Student A	9/10	20	10/12	22	11/2	25	12/5	25
Student B	9/10	15	10/12	14	11/2	17	12/5	19
Student C	9/10	12	10/12	15	11/2	15	12/5	16
Student D	9/10	17	10/12	18	11/2	20	12/5	19
Class average		16		17.25		19.25		19.75

Figure 8.3   Scoring Sheet for Classroom Assessment

Virtually any method classroom teachers use to teach vocabulary can also be used to assess students' vocabulary knowledge. For example, if teachers incorporate word sorts into vocabulary instruction, they can use the same method to assess student learning. It is important to provide students with plenty of practice with the method before it is used as an assessment tool. Additionally, teachers need to be sure that students fully understand what they are being asked to do when they are taking a vocabulary assessment.

Alternative Vocabulary Assessment

Vocabulary assessment includes a broad range of tests that measure different facets of vocabulary knowledge and problem-solving skills. Alternative assessments are used by classroom teachers to monitor progress and inform instruction (see Figures 8.4 to 8.7).

Cloze—words in context, with word bank: students fill in the missing words in the text, using words in a word bank (include more words in the word bank than test blanks).

- Measures receptive word knowledge and the ability to use context to identify words (word bank should include more words than test blanks)
- Example: Select words from the box that make the most sense in the paragraph. Write the appropriate word in the blank (not every word is used).

One morning the children arrived at school and were _____ to find a baby bird sitting in front of their classroom door. The teacher told the children he was _____ that the baby bird fell out of its nest and landed in front of the classroom door. The mother bird cawed _____, diving at the children when they approached the building. The baby bird sat _____, _____ with fear. The teacher called the Animal Rescue Society. They came quickly and picked up the baby bird. The _____ was over and the class settled down to work.

Figure 8.4   Cloze Test

- An alternative that also measures knowledge of morphology provides the root word and asks students to change the form to match the context.

astonish, certain, frantic, upheaval, motionless, quiver

Figure 8.5   Cloze Test Word Bank

Word Sort: students arrange words into categories designated by the teacher.

- Measures conceptual, deep-level word knowledge
- Example: Sort the following words into categories by writing them in the correct boxes: *astonished, frantic, jolt, quivering, cawed, shrill, shuddered, staggered, thunderous, unbearably, lunged, heaved, anxious, cawed.*

Words for Movement	Words for Sounds	Words for Feelings

Figure 8.6   Word Sort

Five-minute vocabulary test—general word knowledge: students are given five minutes to write down as many words as they can think of (proper nouns, numbers, and classroom environmental print do not count).

- Measures lexical access and speed of retrieval

Five-minute vocabulary test—specific topic: students are given five minutes to write down as many words as they can think of about a specific topic in the curriculum (proper nouns, numbers, and classroom environmental print do not count).

Collect as pretest and posttest measures of a unit.

- Measures lexical access and speed of retrieval, and word knowledge related to a specific topic.

Opposites Test

The opposites test measures students' ability to link words with inverse meaning. Although the ability to identify opposites is sometimes used as an indicator of intelligence, we believe that this skill can be taught and measured as part of a vocabulary development program.

Fill in the blanks with the opposite of each word:

1. up _____	young
2. in _____	fat
3. over _____	false
4. little _____	good
5. fast _____	short
6. near _____	night
7. pretty _____	interesting
8. easy _____	slow
9. happy _____	outside
10. boring _____	poor
11. cold _____	after
12. thin _____	down
13. bad _____	narrow
14. rich _____	out
15. wide _____	ugly
16. full _____	hot
17. long _____	far
18. lose _____	sad
19. dark _____	big
20. true _____	light
21. day _____	down
22. soft _____	win
23. old _____	hard
24. before _____	under
25. inside _____	

Figure 8.7 Opposites Test Word Bank

The Metacognitive Test

The Metacogntive Test measures students' vocabulary knowledge and self-monitoring skills. The teacher prepares a text (approximately 200 words) that includes twenty or more challenging words and a multiple-choice vocabulary test based on the same set of words. The students are first given the text. They are asked to read the text and to circle the words they do not know. Once the students have completed the task, the teacher collects the texts and hands out the multiple-choice vocabulary test. The students are instructed to circle the best definition for each word on the test. The vocabulary test questions measure the students' knowledge of the same challenging words found in the text.

The metacognitive test is scored and several key pieces of information are noted. The multiple-choice test score provides information regarding the students' knowledge of the words. The percentage of matches between words circled in the text and words missed on the multiple-choice test indicates the degree to which students are monitoring their word knowledge.

Instruction based on metacognitive methods such as stoplight vocabulary (see Chapter 5) help students improve their self-monitoring skills. When students are given another metacognitive test (similar text and set of multiple-choice questions), an increased percentage of matches demonstrates improved ability to identify unknown words in texts.

The following is an example (excerpt) of a metacognitive test, suitable for students in the fifth grade and up.

Metacognitive Test

Directions: Please read the article below and circle each word you do not understand.

All citizens of the United States are entitled to freedom and equality. But some groups of people have not been treated fairly. Black people were brought to this country as slaves, to do hard manual labor that white people did not want to do. Slaves suffered great hardships and were often abused. Even after slavery was outlawed, African Americans continued to struggle for equal rights . . . .

(The teacher collects papers with circled words and passes out the multiple-choice vocabulary test.)
Directions: Please read each word below and circle the letter next to the best definition of the word.

1. citizens
   A. black people
   B. white people
   C. immigrants
   D. people who are members of a country

2. entitled
   A. have rights
   B. without rights
   C. left behind
   D. treated badly

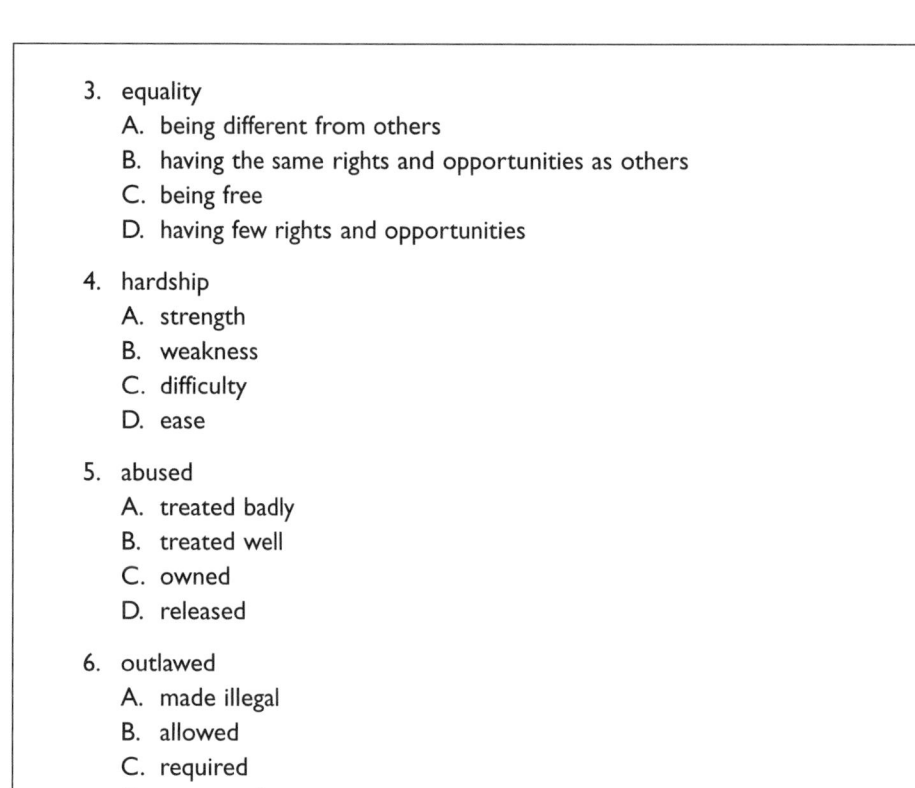

Stoplight Vocabulary Test

Stoplight vocabulary (Lubliner, 2005) is a metacognitive method described in Chapter 5. It can also be used as a metacognitive assessment when grouped with a constructed response vocabulary test. Such a test is constructed as follows: The teacher previews a chapter of the text that the students will be reading and lists challenging words on the stoplight vocabulary sheet. She asks the students to rate their level of word knowledge by coloring in the stoplights: red for an unknown word, yellow for a partially known word, and green for a fully known word. The sheets are then collected and the students are given a constructed response test on the same words. Scoring is based on the match between the stoplight vocabulary rating and the accuracy of the definition (red light—no response, yellow light—partial response, green light—full response). Higher match scores on subsequent stoplight vocabulary tests document students' improved ability to self-monitor their own level of word knowledge. The constructed response segment of the test also provides information regarding students' expressive vocabulary knowledge.

Figures 8.8, 8.9, and 8.10 are examples of a stoplight vocabulary test.

Part 1: Stoplight Vocabulary	

Figure 8.8 Stoplight Vocabulary Symbol Part 1

1. citizen	⬭⬭⬭	4. entitled	⬭⬭⬭
2. equality	⬭⬭⬭	5. abused	⬭⬭⬭
3. hardship	⬭⬭⬭	6. outlawed	⬭⬭⬭

Figure 8.9 Stoplight Vocabulary Test

Source: Lubliner, S. (2005b). *Getting into words: Vocabulary instruction that strengthens comprehension* (pp. 80–88). Baltimore: Paul H. Brookes Publishing Co., Inc. Reprinted by permission.

Follow these steps for stoplight vocabulary

If you don't know the word at all, color the light red. If you have heard of it but aren't sure what it means, color it yellow. If you know the word and can use it in a sentence, color it green (Lubliner, 2005).

Part 2: Constructed Response

Figure 8.10 Part 2: Constructed Response

Write a definition for each of the following words.

1. citizen _____
2. equality _____
3. hardship _____
4. entitled _____
5. abused _____
6. outlawed _____

Clarifying Strategy Self-Report

The clarifying strategy self-report is an assessment that helps identify the strategies that students are familiar with and claim to use, before and after clarifying strategy instruction. The teacher provides students with a blank sheet of

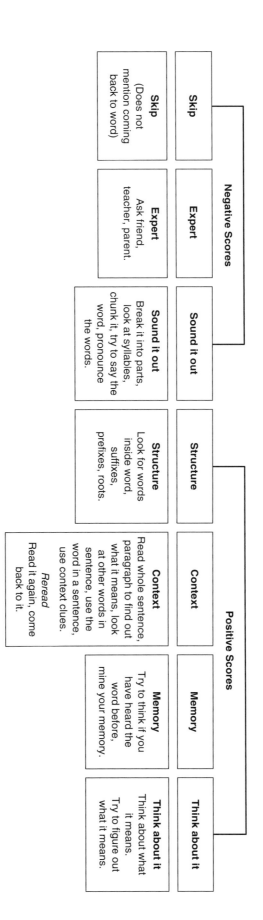

Figure 8.11 Clarifying Strategy Self-Report

paper and asks them to respond to the questions: "What do you do when you're reading and you come to a word that you don't understand? If you don't have a dictionary how do you figure out what the word means?"

Student responses are grouped into categories and the number of responses to each category calculated. The strategy self-report is administered again after students have received clarifying strategy instruction. The goal is to document student awareness and use of effective clarifying strategies: structure, context, memory, and think about it.

Figure 8.11 shows a scoring sheet based on responses collected from ninety-one fifth-grade students before and after clarifying strategy instruction in a twelve-week vocabulary study. A high percentage of students responded that they skip the word, ask someone (expert), or sound it out, before clarifying strategy instruction. These were characterized as negative scores because they were negatively correlated with reading comprehension test scores. The percentage of students who indicated they use structure, context, memory, or think about it, increased after clarifying strategy instruction. These responses were characterized as positive scores because they were positively correlated with reading comprehension scores.

The boxes represent student responses grouped into categories.

Morphological Awareness Test

The morphological awareness test measures students' ability to notice word parts that contribute to the construction of meaning. The teacher develops a short text and asks the students to underline the word parts that have been taught in class. In this third-grade test shown in Figure 8.12 the students are asked to underline prefixes and suffixes. The test can be given with or without a bank of affixes.

Jenny was very unhappy today. She tried to concentrate but she was so distracted she couldn't get anything done. Finally, Jenny gave up. She walked miserably up to the teacher and asked if she could go home. Jenny told the teacher that her dog, Sam was very sick. The vet did not predict that Sam would recover from his illness. Ms. O'Neil was unsure as to what she should do. She made the decision to send Jenny to the office to call her mom.

When Jenny reported to the office, Mrs. Brady, the secretary, was waiting. She smiled happily at Jenny. "Your mom just called, Jenny. The vet was mistaken that your dog's illness was so serious. Sam responded well to the medication and he is going to be fine." Jenny cried with happiness. She hugged Mrs. Brady warmly and skipped back to class as quickly as she could. She couldn't wait to tell everyone the wonderful news about Sam's recovery.

---

un, dis, mis, re, pre, ed, ing, ly, en, able, ion, ness, y, ful

---

Figure 8.12   Word Bank for Morphological Awareness Test

The upper elementary–middle school version of the morphological awareness test measures students' ability to identify Greek and Latin roots in a text. Students are asked to underline each Greek or Latin root they find in the text (see Figure 8.13).

The transcontinental railroad was completed in 1869. There was a great celebration as the president of the Central Pacific Railroad drove a gold spike into a railroad tie. There was a lot to celebrate. Now it was possible to transport goods quickly from one side of the continent to another. Railroad transportation also made it possible for people to travel from place to place. The railroad was part of a new age. Telegraph lines carried news across the country. New buildings were constructed and huge factories made things for growing cities. Construction increased and new cities demanded train stations. Soon railroads expanded across the country. The expansion of the railroads made the development of America possible.

trans, cele, tele, con, com, ex, fac, port, graph, struct, mand(at), plet, poss

Figure 8.13   Word Bank for Transcontinental Railroad Morphological Awareness Test

Word Web Assessment

Words are rarely learned in isolation. Effective instruction provides students with rich interconnected schemata of related words and concepts. These schemata can also be used as the basis of assessment.

A word schema test is constructed as follows: The teacher identifies a set of words and concepts that have been explicitly taught to the students. The teacher may choose to provide a great deal of structure to the assessment or leave the assessment completely open ended. For example, a science unit on the weather could include a word web assessment such as one in Figures 8.14

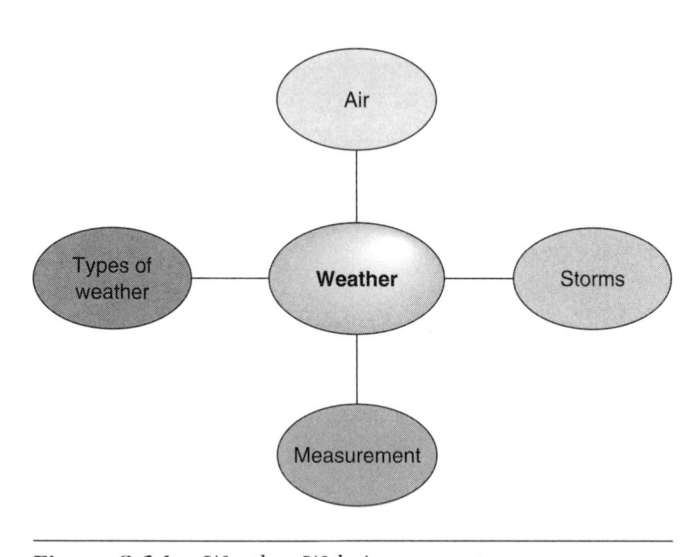

Figure 8.14   Weather Web Assessment

and 8.15. Students could be asked to fill in the Weather Web, using the words in the box.

An open-ended version of the same test could be constructed by asking the students to make their own weather webs using the words in the box and being sure to use categories to organize the big ideas in the webs.

weather vane, hot, cold, dry, anemometer, windy, cloudy, rainy, pressure, sunny, storm, tornado, thunderstorm, lightning, thunder, temperature, hurricane, thermometer, wet, barometer, troposphere, blizzard, warm, atmosphere

Word Sort Assessment

Word schema can also be assessed using a word sort. Either a closed sort (the teacher identifies the categories and the students sort the words) or an open sort (the students identify categories and sort the words) can be used. Figure 8.16 is an example of a closed word sort, used to measure word schema for oceans, mountains, and deserts.

Word Sort Assessment

Sort the following words into the chart below:

addaxes, sandstorm, coral reef, whale, tundra, desiccated, squid, craggy, current, foam, peaks, saguaro, shoals, camels, glacier, alpine, surf, arid, succulent, towering, tsunami, bighorn sheep, euphotic zone, oasis, roadrunners, wolves, summit, anemone, rattlesnake, crepuscular

Ocean Words	Mountain Words	Desert Words
coral reef, whale, squid, current, foam, shoals, surf, tsunami, euphotic zone, anemone	tundra, craggy peaks, glacier, alpine, towering bighorn sheep, wolves, summit	sandstorm, desiccated saguaro, camels, arid, succulent, oasis, roadrunners, rattlesnake

---

Figure 8.15   Word Sort Assessment

Word Concept Diagrams

Another way to assess word schema is to ask students to draw a diagram and describe the relationship between a set of words that represent a set of concepts. For example, we could ask upper-grade students to explain the relationship between words that describe concepts taught in a science unit about volcanoes (see Figure 8.16).

ASSESSING VOCABULARY GROWTH WITH RUBRICS

Teachers often use rubrics to look at growth over time toward a goal. Rubrics give students a clear sense where they are heading and what they need to do to get there. A gymnast or an ice skater knows how judges will rate their performance based on a scoring guide that evaluates both individual elements and overall effect. As they practice, they can keep these criteria in mind. The same is true of rubrics in teaching. They guide students as they develop by providing a clear sense of what is valued and knowledge of how their performance will be assessed. Rubrics can be used to to assess reading, writing, content area information, or any other aspect of your curriculum (Wells & Reid, 2004).

Volcano Assessment

Draw a diagram and explain the relationship between these words having to do with volcanoes: plume, lava, magma, ash, central vent, crater, eruption, ring of fire

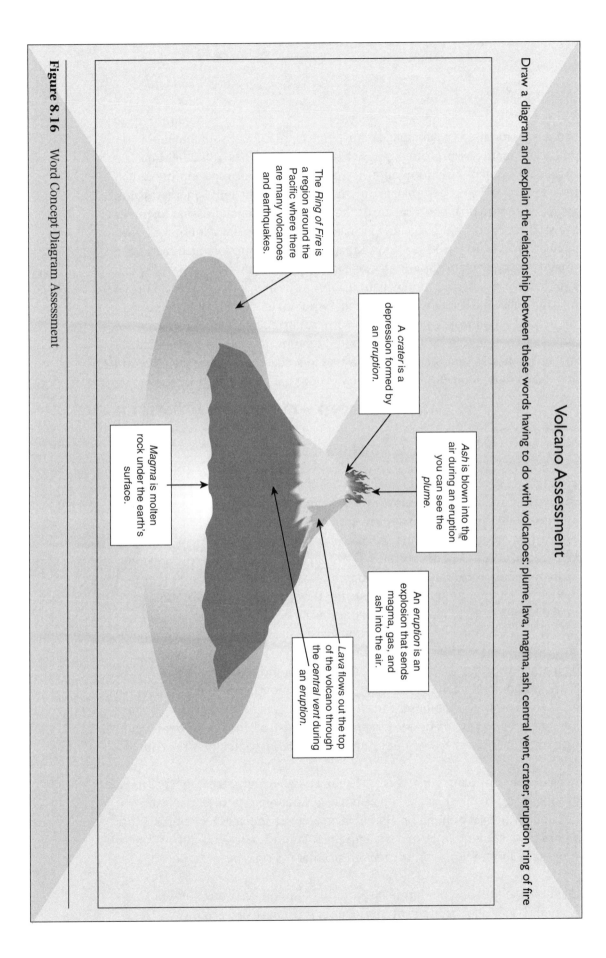

The *Ring of Fire* is a region around the Pacific where there are many volcanoes and earthquakes.

A *crater* is a depression formed by an *eruption*.

Ash is blown into the air during an eruption you can see the *plume*.

An *eruption* is an explosion that sends magma, gas, and ash into the air.

Magma is molten rock under the earth's surface.

Lava flows out the top of the volcano through the *central vent* during an *eruption*.

Figure 8.16   Word Concept Diagram Assessment

When you develop a rubric, it is important to consider your goal. What is it that you think students ought to be able to do at the end of a unit or the end of the year?

Sharing a rubric with students at the beginning of the unit or year eliminates the mystery surrounding what they need to do to obtain a good grade. Many students, especially those who generally do not fare well in schools, do not have a clear understanding of what to do or how to do it. Knowledge of what they are striving to achieve makes it easier for them to reach desired goals.

Involving students in developing a rubric is an even better way to help them understand what you are looking for in their work. In addition, developing the criteria as a class involves metacognitive understanding of how marks are being assigned, and develops a sense of responsibility for the quality of their work. Getting student input into the creation of the rubric allows them to help set the criteria for grading, and gives you additional evidence that they understand the overall goals of your instruction.

Because one goal of this program is to help students become aware of words and to be able to use them in thoughtful communication, we believe that it is also important to assess students' developing word consciousness. The rubric in Figure 8.17 can be used as a guideline to help students pay attention to word consciousness across the curriculum along with other aspects of vocabulary knowledge. In it, we have included the endpoints to give you a sense of the scale. Teachers, and groups of teachers and students, can develop the middle sections given the instructional emphasis and characteristics of the class.

Rubric for Vocabulary Growth

Teachers often ask which type of vocabulary assessment works best. The answer depends on the purpose of assessment. Large-scale assessment entails testing large numbers of students and requires a reliable test that is easy to administer and score. Hence the multiple-choice format is preferable. Classroom assessment on the other hand is more closely aligned to grade-level curriculum and is used to inform instruction. Classroom assessments can be used to assess content knowledge, self-monitoring, and use of metacognitive strategies and to guide student awareness of the ways words can be used to enhance writing. Multiple methods of vocabulary assessments are useful for classroom assessment, ranging from tests based on grade-level texts to assessments that measure students' metacognitive skills to rubrics that help point out performance standards. A nourishing, well-balanced vocabulary development program requires a well-balanced assessment program. The following glossary includes all of the vocabulary assessments discussed in this chapter.

Dimensions of	Undeveloped	2-3-4	Fully Developed
Vocabulary growth	1 At a glance: The student shows little curiosity or interest in words, minimal growth in vocabulary acquisition, minimal risk taking in oral or written communication.		5 At a glance: The student is curious and interested in words, tries to learn new words, and about new words and is willing to try to use sophisticated or academic language in oral and written communication.
Word consciousness	The student shows little interest in word consciousness activities. The student shows little originality or risk taking in word usage. The student lacks awareness of the role of vocabulary in the communication of ideas. There is little recognition of connections between words.		The student is fully engaged with word awareness activities. In both oral communication and writing there is evidence of risk taking to try new ideas. The student uses words appropriately or in original ways. The student is aware of the role of vocabulary in the communication of ideas. The student looks for, and exploits, connections between words.
Oral communication	The student uses limited word choices when communicating with others. The student does not listen effectively to others or attempt to learn words in context. The student does not ask questions about unknown words.		The student is aware that word choice makes a difference, and uses precise word choice when communicating with others. The student listens carefully and attempts to learn words in context. The student asks questions about unknown words.
Written communication	Writing lacks energy and evidence of personal engagement with the topic. Author uses simple language and limited word choice. Author does not attempt to use words appropriate to the discipline. The tone of the writing is flat and the voice of the writer is unclear.		Writing is full of energy and shows evidence of personal engagement with the topic. Words are used accurately and chosen for effect. Word choice is consistent with the discipline. Ideas are presented with voice and style. Author uses techniques such as metaphor or alliteration effectively.
Use of problem-solving strategies in reading	The student ignores new words when reading. The student is unaware of what to do when encountering an unknown word. Student does not use the lessons from the cue cards to understand unknown words.		The student seeks to make sense of new words in reading in a conscious manner. The student applies lessons from the cue cards to understand unknown words.

Figure 8.17 Rubric for Vocabulary Growth

Source: Adapted from J. Scott, B. Skobel, & J. Wells. (2008). *The word conscious classroom: Developing the vocabulary readers and writers need.* New York: Scholastic.

Glossary of Vocabulary Assessments

Assessment of Words

1. *Multiple choice—isolation:* students select the correct synonym to match the target word.

2. *Multiple choice—in context:* students select the correct synonym to match the target word in the sentence.

3. *Fill-in-the-blank—words in isolation with word bank:* students select definitions from a list and fill in the blanks (more definitions than words reduce the likelihood of guessing).

4. *Fill-in-the-blank—words in isolation, constructed response:* students fill in the blank without a list of words to choose from.

5. *Cloze—words in context, with word bank:* students fill in the missing words in the text, using words in a word bank (include more words in the word bank than test blanks).

6. *Cloze—words in context, without word bank:* students fill in the missing words in a text (only exact matches should be accepted).

7. *Five-minute vocabulary test—general word knowledge:* students are given five minutes to write down as many words as they can think of (proper nouns and numbers do not count).

8. *Five-minute vocabulary test—specific topic:* students are given five minutes to write down as many words as they can think of about a specific topic in the curriculum.

9. *Opposites test—students fill in the opposite of each word, using the word bank.*

Assessment of Metacognitive Skills

1. *Metacognitive test:* students circle unknown words in a text and then take a multiple-choice test on the same words.

2. *Stoplight vocabulary test:* student rate level of word knowledge on stoplight vocabulary sheet and then fill in definitions of the same words on a fill-in-the-blank (constructed response) vocabulary test.

3. *Morphological awareness test:* students identify designated word part (prefixes, suffixes, roots, or base words) in a text.

4. *Rubric assessing metacognitive awareness of words:* students are assessed on their awareness of the role of vocabulary in communicating ideas, awareness that word choice makes a difference in writing, their conscious application of lessons regarding the cue cards, and the conscious effort to make sense of new words in reading and to try to use them in writing.

Assessment of Clarifying Strategy Use

1. *Clarifying strategy self-report:* students respond to the prompt, "What do you do when you're reading and you come to a word that you don't understand? If you don't have a dictionary how do you figure out what the word means?"

Assessment of Word Schema

1. *Word web assessment:* students construct a word web demonstrating the relationship between a set of concepts.

2. *Word sort assessment:* students sort words into categories based on conceptual relationships.

3. *Word-concept diagram:* students draw a diagram, label and explain concepts using target words.

Educators have been assessing vocabulary knowledge in much the same way (standardized multiple-choice tests) for decades with very consistent results. Students who enter school with well-developed vocabulary earn high scores on vocabulary tests and students who depend on schools for literacy often score poorly. It is clear that standardized vocabulary tests will not provide all of the assessment data that schools or students need. To help students learn, we need to know what they do and don't understand, and where they need more practice and assistance. Assessment can give us the tools. Researchers are beginning to examine the reliability and validity of alternative measures of vocabulary knowledge (Scott, Hoover, Flinspach, & Vevea, in press). Meanwhile, teachers are developing their own vocabulary assessments that measure students' baseline knowledge, track students' progress, and inform instruction.

Programmatic Change 9

Page Number	Sequence	Description
154	1	Unit planning (unit planning template)
155	2	Grade-level planning
155	3	Schoolwide planning
156	4	Providing and supporting nourishing vocabulary instruction

Figure 9.1 Programmatic Change

Programmatic change requires clear goals and a collaborative effort on the part of a school faculty. When test scores are used to pinpoint failure rather than to inform instruction, little progress can be made. Blaming teachers for poor student performance can result in acrimony and fragmentation as the following vignette illustrates.

Who Is to Blame?

The standardized test scores had been disseminated and the elementary school principal convened a special faculty meeting to discuss the results. The primary teachers preened as the principal praised their strong reading scores. Indeed, the tests confirmed that the school's primary grade students were doing very well in basic reading skills. The fourth and fifth grade teachers sat slumped in their chairs as angry comments flew back and forth. "We would have been fine except for them!" "If the upper-grade teachers were doing their jobs, we would have made adequate yearly progress!" "Thanks to them, we're an improvement school again!"

The principal tried to defuse some of the tension. She reminded the teachers that they were a team and that everyone was responsible for the students' achievement. But it was clear that she shared the primary teachers' frustration with the poor performance of the fourth- and fifth-grade students.

This scenario is acted out in schools across the nation. What is really going on in these schools? Let's take a closer look. Children from less privileged backgrounds enter school with impoverished vocabulary and are fed a steady diet of phonics and decodable texts for the first few years of school. Because the texts used for instruction use a very limited vocabulary, the children appear to be progressing well. Most learn the twenty-six letters, forty or so phonemes, 250 spelling patterns during the primary grades, and seem well on their way to literacy. But something sinister is going on beneath the surface of this idyllic school scenario. Children are receiving almost no vocabulary instruction in the primary classes. This is not a problem for privileged children. They enjoy daily read aloud and extended discourse with their parents, and their vocabulary continues to grow despite lack of instruction at school. But children who depend on schools for literacy are not learning the vocabulary words they need to know and are losing ground every day to their privileged peers. The widening vocabulary gap remains hidden because most of the simple words in primary texts are words most children already know.

Suddenly, around the beginning of fourth grade, there is a huge shift in reading content and the texts are much harder. Upper-grade textbooks and novels are filled with vast numbers of words that children who depend on schools for literacy do not know. Their achievement plummets and, because they are in the upper grades, everyone blames the upper-grade teachers. Who is responsible for what is known as the fourth-grade slump? It is a long story that begins in early childhood.

A vast vocabulary gap exists long before children enter kindergarten and grows larger each year of schooling (Chall, Jacobs, & Baldwin, 1990; Hart & Risley, 1995). Lagging literacy scores in the upper grades are not the sole responsibility of the upper-grade teachers. In fact, these scores can be attributed to inadequate vocabulary instruction at each grade level. Every teacher in the school shares equal responsibility for the downward spiral of students in the upper grades.

Vocabulary malnourishment is similar to other forms of deprivation. It takes a long time for the effects of malnutrition to manifest themselves in weakened bones or stunted growth. When a child is identified as malnourished, it is clear that problem did not occur overnight and cannot be solved with a few good meals. It will take a lengthy period of carefully planned nutritional care to begin to reverse the effects of a starvation diet.

Students require a great deal of vocabulary-enriched instruction if they are to recover from the effects of vocabulary malnutrition. Equally important is changing the diet of younger students so that they do not become malnourished in the first place. This process is challenging and requires a change in mind-set on the part of many teachers, publishers, and literacy experts. One of the most vexing problems that we face is the reliance on publishers for reading instruction. Teachers are pressured to follow the teacher's guide, but the reading programs designed for primary grade students are almost certain to cause vocabulary malnutrition. The emphasis on decoding at the expense of vocabulary in primary grade reading instruction is fostered by literacy experts at the highest level. The widely used Dynamic Indicators of Basic Early Literacy Skills

(DIBELS) test, designed to measure pre-kindergarten through third-grade reading skills, does not include an assessment of vocabulary knowledge. Although
vocabulary is identified as one of the five "big ideas" in literacy, it is likely that
skills that are not deemed important enough to assess will not be taught.
Literacy experts advise teachers to focus on word work in the primary grades,
providing three years of phonics and sight word instruction and only then shift-
ing the emphasis to word meaning (Shanahan, 2006). For children who
depend on schools for literacy, the loss of three years of word learning instruction may be all but impossible to overcome in the upper grades.

Vocabulary malnutrition continues to cause serious reading problems
throughout schooling. Shira recently listened to a struggling tenth-grade
reader who was attempting to read a sixth-grade science text. He began reading with reasonable fluency until he encountered *vapor*, the first of many words
he obviously did not know. The student struggled to decode the word, pronouncing the first consonant with a short *a* sound. When he encountered the
word *humidity*, he paused, sounded out the word, pronouncing the first syllable
hum. As the student struggled with an increasing number of unfamiliar words,
his fluency lagged and he became flustered. When he was asked questions
about the content of the text, his comprehension was extremely poor. Although
the student has received a great deal of remedial reading instruction, he is
unable to read beyond the fifth-grade level and is failing his high school classes.
Had this student been given a rich diet of vocabulary throughout his ten years
of schooling, would it have made a difference? We cannot know for sure, but it
is likely that his literacy development was severely compromised by vocabulary
malnutrition. In this final section of the book, we provide a framework for
nourishing vocabulary instruction, designed to prevent students from arriving
in high school without the vocabulary they need to understand their textbooks.

NOURISHING INSTRUCTION ACROSS THE CURRICULUM AND THROUGHOUT THE SCHOOL

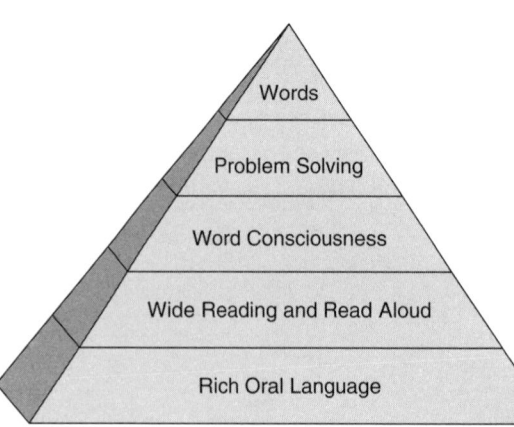

Figure 9.2

Developing a comprehensive vocabulary program takes time and commitment from all of the administrators, teachers, and support staff at a school site. The process begins with a series of faculty meetings, where information about the effects of impoverished vocabulary is shared and goals for vocabulary instruction developed. The entire staff will need to work together to create a vocabulary program that will meet student needs. Planning and implementing the program is a multiyear commitment that begins with the work of grade-level teams.

Step 1: Unit Planning

Teachers begin their work by gathering in grade-level teams to plan instructional units. To increase the efficiency of unit planning, teachers may take individual planning responsibilities or divide into smaller grade-level groups, each responsible for a particular content area. Unit planning entails the selection of vocabulary words from the texts that are used for instruction, based on the principles described in Chapters 4 through 6. Units are planned and vocabulary words identified in each content area, including reading and the language arts, math, science, and social studies. Core vocabulary words (challenging words found in texts) are identified and extended vocabulary words (conceptually related words or words that belong to the same word family) are added to increase the range of vocabulary instruction. Teachers refine the core vocabulary lists that are generated through the use of stoplight vocabulary or the vocabulary knowledge chart (described in Chapter 6). These student self-assessment activities help teachers narrow the core vocabulary list to unknown words (red-light words) that require explicit vocabulary instruction. Teachers use the unit planning template presented in Figure 9.3 to identify methods that will be used to teach vocabulary, script sample classroom discourse to increase vocabulary exposure, identify books related to the content that will be read aloud during the course of each unit, and to select vocabulary assessments that will be used to monitor student learning.

Unit Planning Template

Subject: _____   Text: _____   Chapter: _____   Dates: _____

Content Standards and Objectives	Core Vocabulary	Extended Vocabulary	Instructional Methods	Classroom Discourse	Read Aloud	Assessment

Figure 9.3   Unit Planning Template

A full-sized planning template is provided in Appendix B.

Step 2: Grade-Level Planning

Teachers continue to develop unit plans and meet regularly in grade-level teams to review vocabulary-enriched unit plans. The purpose of these meetings is to ensure that content standards, key concepts, and instructional objectives are integrated with vocabulary goals in each subject area. Over the course of the school year, vocabulary-enriched instructional units are developed to meet grade-level standards in each content area. Individual unit vocabulary lists are compiled, creating a cross-curricular list of core vocabulary words for each grade level.

Step 3: Schoolwide Planning

The second year of planning is crucial to the success of the vocabulary development program. Grade-level core vocabulary lists have been developed, but the important work of increasing the breadth and depth of vocabulary instruction depends on cooperation across grade levels. Schoolwide planning requires a vocabulary team—a committed group of teachers representing each grade level, administrators, and support staff—responsible for implementing a comprehensive vocabulary development program.

Across the Curriculum and Throughout the School

Comprehensive vocabulary development instruction does not take place in a vacuum. It is an essential component of a rich, balanced literacy program. Teaching vocabulary across the curriculum and throughout the school entails constant engagement of children with texts. In addition to reading aloud, teachers make sure that children develop decoding skills, fluency, and reading comprehension proficiency. They plan activities that encourage students to read independently during and outside of school time. An upward spiral begins, as students acquire vocabulary, read more easily, and find reading more enjoyable. The more students read, the more words they learn from texts. When we add the words that are targeted for direct instruction in each subject area to the words acquired incidentally through read aloud and independent reading, the potential for acceleration of vocabulary development becomes clear. We can narrow the vocabulary gap using high-quality trade books and regular instructional materials.

NOURISHING INSTRUCTION IN CONSTRAINED LITERACY SETTINGS

Many teachers, particularly those in low-performing schools, are required to use scripted reading programs that include rigid sequencing guides. If you are one of these teachers, you can still provide nourishing vocabulary instruction. We suggest that you include vocabulary activities in content instruction (math, science, and social studies). Find time to read aloud to students daily and immerse them in rich oral language. You may not be able to avoid overfeeding your students certain components of the literacy curriculum, but you can avoid vocabulary malnourishment with carefully designed instruction.

The following are guidelines, summarizing key concepts discussed in this book.

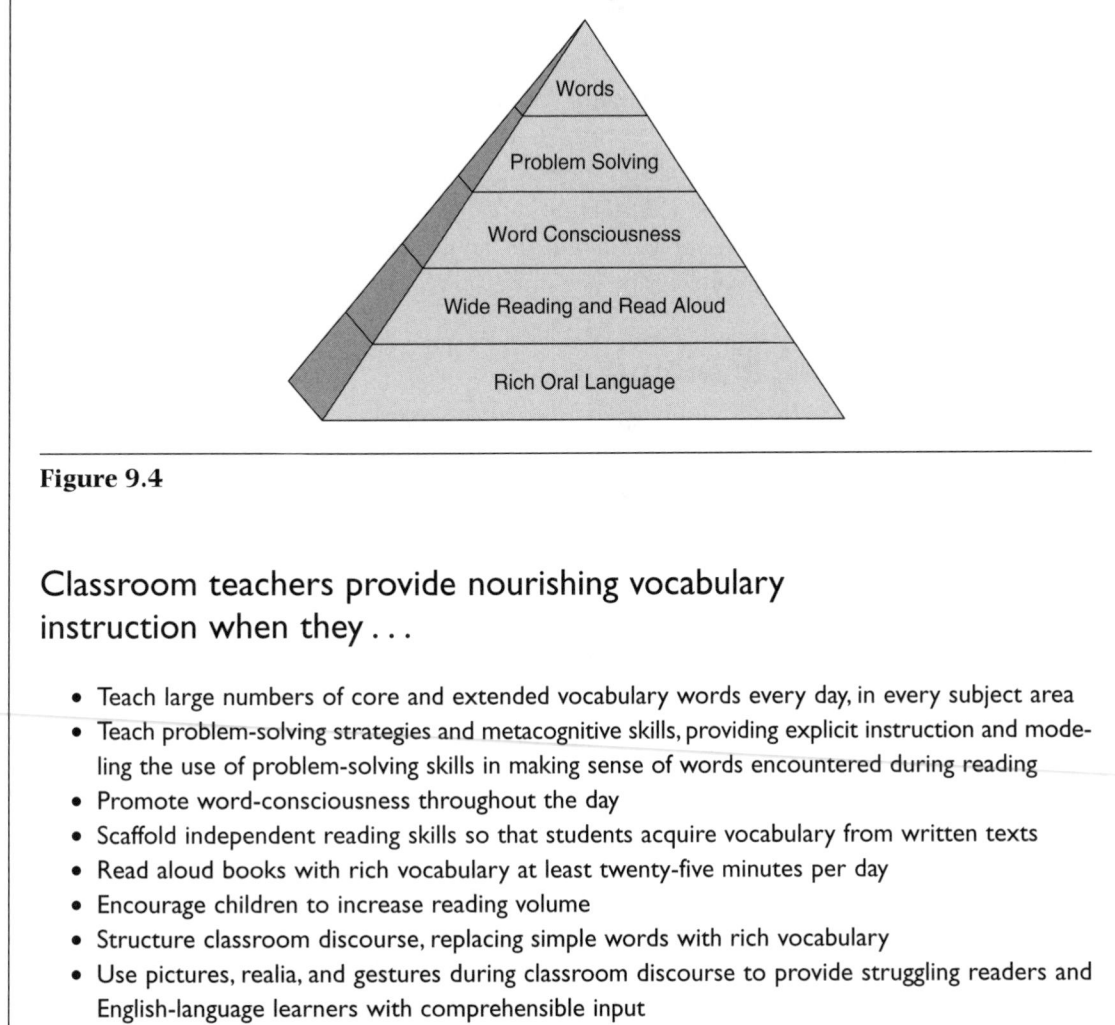

Figure 9.4

Classroom teachers provide nourishing vocabulary instruction when they . . .

- Teach large numbers of core and extended vocabulary words every day, in every subject area
- Teach problem-solving strategies and metacognitive skills, providing explicit instruction and modeling the use of problem-solving skills in making sense of words encountered during reading
- Promote word-consciousness throughout the day
- Scaffold independent reading skills so that students acquire vocabulary from written texts
- Read aloud books with rich vocabulary at least twenty-five minutes per day
- Encourage children to increase reading volume
- Structure classroom discourse, replacing simple words with rich vocabulary
- Use pictures, realia, and gestures during classroom discourse to provide struggling readers and English-language learners with comprehensible input
- Provide multiple exposures to new words, engaging children in the use of rich vocabulary in oral discourse and in writing
- Encourage the playful use of words, and develop enthusiasm for skillful word use
- Encourage students to experiment with language use in a risk-free environment
- Acknowledge the literacy skills students bring to class and build on that foundation

Schools support nourishing vocabulary instruction when they . . .

- Organize grade-level teams to plan systematic vocabulary instruction including vocabulary objectives for instructional units in each subject area
- Articulate grade-level vocabulary objectives, developing a scope and sequence of vocabulary instruction across grade levels
- Support parents in helping their children become life-long readers and writers
- Develop schoolwide reading program including in-class read aloud at every grade level for at least twenty-five minutes per day
- Organize activities designed to encourage outside reading (book fairs, reading nights, and so on)
- Plan staff development programs to encourage best practices in vocabulary instruction

The challenge of implementing a vocabulary development program is substantial. Instructional time is limited and there are many competing demands on teachers' time. It is important that the faculty, administrators, and support staff make a long-term commitment to a comprehensive vocabulary development program such as the one we've developed in this book. Students, particularly those who enter school without an awareness or knowledge of vocabulary terms used in books and schools, may not show immediate progress on standardized tests. However, nutritious vocabulary instruction will result in better educational health. If teachers persevere in embedding vocabulary in all aspects of instruction, we are confident that student achievement will improve and standardized test scores will rise.

The materials and methods included in this book provide a framework designed to accelerate students' vocabulary development. But methods are only ideas until dedicated teachers bring them to life in classrooms. We hope that you will find it helpful in your quest to narrow the vocabulary-related achievement gap. We hope that you will use the methods in this book to nourish students by teaching vocabulary all day, every day, across the curriculum and throughout the school.

Appendix A

REFERENCE MATERIALS FOR TEACHING ENGLISH

Common Errors in English [www.wsu.edu/~brians/errors/]. Written and maintained by a professor of English at Washington State University.

English Zone.com [www.english-zone.com]. A site for English learners with concrete examples and non-examples, lessons, and practice quizzes.

George, J. (1994). *Good grief! Good grammar.* Markham, ON: Pembroke.

Napoli, D. (2003). *Language matters: A guide to everyday questions about language.* Oxford: Oxford University Press.

Read-Write-Think [www.readwritethink.org]. A joint website sponsored by both the International Reading Association and the National Council of Teachers of English. Provides access to high-quality practices and resources linked to standards.

Appendix B

REPRODUCIBLE MATERIALS

Cross-Curricular Planning Matrix

READING-LANGUAGE ARTS	SOCIAL STUDIES	MATH	SCIENCE
Content Standards and Objectives: *Vocabulary Objectives:*	*Content Standards and Objectives:* *Vocabulary Objectives:*	*Content Standards and Objectives:* *Vocabulary Objectives:*	*Content Standards and Objectives:* *Vocabulary Objectives:*
CONNECTIONS ACROSS SUBJECT AREAS			

Figure B.1   Cross-Curricular Planning Matrix

Vocabulary-Enriched Lesson Plan

Lesson Date: _____ Subject: _____ Text: _____ Chapter: _____

Text: _____ Chapter: _____

Standards and Content Objectives:

Vocabulary Objectives:

WORDS Identify words Assess students' vocabulary knowledge	Core Vocabulary: Extended Vocabulary:
SCHEMA Teach key concepts Build word schema	
INSTRUCTIONAL SEQUENCE BEFORE READING DURING READING AFTER READING	
RICH ORAL LANGUAGE	
ASSESSMENT	

Figure B.2   Vocabulary-Enriched Lesson Plan

Scaffolded Discourse Template

Subject	Vocabulary	Scaffolded Discourse
Story content		
Words related to topic		
Problem-solving skills		
Classroom directions		
Other		

Figure B.3 Scaffolded Discourse Template

Read-Aloud Lesson Plan

Lesson Date: _____ Text: _____ Author: _____

Genre: _____ Subject Area: _____

WORDS	
WORD SCHEMA	
INSTRUCTIONAL SEQUENCE BEFORE READING DURING READING AFTER READING	
RICH ORAL LANGUAGE	

Figure B.4 Read-Aloud Lesson Plan

Vocabulary-Enriched Lesson Plan

Lesson Date: _____ Subject: _____ Text: _____ Chapter: _____

Standards:

Content-Vocabulary Objectives:

CORE AND EXTENDED VOCABULARY WORDS	
LESSON INTRODUCTION	
INSTRUCTIONAL SEQUENCE DIRECT VOCABULARY INSTRUCTION: STUDENT ACTIVITIES: USE OF WORDS IN CLASSROOM DISCOURSE: PROBLEM-SOLVING SKILL: HOMEWORK:	
ASSESSMENT	

Figure B.5   Vocabulary-Enriched Lesson Plan

Unit Plan

Subject: _____ Text: _____ Chapter: _____ Dates: _____

	Core Vocabulary Words	Extended Vocabulary Words	Instructional Methods	Classroom Discourse	Problem-Solving Instruction
Content objectives					
Vocabulary objectives					
Assessment					

Figure B.6   Unit Plan

Vocabulary-Enriched Lesson Plan: Secondary

Lesson Date: _____ Subject: _____ Text: _____ Chapter: _____

Standards and Objectives:

Content/Vocabulary Objectives:

Core/Extended Vocabulary Words:

Introduction:

Content and Vocabulary: Instructional Sequence

Direct Vocabulary Instruction:

Student Activities:

Use of Words in Classroom Discourse:

Problem Solving:

Homework:

Assessment:

Figure B.7   Vocabulary-Enriched Lesson Plan: Secondary

Setting/Time Frame/Characters/Plot Organizer

Name: _____ Date: _____

Subject: _____ Text: _____ Chapter: _____

Setting	Time Frame	Characters	Plot
Inference	Inference	Inference	Inference

Figure B.8   Setting/Time Frame/Characters/Plot Organizer

Compare and Contrast Organizer

_____ *and* _____

Name: _____ Date: _____

Description of the Topics			How Are They Similar?	How Are They Different?
Key words				
Questions and answers				

Figure B.9 Compare and Contrast Organizer

Antonym Chart

Name: _____ Date: _____

Antonyms are words that mean the opposite of each other (example: in-out). Fill in the chart, using the list of antoynms in the box below.

Location		Verbs		Time		Description		Description	
in		come		before		ugly		cold	
up		open		late		fat		narrow	
forward		give		day		tall		little	
in front of		break		beginning		good		light	
near		sink		never		young		true	
under		buy		hello		friend		shallow	
inside		laugh		morning		son		best	
above		pull		first		father		dirty	
left		win				interesting		dry	
far		laugh				poor		tight	
to		agree				happy		war	
		give				quiet		fast	
						awake		right	
						king		lucky	
						healthy		smooth	
						nice		inhale	

Antonyms

down below near fix pretty evening backward take exhale night wide mean goodbye after close early hot false push lose big dark worst deep loose peace unlucky clean end wet wrong sad take sick boring enemy mother far daughter asleep bad short noisy always cry disagree go rough queen outside slow thin old rich out right last cry from

Figure B.10   Antonym Chart

Words That Belong Together

Name: _____

Some words belong together and other words don't get along!
These are some examples of words that belong together: ride *in* a car, ride *on* a bus, get *out of* a car, get *off* a bus.

Imagine that you were traveling with your grandfather on a journey to America. What stories would you tell?

I longed for _____

I was excited by _____

I was amazed by _____

I was bewildered by _____

I marveled at _____

I remembered _____

I was reminded of _____

Write your own sentences with words that belong together:

Figure B.11   Words That Belong Together

Mini-Lesson Plan

Students: _____

Shared area of need: _____

Mini-lesson content objectives: _____

Mini-lesson vocabulary objectives: _____

Text materials: _____

Lesson sequence: _____

_____

_____

_____

_____

_____

_____

_____

_____

_____

Assessment: _____

Follow-up: _____

Figure B.12   Mini-Lesson Plan

Classroom Scoring Sheet for Vocabulary Assessment

Grade Level	Test		Test		Test		Test	
Student Name	Date	Score	Date	Score	Date	Score	Date	Score
Class Average								

Figure B.13   Classroom Scoring Sheet for Vocabulary Assessment

Stoplight Vocabulary

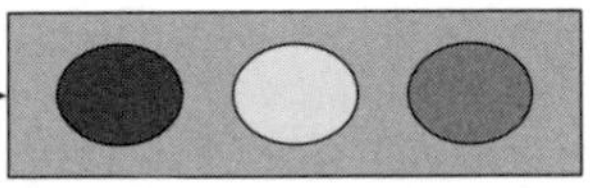

Name: _____

Follow these steps for stoplight vocabulary:

If you don't know the word at all, color the light red. If you have heard of it but aren't sure what it means, color it yellow. If you know the word and can use it in a sentence, color it green. Write a sentence with each green-light word.

1. _____

2. _____

3. _____

4. _____

5. _____

6. _____

7. _____

8. _____

9. _____

10. _____

11. _____

12. _____

Green-light sentences:

_____

_____

_____

_____

_____

_____

_____

_____

_____

_____

Figure B.14 Stoplight Vocabulary

Source: Lubliner, S. (2005b). *Getting into words: Vocabulary instruction that strengthens comprehension* (pp. 80–88). Baltimore: Paul H. Brookes Publishing Co., Inc. Reprinted by permission.

Unit Planning Template

Subject: _____ Text: _____ Chapter: _____ Dates: _____

Content Standards and Objectives	Core Vocabulary	Extended Vocabulary	Instructional Methods	Classroom Discourse	Read Aloud	Assessment

Figure B.15   Unit Planning Template

References

Allington, R., & Cunningham, A. (1996). *Schools that work: Where all children read and write.* New York: HarperCollins.

Anderson, R., & Nagy, R. (1992). The vocabulary conundrum. *American Educator, 16,* 14–18, 44–47.

Anglin, J. M. (1993). Vocabulary development: A morphological analysis. *Monographs of the Society of Research in Child Development,* Serial No. 238, 58, 10.

Ausubel, D. (1963). *The psychology of meaningful verbal learning.* New York: Grune & Stratton.

Ausubel, D. (1978). In defense of advance organizers: A reply to the critics. *Review of Educational Research, 48,* 251–257.

Baumann, J. F., Kameenui, E. J., & Ash, G. (2003). Research on vocabulary instruction: Voltaire redux. In J. Flood, D. Lapp, J. Jensen, & J. R. Squire (Eds.), *Handbook of research on teaching the English Language Arts* (2nd ed.). New York: Macmillan.

Bear, D., Invernizzi, M., Templeton, S., & Johnston, F. (2007). *Words their way: Word study for phonics, vocabulary, and spelling instruction* (4th ed.). Upper Saddle River, NJ: Pearson Education.

Beck, I., & McKeown, M. (1991). Conditions of vocabulary acquisition. In R. Barr, M. Kamil, P. Mosenthal, & P. Pearson, *Handbook of reading research, Vol. II* (pp. 789–814). Mahwah, NJ: Lawrence Erlbaum.

Beck, I., McKeown, M., & Kucan, L. (2002). *Bringing words to life.* New York: Guilford Press.

Beck, I., Perfetti, C., & McKeown, M. (1982). Effects of long-term vocabulary instruction on lexical access and reading comprehension. *Journal of Educational Psychology, 74,* 506–521.

Becker, W. (1977). Teaching reading and language to the disadvantaged—what we have learned from field research. *Harvard Educational Review, 47,* 518–543.

Biemiller, A. (2001). *The relationship between vocabulary assessed with picture vocabulary methodology, same words with sentence context method, root word inventory, and reading comprehension.* Paper presented at the annual conference of the Society for Scientific Study of Reading, Boulder, CO.

Biemiller, A. (2004). Teaching vocabulary in the primary grades: Vocabulary instruction needed. In J. Baumann & E. Kame'enui (Eds.), *Reading vocabulary: Research to practice.* New York: Guilford Press.

Biemiller, A. (2005). Size and sequence in vocabulary development: Implications for choosing words for primary grade vocabulary instruction. In A. Hieber & M. Kamil (Eds.), *Teaching and learning vocabulary: Bringing research to practice* (pp. 223–242). Mahwah, NJ: Lawrence Erlbaum.

Biemiller, A., & Slonin, N. (2001). Estimating root word vocabulary growth in normative and advantaged populations: Evidence for a common sequence of vocabulary acquisition. *Journal of Educational Psychology, 93,* 498–520.

Blake, M. (2004). *Monsters of the deep.* Chicago: Wright Group/McGraw-Hill.

Brown, A., & Palinscar, A. (1985). *Reciprocal teaching of comprehension strategies: A natural history of one program for enhancing learning* (Technical Report No. 334). Urbana: University of Illinois, Center for the Study of Reading.

Brown, A., & Palinscar, A. (1986). *Guided cooperative learning and individual knowledge acquisition* (Technical Report No. 1372). Washington, DC: Department of Education.

Chall, J. S., Jacobs, V. A., & Baldwin, L. E. (1990). *The reading crisis: Why poor children fall behind.* Cambridge, MA: Harvard University Press.

Cooper, S. (1986). *Greenwitch.* New York: Simon & Schuster.

Coxhead, A. (2000). A new academic word list. *TESOL Quarterly, 34,* 213–238.

Cummins, J. (1994). Primary language instruction and the education of language minority students. In C. Leyba (Ed.), *School and language minority students: A theoretical framework.* Los Angeles: Evaluation, Dissemination and Assessment Center, California State University, Los Angeles.

Dale, E., & O'Rourke, J. (1981). *The living word vocabulary.* Chicago: World Book/Childcraft International.

Dickinson, D., & Tabors, P. (2001). *Beginning literacy with language.* Baltimore: Paul H. Brookes Publishing.

Durkin, D. (1978–1979). What classroom observations reveal about reading comprehension instruction. *Reading Research Quarterly, 14,* 481–533.

Education Data Partnership (2005). http://www.ed-data.k12.ca.us.

Elley, W. (1989). Vocabulary acquisition from listening to stories. *Reading Research Quarterly, 24,* 174–187.

Fleischman, S. (1995). *The thirteenth floor: A ghost story.* New York: Greenwillow Books.

Gándara, P., Rumberger, R., Maxwell-Jolly, J., & Callahan, R. (2003, October 7). English learners in California schools: Unequal resources, unequal outcomes. *Education Policy Analysis Archives, 11*(36).

Graves, M. F. (1986). Vocabulary learning and instruction. In E. Z. Rothkopf & L. C. Ehri (Eds.), *Review of research in education* (13, pp. 49–89). Washington, DC: American Educational Research Association.

Graves, M. F. (2000). A vocabulary program to complement and bolster a middle grade comprehension program. In B. M. Taylor, M. F. Graves, & P. van den Broek (Eds.), *Reading for meaning: Fostering comprehension in the middle grades.* Newark, DE: International Reading Association.

Graves, M. F. (2004). Teaching prefixes: As good as it gets. In J. Baumann & E. Kame'enui (Eds.), *Reading vocabulary: Research to practice.* New York: Guilford Press.

Graves, M. F., & Watts-Taffe, S. M. (2002). The place of word consciousness in a research-based vocabulary program. In A. E. Farstrup & S. J. Samuels (Eds.), *What research has to say about reading instruction* (3rd ed., pp. 140–165). Newark, DE: International Reading Association.

Hammer, P. (1979). What is the use of cognates? ERIC Document Reproduction Service ED 180 202. Washington, DC: U.S. Department of Health, Education, and Welfare.

Hart, B., & Risley, R. T. (1995). *Meaningful differences in the everyday experiences of young American children.* Baltimore: Paul H. Brookes Publishing.

Hayes, D., & Ahrens, M. (1988). Vocabulary simplification for children: A special case of "motherese"? *Journal of Child Language, 13*(2), 395–410.

Hennessy, B. G. (1990). *The dinosaur who lived in my backyard.* New York: Puffin.

Kintsch, W. (1998). *Comprehension: A paradigm for cognition.* Cambridge, UK: Cambridge University Press.

Kintsch, W., & van Dijk, T. (1978). Toward a model of text comprehension and production. *Psychological Review, 85,* 363–394.

Klingner, J. K., & Vaughn, S. (1996). Reciprocal teaching of reading comprehension strategies for students with learning disabilities who use English as a second language. *Elementary School Journal, 96,* 275–293.

Krashen, S. (1994). Bilingual education and second language acquisition theory. In C. Leyba (Ed.), *School and language minority students: A theoretical framework.* Los Angeles: Evaluation, Dissemination and Assessment Center, California State University, Los Angeles.

Lasky, K. (1981). *The night journey.* New York: Puffin Books.

Lovgren, S. (2005). Leprosy was spread by colonialism. *National Geographic News,* Retrieved October 7, 2006, from http://news.nationalgeographic.com/news/2005/05/0512_050512_leprosy.html.

Lubliner, S. (2001). *A practical guide to reciprocal teaching.* Bothell, WA: Wright Group/McGraw-Hill.

Lubliner, S. (2005a). "Go look it up": Dictionary instruction revisited. *The California Reader, 38*(4).

Lubliner, S. (with Smetana, L.). (2005b). *Getting into words: Vocabulary instruction that strengthens comprehension.* Baltimore: Paul H. Brookes Publishing.

Lubliner, S., & Smetana, L. (2005). Effects of comprehensive vocabulary instruction on title I students' metacognitive word-learning skills and reading comprehension. *Journal of Literacy Research, 37,* 163–200.

McKeown, M. (1993). Creating definitions for young word learners. *Reading Research Quarterly, 27,* 16–33.

McKeown, M., Beck, I., Omanson, R., & Perfetti, C. (1983). The effects of long-term vocabulary instruction on reading comprehension: A replication. *Journal of Reading Behavior, 15*(1), 3–18.

McKeown, M., Beck, I., Omanson, R., & Pople, M. (1985). Some effects of the nature and frequency of vocabulary instruction on the knowledge and use of words. *Reading Research Quarterly, 20*(5), 522–535.

Miller, C. A., & Gildea, P. M. (1987). How children learn words. *Scientific American, 257*(3), 94–99.

Nagy, W. (1985). *Vocabulary instruction: Implications of the new research.* Paper presented at the National Council of Teachers of English, Philadelphia, PA.

Nagy, W. (1988). *Vocabulary instruction and reading comprehension* (Technical Report No. 431.) Urbana: University of Illinois Center for the Study of Reading.

Nagy, W., & Anderson, R. (1984). How many words are there in printed school English? *Reading Research Quarterly, 19*(3), 304–330.

Nagy, W., Anderson, R., & Herman, P. (1987). Learning word meanings from context during normal reading. *American Educational Research Journal, 24*(2), 237–270.

Nagy, W., & Herman, P. (1987). Breadth and depth of vocabulary knowledge: Implications for acquisition and instruction. In M. McKeown & M. Curtis (Eds.), *The nature of vocabulary acquisition* (pp.19–35). Hillsdale, NJ: Lawrence Erlbaum.

Nagy, W., & Scott, J. (1991). Word schemas: Expectations about the form and meaning of new words. *Cognition and Instruction, 7*(2), 105–127.

Nagy, W., & Scott, J. (2000). Vocabulary processes. In M. L. Kamil, P. B. Mosenthal, P. David Pearson, & R. Barr (Eds.), *Handbook of reading research* (Vol. III, pp. 69–284). Mahwah, NJ: Lawrence Erlbaum.

Nash, R. (1997). *NTC's dictionary of Spanish cognates.* Chicago: NTC Publishing Group.

Nation, I. S. P. (2001). *Learning vocabulary in another language.* Cambridge, UK: Cambridge University Press.

National Institute of Child Health and Human Development (NICHHD). (2000). *Report of the National Reading Panel. Teaching children to read: An evidence-based assessment of the scientific research literature on reading and its implications for reading instruction* (NIH Publication No. 00–4769). Washington, DC: U.S. Government Printing Office.

Oxford English dictionary [2nd CD-Rom ed.]. (2004, December 10). New York: Oxford University Press.

Palincsar, A. (1983). *Reciprocal teaching of comprehension-monitoring activities* (Report No. US-NIE-C-400–76–0116). Washington, DC: U.S. Department of Education.

Palincsar, A. (1984). *Reciprocal teaching: Working within the zone of proximal development.* Paper presented at the Annual Meeting of the American Educational Research Association, New Orleans, LA.

Palincsar, A. (1985). *The unpacking of a multi-component, metacognitive training package.* Paper presented at the Annual Meeting of the American Educational Research Association, Chicago.

Palincsar, A. (1986). The role of dialogue in providing scaffolded instruction. *Educational Psychologist, 21*(1&2), 73–98.

Palincsar, A., & Brown, A. (1983). *Reciprocal teaching of comprehension monitoring activities.* Bethesda, MD: National Institute of Health and Human Development.

Palincsar, A., & Brown, A. (1984). Reciprocal teaching of comprehension fostering and monitoring activities. *Cognition and Instruction, 1*(2), 117–175.

Pearson, P. D., Hiebert, E. H., & Kamil, M. L. (2007). Vocabulary assessment: What we know and what we need to know. *Reading Research Quarterly, 42*(2), 282–296.

Penno, J., Wilkinson, I., & Moore, D. (2002). Vocabulary acquisition from teacher explanation and repeated listening to stories. Do they overcome the Matthew effect? *Journal of Educational Psychology, 94*(1), 23–33.

Poe, E. A. (2002). *The Raven and other poems.* New York: Scholastic Paperbacks.

Pringle, L. P. (1995). *Dinosaurs, strange and wonderful.* Honesdale, PA: Boyds Mills Press.

Robbins, C., & Ehri, L. (1994). Reading storybooks to kindergarteners helps them learn new words. *Journal of Educational Psychology, 86*(1), 54–64.

Rosenshine, B., & Meister, C. 1994. Reciprocal teaching: A review of the research. *Review of Educational Research, 64*(4), 479–530.

Roser, N., & Juel, C. (1982). Effects of vocabulary instruction on reading comprehension. In J. A. Niles & L. A. Harris (Eds.), *Yearbook of the National Reading Conference (31): New inquiries in reading research and instruction* (pp. 110–118). Rochester, NY: National Reading Conference.

Say, A. (1993). *Grandfather's journey.* New York: Houghton Mifflin.

Scarcella, R. (2002). Some key factors affecting English learners' development of advanced literacy. In M. J. Schleppegrell & M. C. Colombi (Eds.), *Developing advanced literacy in first and second languages.* Mahwah, NJ: Lawrence Erlbaum.

Schatz, E., & Baldwin, R. (1986). Context clues are unreliable predictors of word meaning. *Reading Research Quarterly, 21*(4), 439–453.

Schwanenflugel, P. J., Stahl, S. A., & McFalls, E. L. (1997). Partial word knowledge and vocabulary growth during reading comprehension. *Journal of Literacy Research, 29(4),* 531–553.

Scott, J. A. (2004). Scaffolding vocabulary learning: Ideas for equity in urban settings. In D. Lapp, C. Block, E. Cooper, J. Flood, N. Roser, & J.Tinajero (Eds.), *Teaching all the children: Strategies for developing literacy in an urban setting* (pp. 275–293). New York: Guilford Press.

Scott, J. A., Hoover, M., Flinspach, S., & Vevea, J. (2007). *A multiple level vocabulary assessment tool: Measuring word knowledge based on grade level materials.* Paper presented at the National Reading Conference, Austin, TX.

Scott, J. A., Jamieson-Noel, D., & Asselin, M. (2003). Vocabulary instruction throughout the day in twenty-three Canadian upper-elementary classrooms. *The Elementary School Journal, 103*(3), 269–286.

Scott, J. A., Lubliner, S., & Hiebert, E. H. (2006). Constructs underlying word selection and assessments tasks in the archival research on vocabulary instruction. In C. M. Fairbanks, J. Worthy, B. Maloch, J. Hoffman, & D. Schallert (Eds.), *National Reading Conference yearbook.* Fort Worth, TX: Texas Christian University Press.

Scott, J. A., & Nagy, W. (1997). Understanding the definitions of unfamiliar verbs. *Reading Research Quarterly, 32*(2), 184–200.

Scott, J. A., & Nagy, W. (2004) Developing word consciousness. In J. Baumann & E. Kame'euni (Eds.), *Vocabulary instruction: Research to practice.* New York: Guilford Press.

Scott, J. A., Skobel, B., & Wells, J. (2008). *The word conscious classroom: Building the vocabulary readers and writers need.* New York: Scholastic-Theory into Practice Series.

Shanahan, T. (2006). Developing fluency in the context of effective literacy instruction. In T. Razinski, C. Blachowicz, & K. Lems (Eds.), *Fluency instruction: Research-based best practices.* New York: Guilford Press.

Snow, C., & Kim, Y. (2007). Large problem spaces: The challenge of vocabulary for English language learners. In R. Wagner, A. Muse, & K. Tannenbaum (Eds.), *Vocabulary acquisition: Implications for reading comprehension.* New York: Guildford Press.

Stahl, S. (2003). How words are learned incrementally over multiple exposures. *American Educator, 27*(1), 18–19.

Stahl, S., & Nagy, W. (2006). *Teaching word meanings.* Mahwah, NJ: Lawrence Erlbaum.

Stanovich, K. E. (1986). Matthew effects in reading: Some consequences of individual differences in the acquisition of literacy. *Reading Research Quarterly, 21,* 360–406.

Swanborn, M. S. L., & de Glopper, K. (1999). Incidental word learning while reading: A meta-analysis. *Review of Educational Research, 69*(3), 261–285.

Templeton, S., Johnston, F., Bear, D., & Invernizzi, M. (2006). *Words their way: Word sorts for derivational relations spellers.* Upper Saddle River, NJ: Pearson Education.

Watanabe, Y. (1997). Input, intake and retention: Effects of increased processing on incidental learning of foreign vocabulary. *Studies in Second Language Acquisition, 19,* 287–307.

Watts, S. (1995). Vocabulary instruction during reading lessons in six classrooms. *Journal of Reading Behavior, 27,* 399–424.

Wells, J., & Reid, J. (2004). *Writing anchors: Explicit lessons that identify criteria, offer strategic support, and lead students to take ownership of their writing.* Markham, ON: Pembroke Publishers.

West, M. (1953). *General service list of English words.* London: Longman Group.

White, T., Sowell, J., & Yanagihara, A. (1989). Growth of reading vocabulary in diverse elementary schools. *Reading Teacher, 42,* 343–354.

Zeno, S. M., Ivens, S. H., Millard, R. T., & Duvvuri, R. (1995). *The educator's word frequency guide.* New York: Touchstone Applied Science Associates, National Institute of Child Health and Human Development.

Index